MARKET POWER AND PRICE LEVELS IN THE ETHICAL DRUG INDUSTRY

MARKET POWER
AND
PRICE LEVELS
IN THE
Ethical Drug Industry

by Hugh D. Walker

INDIANA UNIVERSITY PRESS

BLOOMINGTON · LONDON   1971

TO THE
MEMORY OF MY FATHER

Acknowledgments

This book is a revision of my dissertation presented in 1967 to Vanderbilt University for the Ph.D. in economics. I am indebted to James McKie, Fred Westfield, James Worley, and Nicholas Georgescu-Roegen for guidance and advice, and to the Earhart Foundation and the Canada Council for financial support. Elton Hinshaw, Howard W. Nicholson, and Leonard Gilday read parts of the manuscript as it was being revised and made helpful comments on content and style. I am particularly grateful to Walter Albee, monograph editor of the Indiana University Press, and to his assistant, Sandy Mathai, for their effort and patience in transforming the style of a dissertation into that of a book.

Contents

The chemical signs used on the chapter openings of this book were reproduced from Rudolph Koch's Book of Signs *with the permission of Dover Publications, Inc., New York. (See p. 257 for explanation of symbols.)*

Tables

x   Tables

CHAPTER ONE

Introduction

Until the middle 1930s the ethical drug industry was a relatively static industry supplying medicinal chemicals to the pharmacist, who then compounded them into the medications prescribed by the physician. New therapeutic agents entered the product lines of the firms when investigators—often European—discovered them. The remarkable medical progress wrought by the sulfa drugs in the late 1930s, and experience with large-scale research during World War II, changed the outlook of the industry. By the middle 1940s new products were being developed in the laboratories of the industry, and the introduction of new, and often better, drugs became the vehicle of rivalry. In the following decade the success of the industry in discovering and introducing significant new drugs was so spectacular that other dimensions of its performance were largely immune to criticism. This very success, however, ultimately created difficulties. Although new products were successful in dealing with previously intractable diseases, patients were often required to continue drug therapy for long periods of time. Moreover, the newer drugs were often expensive, and as many of the patients were elderly people with small resources, the impact of the prices of these drugs upon the incomes of patients assumed considerable importance.

Significant public criticism of the industry's performance can be said to have begun on December 7, 1959, when the Subcommittee on Antitrust and Monopoly of the Senate Judiciary Committee began, under the chairmanship of the late Senator Estes Kefauver, hearings on "administered prices in the drug industry." The hearings continued intermittently for the next nine months and led Senator Kefauver to introduce remedial legislation.

Not only did these hearings represent a landmark in the public's attitude toward the industry, but they also made accessible for the first time significant amounts of information about the industry. Many of the major firms in the industry had been, until very recently, closely controlled family enterprises with an instinctive sense of the high purpose of their undertaking and little disposition to make information about their operations public. Others were divisions of large chemical firms, and still others were subsidiaries of large European firms for which separate information on drug prices was not available. An active trade association, founded in 1957, began to collect and disseminate information about the industry only in response to the Senate hearings. No major legal action had arisen that would have yielded court records useful to an economist wanting to study the industry. Until the publication of the hearings, professional economists had been unable to study the industry because of lack of information.

The hearings did, however, generate some interest. In 1962, the first article concerning the U.S. pharmaceutical industry ever to appear in a professional economic journal was published. Four years later, the total academic publication on the industry consisted of six articles and a few chapters in books concerned with the economics of health. On the whole, the authors have found the performance of the industry to be open to criticism. Thus, Seymour Harris has written:

Many are concerned that an industry which comes close to being a public utility achieves the highest profits in relation to sales and investment of any industry; is highly concentrated in its control of the market; reveals serious monopolistic trends; increases the cost to consumers by differentiating the product at a dizzy pace, with the differentiated product usually similar to or identical with existing products; and greatly inflates the cost through record expenditures on selling. The competition among companies to overwhelm the doctors by repetitious and often misleading advertising, and a failure to give as much publicity to the bad side effects as to the immediate beneficial effects, are unfortunate. Thus competition forces even highly moral firms to become less ethical in their behavior. In the drug industry the relation of labor to total costs is minimal; and like the soap and tobacco industries, using similar selling techniques, their relation of labor to value added is a minimum—selling expenditures and profits are the large items in gross receipts.

The cost of drugs is too high. I say this, though I am aware that the research contributions of the industry are important and that the lives saved, the suffering averted, and the acceleration of recoveries are worth more than the $4 billion spent on drugs. But the cost could be substantially less.[1]

In the earliest appraisal of the information contained in the hearings, Henry Steele has recommended that:

Uncompromising measures, rigorously enforced, are indicated in order to halt, and in time remedy, the existing misallocation of resources in excessive selling efforts, duplicative research and product development programs, and exceptionally high profit levels—all of which are characteristic of the industry and much of which is paid for by individuals who can ill afford to do so.[2]

The purpose of this study is to estimate the benefits and the costs which might be expected to result from the removal, or redistribution, of market power in the industry. The principal sources of market power are the peculiar protection enjoyed by drug manufacturers because of the brand names used in the ethical drug industry and the provision of patent protection for the more recently introduced drugs. Brand names and patent protection permit firms to charge prices which are very much higher than the prices that would exist in the absence of market power. The benefits of a public policy that removed those sources of market power in the drug industry would be the reduction of price levels and, under the assumption of price inelasticity of demand in the industry, the reduction of aggregate expenditures by the public for approximately the same basket of goods. The major cost of a public policy arises from the possibility that the removal of a significant degree of market power might impair the willingness or the capacity of the industry to engage in research, and thus might reduce the flow of useful discoveries from the industry.

The structure of the ethical drug industry

The drug industry is customarily classified into two sectors: the ethical drug industry, which can be subdivided into prescribed drugs and over-the-counter drugs; and the proprietary drug industry. Prescribed drugs are those which require a physician's prescription before they can be purchased by the consumer. Since the power of deciding which, if any, drug the patient may purchase resides with the physician, producers of ethical drugs promote their products to doctors, not to the general public. Over-the-counter drugs (e.g., some specialized vitamin preparations and some specialized antacid preparations for the treatment of gastro-intestinal disorders) are considered to be safe for self-medication when the consumer follows the directions that accompany the product, and hence may be purchased without a prescription. These drugs, however, are typically therapeutic agents for conditions requiring the supervision of a physician, and thus they too are promoted only to the physician.* While the patient may purchase over-the-counter drugs on his own initiative, he usually learns of and purchases these drugs only on the advice of a physician. Moreover, in recommending a particular over-the-counter drug, the physician may write the name of the drug on a prescription blank, leading the consumer to regard the drug as one requiring a prescription.

Proprietary drugs (for example, aspirin) are those which the Food and Drug Administration has judged to be safe for self-medication by the consumer when the directions accompanying the product are adhered to. Like over-the-counter drugs proprietary drugs can be purchased without a prescription, but, unlike over-the-counter drugs, proprietary drugs are advertised intensively to the general public. The proprietary segment of the drug industry is quite different from the ethical segment. The use of brand names and the existence of patents are not so important as structural determinants in the proprietary industry as they are in the ethical drug industry, and the question of equity is not a significant issue in the

* Since over-the-counter drugs comprise a very small proportion of the ethical drug industry, the term "ethical drugs" will hereafter be used to refer both to prescribed drugs and over-the-counter drugs.

proprietary-drug industry. The possible public policies of removing brand names and removing patents* are not particularly relevant for improving market performance in the proprietary drug industry, and this segment of the drug industry will not be dealt with further.

It is estimated that the ethical drug industry consists of approximately 520 firms.† For the purpose of the present study, the 33 largest firms in the ethical drug industry are defined to be "large firms." The selection of 33 firms to comprise the "majors" in the industry was forced by the way in which much of the information in the Senate hearings was presented. It would have been preferable to have data on approximately the 20 largest firms, but this was not possible. The characteristics of the large firms are: (a) sales greater than $10 million in 1959; (b) intensive promotion of their products to physicians; and (c) an announced preoccupation with research and development. These characteristics—although they do not provide a dichotomy between the "large firms" and other firms in the industry—are much more descriptive of the large firms than of the others. A profile of the operations of the large firms is provided by Table I-1 showing the proportional allocation of total revenues to various activities. It will be noted here that the percent of expenditure on research and development is substantially lower than that on selling.

* These two policies and the policy of removing both brand names and patents are those that will be considered in this study.

† The Pharmaceutical Manufacturers Association states that there are "approximately 700 firms" and the Census of Manufactures for 1958 reports 110 firms in S.I.C. group 2831 (Biological Products), 120 firms in S.I.C. group 2833 (Medicinals and Botanicals), and 1,062 firms in S.I.C. group 2834 (Pharmaceutical Preparations). As the Census makes no distinction between ethical drugs and proprietary drugs, many of the firms identified by the Census would undoubtedly be proprietary firms. If the membership of the industry is taken to be the 141 firms which belonged to the Pharmaceutical Manufacturers Association in 1961, plus all other firms identified by examining each ethical drug and determining which firms produce it, as reported in *Drug Topics Red Book,* the total number of firms in the industry is estimated to be about 520. Data compiled from the following sources: Pharmaceutical Manufacturers Association, *Prescription Drug Industry Fact Book* (Washington, D.C., 1962), pt. 1, p. 2—hereafter cited as *Fact Book; Concentration Ratios in Manufacturing Industries: 1958* (Washington, D.C., 1963), pp. 132–33; *Drug Topics Red Book: 1962* (N.Y., 1961)—hereafter cited as *Red Book.*

The remaining firms in the industry are defined, within this study, to be "small firms." This group can be subdivided into two sub-groups: (a) "small firms selling their products under brand names" and (b) "small firms selling their products under generic names." The first group is taken to be all the members of the Pharmaceutical

I-1.   DISTRIBUTION OF 1958 SALES
DOLLAR FOR 22 LARGE FIRMS[a]
(Ethical drugs only)

	Percent of 1958 Sales Dollar
Cost of goods sold	32.1%
General and administrative	10.9
Selling	24.8
Research and development	6.3
Taxes	12.8
Net income	13.0
Total revenues	100.0

[a]U.S., Congress, Senate, Subcommittee on Anti-trust and Monopoly of the Committee on the Judiciary, *Report, Administered Prices: Drugs*, 87th Cong., 1st sess., 1961, S. Rept. 448, p. 31, Table 9.

Manufacturers Association which do not belong to the group of 33 large firms. In 1961, the Association had 141 members; thus the number of small firms selling under brand names is taken to be 108. They typically produce a few specialties which the firm promotes under its own brand names to the medical profession. These firms do engage in some research and development, but differ from the large firms in emphasizing development more than research.

We have been able to identify 379 "small firms selling under generic name."* Although these firms manufacture some of their

* The significance of the difference between brand names and generic names is treated in detail in Chapters II, III, and IV. For the present, consider the generic name to be equivalent to the chemical name of a drug, and the brand name to be an optionally assigned trademark for the drug.

own output, they generally purchase drugs in bulk form from the large firms and repack them in dosage form for sale to pharmacists, hospitals, and public agencies under generic names. This group of firms does not promote its products to physicians and does not engage in any significant amount of research and development. As will be explained in Chapter III, these firms are assumed to have no market power in the industry.

The difficulty of estimating the total sales of the ethical drug industry is that information about the small firms selling under generic names cannot be readily obtained.* The only available information seems to be that provided by the Food and Drug Administration on the sales in 1959 of 44 of the estimated 379 small firms. These 44 firms had total sales of $25.7 million, or mean sales of $585,000.[3] Multiplying the mean sales per firm by the total number of firms provides an estimate of the total sales of this group of firms in 1959 of $221.7 million.

The Pharmaceutical Manufacturers Association reports that in 1959 its member firms—large firms and small firms selling under brand names—had domestic sales of ethical drugs in final dosage form of $1,850 million, and corresponding sales in 1961 of $1,954 million.[4] This is an increase of 5.6 percent over the two-year period. If the sales of small firms selling drugs under generic names can be assumed to have grown at the same rate over the period, then the estimate of total sales for this group of firms in 1961 is $234.2 million. Total domestic sales of human ethical drugs in final dosage form for the industry in 1961 are estimated to have been $2,188 million.

The Pharmaceutical Manufacturers Association estimates that the 33 largest firms in the industry accounted for 80 percent of the industry's sales in 1961;[5] the sales of this group of firms are therefore estimated to have been $1,750 million. The remaining firms in the Association, small firms selling under brand names, are esti-

* The reader should understand that no data were available to the author for the dollar volume of the sales of individual drugs. Estimated sales of individual drugs are therefore projections of data for the sales of groups of drugs. Prices of individual drugs were known, however, and these prices are used extensively in estimating the effects of policies to reduce market power. The assumptions and procedures used in deriving these estimates are explained in the appendices at the back of the book.

mated to have had sales in 1961 of $204 million. In summary, the
sales of the different classes of firms in the industry are estimated
to have been distributed as shown in Table I-2.

I-2.   DISTRIBUTION OF 1961 DOMESTIC SALES OF
ETHICAL DRUGS BY CLASS OF FIRM

	Number of firms	Total sales in $ millions	Percentage of total sales
Large firms	33	$1,750	80.0%
Small firms selling under generic name	379	234	10.68
Small firms selling under brand name	108	204	9.32
Totals	520	$2,188	100.0%

The nature of the demand for ethical drugs

Under the present laws governing the dispensing of ethical drugs,
a consumer can enter a particular ethical drug market only after he
has received a physician's prescription for the drug. Once in possession of a prescription, the typical, though not inevitable, consumer response is to regard the consumption of the drug as essential
to his health and comfort, and possibly even imperative for the
maintenance of life itself. Thus, once a physician has prescribed a
drug, the preference structure of the patient may become such that
there is no possibility of substitution between the drug and any
other commodity; in such a case, the marginal utility derived from
the consumption of the required dosage of the drug approaches
infinity.

In writing a prescription, the physician almost invariably specifies
the quantity that the patient is to consume. Larger quantities consumed in the same period of time will, generally, confer no additional therapeutic benefits; in many cases, consumption of larger

quantities than those recommended would be harmful. The relationship between improved health and drug inputs is relatively rigid. In general, improvement in health cannot be shifted to a higher level or made to occur at a faster rate by an increased rate of drug consumption.

This implies that the patient is unlikely to purchase greater quantities of a particular drug if prices decline—even by substantial amounts. Given the restrictions upon consumer choice in the ethical drugs market, a decrease in the price of drugs is not in itself likely to increase the quantity demanded by bringing new consumers into the market. Thus, since price decreases are expected to have insignificant effects in the direction of increasing quantity demanded, the demand function for drugs is expected to be highly inelastic for price reductions.

Similarly, demand is expected to be highly price inelastic for price increases. A typical statement of this relationship is the following:

Since drugs are concerned with life and health it is not at all clear that members of society can make rational choices between drugs and other commodities or between various drugs. . . . A desperately ill man in need of a drug that may save his life or cure his unbearable pain is not likely to be in the mental frame of mind required for rational choice between the drug in question and alternative consumer goods on a price basis.[6]

In this case the argument rests upon the very high marginal disutility which the consumer will experience from foregoing consumption of the drug.

Much the same type of argument holds with respect to the influence of consumer income upon quantity demanded. Changes in income would be expected to have a negligible influence upon the demand for almost all drugs. The marginal utility derived from a prescribed drug will be higher than the marginal utility of expenditures on other goods and services for any level of income. Indeed, there are instances recorded in the Subcommittee hearings of persons from low-income groups who have gone without food for several days in order to purchase drugs. For a consumer to buy a drug which has been prescribed for him, it is sufficient, except in very rare cases, that he have enough money to make the purchase.*

Data relating the consumption of ethical drugs to the standard economic variables in a demand function are very sparse. What little information is available lends support to the hypothesis that quantity demanded is essentially independent of price and income. The Health Information Foundation and the National Opinion Research Centre of the University of Chicago conducted, in 1958, a joint survey of the utilization of medical services and facilities by 9,564 members of 2,941 families.[7] The results included data relating family expenditures on prescribed drugs to family income levels. This information can be used to estimate the income elasticity of demand for prescribed drugs. In Table I-3 the arc-elasticity measure of income elasticity of demand is computed between the mean family income for each successive pair of income groupings and the mean family expenditures on prescribed drugs for the corresponding ranges of income. The corresponding income elasticities for all medical expenditures are shown for comparison. Prescribed drug expenditures are seen to be highly inelastic in relation to income, and, with the exception of the highest income group, the inelasticity increases as income increases. The same relationship is observed for expenditures on all personal health services, although, as would be expected, the inelasticity is not so great here as it is for prescribed drugs.†

Standard economic theory suggests that the demand for drugs would be highly inelastic in relation to price and income, and the only available estimates of price and income elasticities do not indicate that this hypothesis should be rejected. It would therefore seem that family income is not significant in an explanation of drug expenditures.‡

* It may be that persons in higher income groups purchase more *different* drugs than do persons in lower income groups. The determining variable in this case, however, is that the former are more likely to visit a physician for any given complaint, and, as a result, receive a greater number of prescriptions.

† The amount of medical care received without cost or at reduced rates was treated as a proxy variable; this item is also statistically insignificant.

‡ Of additional interest here is the fact that the Commission on the Cost of Medical Care used the same data in investigating the demand for medical care and for its components. American Medical Association, *Report of the Commission on the Cost of Medical Care*, 4 vols. (Chicago, 1964), I: 55–57.

I-3. DISTRIBUTION OF FAMILY MEDICAL EXPENDITURES AND FAMILY DRUG EXPENDITURES IN 1958 ACCORDING TO LEVEL OF FAMILY INCOME[a]

Mean Family Income	Mean Gross Personal Health Expenditures per Family	Estimated Income Elasticity of Demand for Personal Health Expenditures	Mean Gross Personal Health Expenditures per Individual	Gross Health Expenditures as Percent of Family Income	Mean Gross Expenditures for Prescribed Drugs per Family	Estimated Income Elasticity of Demand for Prescribed Drugs	Mean Gross Expenditures for Non-Prescribed Drugs per Family	Non-Prescribed Drug Expenditures as Percent of Prescribed Drugs	Prescribed Drug Expenditures as Percent of Gross Health Expenditures	Prescribed Drug Expenditures as Percent of Family Income
All groups ($5,346)	$294		$ 94	5.5%	$40		$20	50.0%	13.6%	0.75%
Under $2,000 ($1,269)	$165	.156	$ 75	13.0%	$30		$12	40.0%	18.2%	2.37%
$2,000-$3,499 ($2,690)	$226	.199	$ 80	8.4%	$35	.077	$17	48.6%	15.5%	1.30%
$3,500-$4,999 ($4,484)	$287	.079	$ 88	6.4%	$40	.067	$18	45.0%	13.9%	0.89%
$5,000-$7,499 ($6,222)	$336	.100	$ 95	5.4%	$41	.012	$21	51.2%	12.2%	0.66%
$7,500 and over ($10,538)	$411		$119	3.9%	$52	.118	$27	51.9%	12.7%	0.50%

[a]Odin W. Anderson et al., *Changes in Family Medical Expenditures and Voluntary Health Insurance: A Five Year Resurvey* (Cambridge, Mass., 1963), pp. 39-56.

Purpose of the study

The ethical drug industry may safely be characterized as one which has been, since the end of World War II, highly progressive. On most indices of research-and-development effort, the industry ranks at or near the top. The medical significance of many of the new products that have come from the industry in the past twenty years is certainly obvious. On the other hand, the large firms in the drug industry appear to possess very considerable amounts of market power. As a group, they have earned profits which are much above the level of "all manufacturing," and they have been able to maintain these profit levels over long periods of time. For products which are at least nominally identical, the large firms are able to charge prices which are approximately twice as great as the prices charged by small firms. Thus, although the industry appears to be progressive, its performance seems to be unsatisfactory otherwise.

If the demand for drugs is perfectly inelastic in relation to income and price, there can be no criticism that the industry allocates resources inefficiently, in the rigorous use of the term. Nevertheless, there may still exist "oligopolistic wastes" in the form of excessive promotion and selling effort. A policy which imposed price competition on the industry could eliminate these wastes; and if vigorous price competition in the industry eliminated the permanent excess profits in the industry, such a policy would redistribute income from stockholders to consumers.

It has been a popular hypothesis that some degree of market power must be accepted as the price of progressive results from an industry. The purpose of this study is to compare the ramifications of market imperfections in the ethical drug industry with the progressive results. Would it be possible to improve the performance of the industry without, at the same time, impairing its incentive or capacity to engage in research? If so, what is the approximate amount of "excess" monopoly power in the industry? If not, is there some combination of policies to remove market power and restore incentives which could result in a net social gain? This study seeks to provide answers to these questions.

Chapter III is a discussion of the determinants of the industry's structure. It is concluded that market power in the drug industry arises principally from two sources. The first of these sources is the power vested in the physician to select not only the particular drug which a consumer may purchase but also the manufacturer of the drug. Once the physician has specified a particular firm, either explicitly or implicitly (by the use of a brand name unique to the firm), then under the provisions of the state laws governing "substitution" of drugs, neither the consumer nor the pharmacist may select the product of any other manufacturer of the same drug. Each large firm mounts a substantial promotional effort designed to induce the physician to prescribe its particular brand of a drug. The second source of market power is the existence of patents on most of the recently introduced drugs.

Appropriate public policies to reduce market power appear to be those which would eliminate the sources of market power. Three such policies are considered. The first is a policy which would remove the restrictions upon the consumer's freedom to select the manufacturer of a prescribed drug. It is convenient to refer to this policy as "the removal of brand names." It should be understood, however, that this is simply the name of the policy; the policy itself would guarantee consumers that the products of all sellers of a given drug were therapeutically acceptable, and would permit the consumer to select the manufacturer of a drug prescribed for him. The policy would thus remove the incentive and the power of the physician to specify the seller. The second policy is one which would remove patent protection on drugs. The third policy would combine the first two policies.

The assessment of market power requires an examination of the issue of whether observed price differences among drugs that are nominally identical reflect corresponding quality differences in the product. This issue is discussed in Chapter IV, where it is concluded that there is no convincing evidence to support the claims (a) that firms selling at lower prices are selling an inferior product or (b) that firms selling at higher prices are selling a superior product.

Chapter V discusses variations in prices charged by different types of firms for the same drug. Descriptive measures of these price relationships are used to determine which characteristics of a drug are important for the estimation of the effects of a particular policy, and the values obtained are used as parameters in the models that have been set up to represent the policies considered.

Chapter VI is the core of the study. Here the consequences of each policy are studied, and in the related appendices estimates are made of the effects of each policy upon the sales of each type of firm. Subsequently, estimates of the effects of the policies upon various types of drugs are made. The principal conclusions of this chapter are that the removal of brand names would reduce the annual sales of the industry by $228 million, that the removal of patent protection would reduce annual sales by $274 million, and that the removal of both brand names and patent protection together would reduce the annual sales by $617 million.

Chapter VII is a brief discussion of the probable reactions of retail pharmacists to the introduction of each of the policies, and of the probable effect of the reduction in manufacturers' sales upon the consumer.

Descriptive material on the research-and-development effort of the industry is presented in Chapter VIII. It is concluded that the industry's investment in research and development has been socially productive and that continuation of this type of research is highly desirable.

In Chapter IX estimates are made of how the industry might be expected to adjust its operations to each of the policies. It is concluded that although the removal of brand names would not impair the incentives or the capacity of the large firms to engage in research and development, the removal of patents, either alone or in combination with brand names, would probably do so. Thus, if either of the second or third policies were introduced, alternative means of financing research and development would have to be developed. If the alternative is a government subsidy for the performance of research, the net benefits resulting from the introduction of the removal of brand names is estimated to be $228 million annually, the net benefit from the removal of patents to be $82 million annually, and the net benefit of the removal of both together to be $425 million annually. It is concluded that there are public policies which could significantly improve the performance of the industry and that these policies could yield a significant net social benefit.

CHAPTER TWO

Description of the Data

The discussion of the static allocative efficiency of the industry is based upon price relationships observed to exist among various types of firms in 1961. This year was chosen as the period for which data would be collected as it appeared to be the year for which the greatest amount of supporting information was available. The price data were obtained for drugs that met the following criteria:

1) The drug was in normal commercial use in 1961—in other words, was available through the usual industry channels and was not used solely for the purpose of investigation or experimentation. At one extreme, the list contains drugs which, in 1961, had only very recently passed from the experimental stage, and, at the other extreme, those which have been available since the beginning of rational therapeutics.

2) Only drugs which are single chemical entities are considered. Ethical medications which are combinations of drugs, considered themselves to be single chemical entities are not included. Combinations were excluded because the number of instances in which two firms produce combinations for which prices could be meaningfully compared is quite low; and the effort required to collect the data would not have been justified by the small amount of usable information that would have been obtained.

3) Single chemical entities which are radioactive materials or which are used exclusively for diagnostic purposes are not included. Radioactive drugs are excluded on the following grounds: This segment of the industry is subject, to some extent, to the regulation of the Atomic Energy Commission; the number of firms operating in this area is limited, and there appear to be no small firms; and, price information concerning these drugs is incomplete. Diagnostics were excluded because they constitute a different market from therapeutic or immunological drugs and because many diagnostics are radioactive.

4) Drugs which were introduced into commercial use in 1961 were excluded. With the available sources of information, data concerning these drugs would have been incomplete.*

5) Only drugs produced for human consumption were considered; all veterinary preparations were excluded.

Subject to the restrictions just noted, drugs listed in any of the following reference sources were included:

a) *New and Nonofficial Drugs: 1962*

Council on Drugs of the American Medical Association, *New and Nonofficial Drugs: 1962* (Philadelphia: J. B. Lippincott Co., 1962). This reference gives an evaluation of each drug "proposed for use in or on the human body for the diagnosis, prevention or treatment of disease, whether or not their usefulness has been established." Inclusion in this compendium is ". . . limited to individual drugs generally available in the United States which have not been included in [official compendia of drugs] for a prior cumulative period of more than twenty years."

b) *Review of Drugs: 1941–1961*

Pharmaceutical Manufacturers Association, *Review of Drugs, 1941–1961: Single Chemical Entities Introduced in the United*

---

* Throughout the study the term "1961 sales" is used although drugs introduced in 1961 have been excluded. This term should be understood to mean the basket of goods available at the beginning of 1961 evaluated at the prices prevailing in the middle of 1961.

States (Washington, D.C.: Pharmaceutical Manufacturers Association, 1962). Listing presents major products from 1941–1948; from 1949 through 1961 all products marketed have been included.

c) Two standard textbooks on pharmacology:

Harry Beckman, *Pharmacology: The Nature, Action and Uses of Drugs* (second edition; Philadelphia: W. B. Saunders Co., 1961).

Arthur Grollman, *Pharmacology and Therapeutics* (fifth edition; Philadelphia: Lea & Febiger, 1962).

Ultimately 656 drugs were included in the study, and the majority of the drugs were listed in all sources. The textbooks listed those which had been available for more than twenty years, which were official (i.e., recognized by the *U. S. Pharmacopeia,* the *National Formulary,* or *Accepted Dental Remedies*), and which were probably well known to practicing physicians. The other two sources ("a" and "b") did not always list the same drugs, and included some that had only recently become available and whose merit was not sufficiently well established to warrant their inclusion in a standard textbook.

Information concerning 1961 prices was obtained for each drug from *Drug Topics Red Book: 1962,* the standard price catalogue of the retail drug trade. The mean and the variance of the prices charged to the retail pharmacist by each of four classifications (to be explained in the next chapter) of manufacturing firm were computed for each drug. Most drugs are sold under a variety of sizes and dosage forms. Prices were therefore obtained for the one size and dosage form which yielded the largest number of observations. Thus, if more firms sold a particular drug in the form of 50-mg. uncoated tablets in bottles of 1,000 tablets than in any other form, data were obtained for only this dosage and size. The reader should understand that prices have been collected only for formally homogeneous entities; prices for capsules and tablets have not been mixed together, and variations such as enteric coatings or sustained release preparations have not been included with unadorned preparations.

Generic names and brand names

Most drugs are chemically synthesized substances and have chemical names to identify them. The substances and names are often complex. Consider the following:

a) 10–(3–Dimethylaminopropyl) phenothiazine hydrochloride;
b) 5–Acetylaminor–4 methyl–Δ^2–1,3,4–thiadiazoline–2–sulfon-amide;
c) 4–Dimethylamino–1,4,4a,5,5a,6,11,12a–octahydro–3,6,10, 12,12a–pentahydroxy–6–methyl–1,11–dioxo–2–naphthacenccar-boxamide hydrochloride.

It is hardly surprising that a supplementary terminology has been developed for the identification of drugs. Instead of being referred to by their chemical names, drugs are referred to by their generic names. The generic names of the above drugs are: (a) promazine hydrochloride; (b) methazolamide; (c) tetracycline hydrochloride. When a chemical substance is discovered to have some useful pharmaceutical properties, the discoverer assigns a generic name to it.[1] If this substance becomes an accepted drug, firms (assuming that no patents exist) may produce the drug and sell it as a substance to be identified only by its generic name. If a physician prescribes this drug by writing its generic name upon a prescription blank, a firm takes its chances that the pharmacist will select its product rather than that of some other firm in filling the prescription. A firm may, however, assign a trademark or brand name to the substance. For example, the brand names used by the firms selling tetracycline are: Achromycin (Lederle); Panmycin (Upjohn); Polycycline (Bristol); Steclin (Squibb); and Tetrabon (Pfizer). The significance of brand names is that they have a legal status provided by the anti-substitution laws which govern the dispensing of prescriptions in almost all states. If, in prescribing tetracycline, the doctor uses a brand name on the prescription blank, then the pharmacist may not legally fill the prescription with any drug other than the product of the manufacturer using the brand name specified in the prescription. It does not matter that there are other manufacturers selling the drug under other brand names or that there may be still other firms selling the drug under its generic name; to substitute the product of these other manufacturers for the product of the manufacturer using the brand name in question is a violation of the anti-substitution laws for which the pharmacist may lose his license. Accordingly, if a firm markets a drug using a brand name, and can induce the physician to specify the drug by using that name, the firm becomes a monopolist in respect to the filling of that prescription.

A large firm may sell a particular drug under a brand name, or it may decline to assign a brand name and choose to sell the drug under its generic name. Small firms have been classified into two groups: (a) those which sell all of their output under generic names, and (b) those which sell all of their output under brand names.* With respect to a particular drug, each selling firm will fall into one, and only one, of the following classifications of "firm types":

    1) Small firm selling the drug under its generic name;
    2) Small firm selling the drug under a brand name;
    3) Large firm selling the drug under its generic name;
    4) Large firm selling the drug under a brand name.

If a drug is sold by only one firm, there will be only one type of firm selling the drug; if a drug is sold by four or more firms, then it is possible that all four types of firm will be selling the drug. Notice that for large firms, this classification does not provide a once-and-for-all classification of a firm with respect to all drugs; it merely classifies the firm with respect to one particular drug.

If a firm is the only seller of a drug, then that firm is a monopolist in the market for that drug. (From the viewpoint of the consumer, this is pure monopoly, since the consumer can purchase only the drug specified in the prescription. From the viewpoint of the prescribing physician, the situation may or may not represent pure monopoly. If there are no other drugs which are close substitutes for the drug in question, the firm is a pure monopolist; if there are many other drugs which are close substitutes, the firm is only one of many monopolistic competitors.)

A drug may be sold by more than one firm; in this case, the firms may be all of the same type or they may be of different types. Each

* It should be added here that small firms sell under one or the other, never both.

drug will fall into one, and only one, of the following "market structures":

1) A market in which the drug is sold by only one firm;
2) A market in which the drug is sold by more than one firm, all the firms being of the same type;
3) A market in which the drug is sold by more than one type of firm.

Table III–3, on p. 32, classifies the 656 drugs according to the market type into which each drug falls and according to the types of firm which sell each drug. The entries in the table represent the number of drugs falling into each cross-classification. The first percentage figure in each cell is the percentage of the column total (total number of drugs sold by each type of firm) represented by the cell entry. For example, of the 157 drugs sold by small firms selling under brand names, 51 drugs, or 32.5 percent, were sold in markets in which there was only one firm. Similarly, of the 450 drugs sold under brand names by large firms, 133 drugs, or 29.6 percent, were sold in markets in which there was at least one other type of firm. The second percentage figure in each cell is the percentage of the row total (total number of drugs sold under each market structure) represented by the cell entry. (In the case of drugs sold by more than one type of firm, each drug will be counted in at least two columns; therefore, the total of cell entries will not equal the total for the row, and the percentage figures will not add to 100.) For example, of 377 drugs sold by only one type of firm, 51 drugs, or 13.5 percent, were sold by a small firm under a brand name. Similarly of the 227 drugs which were sold by more than one type of firm, 133 drugs, or 58.6 percent, were sold by large firms using a brand name.

The classification of drugs by type of drug

Each drug is classified into one, and only one, of forty different categories, or minor groups, which indicate the general usage of the drug. From a therapeutic viewpoint, drugs classified into the same minor group are, to some extent, substitutes for one another. Because of the subsequent cross-classification of drugs on the basis of type and some other attribute, it is not possible to use the minor groups for analytical purposes because the number of drugs in each cell of the cross-classification would be too small. Some aggregation of the minor groups is necessary if the data are to be presented and discussed with any generality. These forty minor groups are therefore classified into twelve major groups. Eleven of the major groups represent collections of drugs with the same general type of action (for example, anti-infectives), or which have their principal effect upon a particular system (for example, drugs affecting the central nervous system). The remaining major group includes minor groups which cannot be meaningfully classified in any other major group.

Table II-1 identifies the minor and major groups and shows the number of drugs falling into each group. Each group is assigned a two- or three-digit number, and, hereafter, drug types are referred to only by this number. (See Appendix B, pp. 169–78, for an analysis of the sales of drugs by type and estimates of the effect on sales, by drug type, of each of three policies—removal of brand names, patents, and both brand names and patents.)

Drugs can also be classified according to the way in which they are administered. In this classification each drug is put into one, and only one, of the following categories: (a) orally administered drugs; (b) parenterally administered drugs—injectables; (c) immunological serums (which are included in this group regardless of the method of administration); and (d) bulk drugs, i.e., drugs which are supplied to the pharmacist in bulk form and which he then compounds into a dosage form. These four groupings are of interest because they tend to identify the type of purchaser who is likely to buy the drug. Consider only drugs which are administered outside a hospital. Parenterally administered drugs are usually purchased by the physician from the pharmacist or drug wholesaler, and are subsequently administered—resold—to the patient by the physician. The term "parenteral" may be misleading; what is actually classified under this heading are drugs which the physician, rather than the patient, would purchase. Thus, general and local anaesthetics, whether or not they are actually administered parenterally, are classified as parenterals because the patient is unlikely to purchase them directly. Drugs which are classified as orally administered drugs are those which the patient is likely to purchase directly from the pharmacist. This classification includes, there-

Type of drug by
numerical symbol   *Number of drugs in use in 1961*

10	Drugs affecting the blood and blood-forming organs		
	Hematinics	9	
	Anticoagulants	14	
	Hemostatics	7	
	Miscellaneous agents	8	
		38	38
20	Drugs affecting the heart		
	Stimulants of cardiac muscle	9	
	Depressants of cardiac muscle	4	
	Coronary disease vasodilators	18	
		31	31
30	Drugs affecting the blood vessels		
	Vasodilators in hypertension	16	
	Vasodilators in peripheral vascular disease	9	
	Miscellaneous agents	8	
		33	33
40	Drugs affecting the central nervous system		
	Analgesics	26	
	Sedatives and hypnotics	28	
	Analeptics	44	
	Anticonvulsants	12	
	General anesthetics	11	
	Local anesthetics	23	
	Miscellaneous agents	17	
		161	161
50	Drugs affecting the autonomic nervous system		
	Parasympathomimetic agents and cholinesterase inhibitors	11	
	Cholinergic blocking agents	24	
	Sympathomimetic agents	28	
		63	63
			326

Type of drug by numerical symbol		Number of drugs in use in 1961	
60	Drugs affecting the kidneys		
	Diuretics and uricosurics	27	27
70	Drugs affecting the gastro-intestinal system		
	Antacids	9	
	Miscellaneous agents	8	
		17	17
80	Anti-infective agents		
	Antibiotics	41	
	Chemotherapeutic agents	54	
	Miscellaneous agents	12	
		107	107
90	Agents for constituent replacement		
	Enzymes	7	
	Hormones	63	
	Insulin	8	
	Vitamins	14	
		92	92
100	Antihistamines		
	Antihistamines	28	28
110	Skeletal muscle stimulants and depressants		
	Skeletal muscle depressants	15	
	Agents affecting uterine muscle	5	
	Miscellaneous agents	2	
		22	22
120	Miscellaneous agents		
	Gold preparations	4	
	Thyroid depressants	5	
	Anti-neoplastic agents	8	
	Agents affecting pupil size and visual accommodation	3	
	Agents affecting idiopathic dermatoses	4	
	Immunologic agents	13	
		37	37

$$326 + 330 = 656$$

fore, not only drugs in the form of tablets and capsules, but also ointments, eye drops, etc. What distinguishes the immunological serums is that each batch must be certified by the Public Health Service before it can be marketed. They differ in this respect from drugs that are subject to the jurisdiction of the Food and Drug Administration. Apart from a small group of drugs referred to as "certifiable antibiotics," the Food and Drug Administration does not inspect each batch of drugs. Drugs classified as bulk drugs are those for which the pharmacist prepares the dosage form.

Classification of drugs by year of introduction

A detailed classification of drugs by the year of introduction (the year in which any given drug was made available for sale and consumption) is set forth in Appendix C, pp. 179–92. For the purposes of the present discussion, it will be sufficient to observe that the duration of patent protection is seventeen years and that the year 1944 marks the limit of patent protection. The significance of the year is, of course, that it enables us to distinguish between those drugs which, having been introduced after 1944, are probably still protected by patents and those which, having been introduced before 1944, are probably not.

CHAPTER THREE

Market Power in the Ethical Drug Industry

The possession of market power by a firm in a particular market means that the firm "can behave in a manner different from the behavior that a competitive market would enforce on a firm facing similar cost and demand considerations."[1] The most pointed evidence that large firms in the drug industry possess market power is that, for products which are therapeutically homogeneous, they are able to charge higher prices than those charged by smaller firms.* As an example, consider the drug "reserpine," which CIBA introduced into clinical practice in 1953. (Although the firm received a patent for the drug, it chose to license other firms to produce the drug.) Table III-1 exhibits the prices charged by the types of firm which produced the drug in 1961.

---

* Since only single chemical entities are considered, the only way in which the products of competing sellers could fail to be therapeutically homogeneous is through the existence of quality differentials. The contention that products of competing sellers are therapeutically homogeneous is very important; if the products do not have this characteristic, and if higher quality is found to be associated with higher prices, then it can be argued that the first requires the second. The question of homogeneity is sufficiently critical to deserve a separate chapter and is considered in detail in Chapter IV. For the present, the argument proceeds as though the conclusions of that chapter—that the products are homogeneous—have been established.

The mean price charged by the five large firms which sold reserpine under their own brand names is 6.35 times greater than the mean price charged by the 72 small firms which sold the same

III-1.   MEAN PRICES CHARGED IN 1961 FOR 1,000 TABLETS
          OF RESERPINE ACCORDING TO TYPE OF FIRM
              (One tablet = 0.25 mg.)

Type of firm	Number of firms selling in dosage form[a]	Mean price charged by type of firm
Small firm Generic name	72	$5.661
Small firm Brand name	20	14.893
Large firm Generic name	0	—
Large firm Brand name	5	35.960

[a]Note that the number of firms refers only to the number of firms selling the particular dosage form. Some firms not included in these figures sell the drug in other dosage forms, such as 0.1 mg. Reserpine was not produced by any large firm which sold the drug under its generic name.

quantity of the same drug under its generic name. Further, not all the prices charged by small firms selling the drug under its generic name are the same; several firms sold the drug at a price of $1.50, the minimum observed price. If the mean price charged by large firms selling the drug under brand names is compared to the minimum price charged by small firms selling under the generic name, the price charged by the former type of firm is seen to be approximately 24 times greater.

On the whole, for drugs which are sold both by large firms selling the drug under brand names and by small firms selling the drug under generic names, the former charge a price 2.14 times greater than the latter for the same quantity of the same drug. (This finding is also taken up in detail in Chapter V.)

The second indication of market power in the pharmaceutical industry is the persistence of excess profits. Data concerning profits

III-2.   MEDIAN RATES OF RETURN ON INVESTED CAPITAL
FOR SELECTED INDUSTRIES (MEMBERSHIP IN INDUSTRIES IS
RESTRICTED TO FIRMS IN THE LARGEST 500)[a]

Industry	1964	1963	1962	1961	1960
	%	%	%	%	%
Pharmaceuticals	16.3	14.7	14.4	15.8	15.5
Soap and cosmetics	14.7	14.8	16.2	15.5	15.8
Tobacco	12.3	13.1	13.1	11.4	11.7
Aircraft and parts	11.8	10.1	11.1	11.6	11.0
Motor vehicles and parts	12.5	11.1	10.7	7.2	9.0
Appliances and electronics	11.9	9.7	9.9	8.8	10.3
Glass, cement, etc.	10.5	9.1	9.7	9.8	10.2
Mining	11.8	9.6	9.6	9.3	9.4
Rubber	10.6	9.0	9.6	10.7	10.4
Chemicals	12.1	10.2	9.5	8.3	9.9
Lumber and wood[b]	—	11.5	9.2	5.6	6.4
Publishing and printing	12.6	11.8	9.0	9.2	9.5
Machinery[b]	—	9.0	8.8	8.6	8.8
Petroleum refining	9.0	9.5	8.5	8.4	8.6
Food and beverages	9.8	8.8	8.4	8.5	8.9
Paper and allied products[b]	9.6	7.6	8.0	7.1	8.4
Apparel	11.0	9.8	7.4	8.8	9.1
Metal products	9.6	7.8	7.4	6.9	6.1
Textiles	8.6	6.8	7.1	6.1	8.3
Metal manufacturing	9.1	7.5	6.5	6.7	6.6
Shipbuilding and railroad equipment	9.4	6.7	4.0	6.7	6.6
All Industry (Median for 500 largest firms)	10.5	9.1	8.9	8.3	9.1
Ratio of pharmaceuticals to all industry	1.55	1.62	1.62	1.90	1.71

[a]"The Fortune Directory: The 500 Largest U.S. Industrial Corporations," *Fortune Magazine,* 1960-65.

[b]"Lumber and wood" and "Machinery" classifications were discontinued in 1964; the former is grouped in "Paper and wood products."

in the ethical drug industry are less than completely satisfactory because all published sources of data group together ethical drugs and proprietary drugs. Further, to the extent that firms which are primarily pharmaceutical firms engage in non-drug operations, profits from these activities will be included in overall profits.†

The *Fortune* annual survey of the 500 largest industrial firms has, since 1960, presented a summary of financial returns for the firms in the pharmaceutical industry. A comparison of the pharmaceutical industry with other industries during the period 1960–64 is shown in Table III–2 (p. 27). During this period, the median rate of return in the pharmaceutical industry was never less than the second highest and in two of the five years it was the highest. In none of the five years was the median rate of return in the pharmaceutical industry less than 1.55 times greater than the median rate of return for all firms in the survey.

The First National City Bank of New York publishes, annually, data on the rate of return on net assets for approximately 45 industries. This information is obtained from annual reports and thus relates to domestic, publicly owned companies. In the period 1956–63, the pharmaceutical industry was never less than the second most profitable and in six of the eight years was the most profitable. During these years, the mean rate of return for pharmaceutical firms included in the survey was not less than 1.62 times greater than the mean rate of return for all manufacturing firms in the survey.

Since the second quarter of 1956, the Federal Trade Commission and the Securities and Exchange Commission have published quarterly data for rates of profit (after taxes) on shareholders'

† For two reasons, this is probably not a serious problem. First, in the 1958 Census of Manufactures the specialization ratio for the primary product was given as 0.88 (and the coverage ratio 0.94) for the industry identified with preparation of pharmaceuticals (industry code 2834). More significantly, the pharmaceutical industry has typically had profit rates which are higher than any other industry. If a pharmaceutical firm is diversified, the profits from activities not directly related to the manufacturing of drugs as such would probably reduce the firm's average rate of return. Complete separation of pharmaceutical manufacturing from other activities (for example, toiletries, proprietary preparations, and chemicals) would probably—in the case of a diversified firm–show profit rates higher than those observed for firms whose primary but not exclusive interest is drugs.

equity in the drugs-and-medicines industry (Standard Industrial Classification 283). In the period beginning with the second quarter of 1956 and ending with the fourth quarter of 1964, the median ratio of profit rates in the pharmaceutical industry to profit rates in all manufacturing industries was 1.72. Individual values of this ratio ranged from 1.27 to 2.76.

Factors in market power

Market power in the ethical drug industry is attributable to the lack of consumer choice, to the established preferences of physicians for large firms, and to barriers that prevent entry into the submarkets occupied by large firms that result from the scale of selling activities and the degree of resource control conferred by patents. These factors are now taken up in turn.

The position of the consumer

A unique feature of the ethical drug industry is the almost complete absence of consumer sovereignty. Drugs designated by the Food and Drug Administration as "bearing the prescription legend" (or, stronger still, as "bearing the narcotic legend") require a physician's authority for their purchase. Once in possession of this authority—a prescription—the consumer is restricted to the particular drug which the physician has specified, even though there may be other drugs with identical therapeutic properties. If the physician has identified the manufacturer, either explicitly or implicitly, by the use of a brand name unique to the firm, the consumer's latitude is further restricted to the specified firm by state laws on substitution. The consumer does not have the usual option, available to him in other markets, of buying close substitutes.

Nor, in most cases, does the consumer have the other usual option—that of remaining out of the market. If the drug is essential to the patient's continued good health, then the consumption of the drug confers more satisfaction than any other purchase that he could make. But, even if the drug is not essential—and the patient may be unable to judge this—remaining out of the market means that he may derive no benefit from the investment he has made by consulting a physician. For the most part, the consumer purchases a drug if, and only if, he has a prescription. Price plays a very small role in his decision to enter the market, and none at all in his selection of the particular drug.

The occasions on which the consumer does have some choice in the selection of the manufacturer require the following conditions: (1) The doctor must not specify the firm; instead, he must use the generic name of the drug in writing his prescription; (2) there must be more than one seller of the drug; and (3) the consumer must know under what conditions (i.e., *1* and *2*) he has a choice of manufacturer. For the choice to be meaningful, the various sellers in the market must not charge a single price, and the consumer must have sufficient familiarity with the market to know what prices are available.

It is unlikely that consumers are able to recognize very many of the occasions on which they have a choice of seller. Apart from the comments which could be made about the legibility of the average physician's handwriting, consumers are not well versed in the various brand and generic names. If the consumer fails to recognize an opportunity to choose the seller, the option to choose the seller passes, by default, to the pharmacist. There is little reason to expect that the pharmacist will exercise a choice in the best interests of the consumer: the consumer wishes to minimize his expense; the pharmacist wishes to maximize his profit. Since the pharmacist typically prices his products by adding a fixed percentage mark-up to the cost of goods sold, the higher the cost of the drug to him, the greater the gross income he will derive from its sale. (There are undoubtedly occasions when the opportunity of choosing the seller permits the pharmacist to dispose of a lower-priced product which, he predicts, he would otherwise have trouble selling.) On most occasions, if the patient has an opportunity to choose the firm, but does not take advantage of the opportunity, he pays no less than he would have if the physician had prescribed a product sold under a brand name by a large firm.

When the consumer is restricted by the doctor's prescription to the product of a specified firm, he may still take his prescription from one pharmacy to another, requesting price quotations; but even in states where drugs are not covered by "fair trade" laws, the bids will probably not be significantly different. The large numbers of drugs and brands of drugs carried by the pharmacist make any sort of independent price policy difficult. As a result, the pharmacist typically determines his price for a particular product by looking up the cost of the drug to him in a price catalogue and adding a percentage mark-up to this cost. As the price catalogue is standard in the retail drug trade and as the mark-up tends to be standard, at least within a geographical area, the patient will receive quite similar price quotations. Also, price competition among individual pharmacists comes under the strongest condemnation by other pharmacists and by the state associations.

The consumer's position in the market is likely to be one of passivity. For the most part, he is deprived of any choice other than that of canvassing the retail sellers. Since retail sellers are likely to quote similar prices, the marginal cost of obtaining an additional bid is likely to be greater than the expected benefit of the bid, and, after several experiences of this type, the consumer will probably discontinue his shopping.

The role of the physician

The physician acts as a consultant to and purchasing agent for the patient. In his former capacity, the physician decides upon the appropriate drug; in his latter capacity, he may decide which of the firms selling the drug will be selected to fill the prescription. There are many drugs for which there is no choice of manufacturer; of the 656 drugs that make up the drug "population" referred to in this study, 57.5 percent are produced by only one firm (Table III-3, p. 32). However, in the remaining cases, where there is a choice of firm and the physician could, therefore, pass the option of making the choice along to the consumer, he rarely does so. There are several possible reasons for this behavior.

The physician is generally not well informed about the price of drugs and thinks that the patient would derive no significant economic benefit from exercising the option of selecting the firm. The professional sources of information about drugs, such as journal articles and *New and Nonofficial Drugs,* make no mention of drug prices, although the former source may, on the rarest of occasions, refer to the drug as being "expensive." The doctor's immediate source of information in a prescribing situation is the *Physician's Desk Reference*[2]—a compendium of entries that is prepared and

III-3. CLASSIFICATION OF NUMBER OF DRUGS ACCORDING TO THE NUMBER OF SELLING FIRMS, SIZE
OF SELLING FIRM, AND USE OF BRAND OR GENERIC NAME IN SELLING

	Small Firm Generic Name	Small Firm Brand Name	Large Firm Generic Name	Large Firm Brand Name	Total
Drug produced by only one firm	15 6.61%[a] 3.98%[b]	51 32.48% 13.53%	18 13.04% 4.78%	293 65.11% 77.72%	377 57.47%
Drug produced by only one type of firm but by more than one firm	18 7.93% 34.31%	6 3.82% 11.54%	4 2.90% 7.69%	24 5.33% 46.15%	52 7.93%
Drug produced by more than one type of firm	194 85.46% 85.46%	100 63.69% 44.05%	116 84.06% 51.10%	133 29.56% 58.59%	227 34.60%
Total number of drugs produced by type of firm	227	157	138	450	656
Percent of all drugs produced by type of firm	34.60%	23.93%	21.04%	68.59%	100.00%

[a]This figure indicates that the number of drugs produced by only one firm is 6.61 percent of the total number of drugs produced by small firms (227) selling under generic names.

[b]Means that the number of drugs produced by only one firm is 3.98 percent of all the drugs (377) produced by only one firm.

32

financed mainly by the large firms. (The small firms which sell drugs under their generic names are not represented in this manual.) In their entries in the *Physician's Desk Reference,* the large firms make no mention of the cost of their drugs. Sales representatives are apparently instructed not to volunteer information about prices. The small firms, whose principal appeal to the doctor would be price, generally do not employ salesmen to visit doctors; in the rare cases where they do, these salesmen have difficulty in gaining access to the physician. The small firms may resort to direct-mail techniques to advise the physician of their relatively low prices, but here they must compete with the enormous volume of material which the large firms send out. Small firms appear to be inhibited from making direct-mail appeals by the fear that if they compare their prices with the prices of drugs identified by brand names, they may cause the large firms to take legal action. Apparently the small firms believe that advertising of this kind could be construed as infringement of a trade mark.

Large firms attempt to induce physicians to prescribe drugs according to their brand names. They advertise their products extensively to the physician, advising him to prescribe the product of a firm whose "reputation" he knows, attributing all sorts of dangers to prescribing the product of an unknown firm, or of permitting the patient to make such a choice. Large firms perform research and development, whereas small firms do not. Doctors think that firms which engage in such socially desirable activity should receive the support of the medical profession and some prescribe the products of the large firms on this ground.

In many instances the doctors may not know that there is a choice of sellers, and even when they do, they may be reluctant to refrain from specifying the seller. If they do not specify the seller, the pharmacist becomes responsible for making the choice, and many doctors undoubtedly believe that they are better qualified to select the firm than the pharmacist is.

Generic names, though a considerable simplification over the chemical names, are, nevertheless, often awkward and difficult to remember. By comparison, brand names are usually short, catchy, and easy to remember. In the actual writing of the prescription, the use of brand names saves the doctor some time.[3]

On occasion, the patient may bring suit against the physician for prescribing an inappropriate drug.[4] In such a case, the physician may receive more legal assistance from a large firm than he would from a small firm. As doctors are often not perfectly certain about the proper use of drugs, they may regard prescribing the products of large firms as a form of malpractice insurance.

It is also possible that some patients may not wish to purchase less expensive drugs. Most patients, in consulting a physician, like to think that they are not wasting their time or the physician's. The patient who is told to "take two aspirin and go to bed" often feels that the physician has not taken his complaint seriously. On the other hand, the same patient given a prescription for the same complaint feels that he has been well treated. Casual empiricism suggests that patients associate high prices with complicated or serious illnesses. To the extent that they wish to believe that their judgment in deciding to consult a physician was correct, the high prices of prescribed drugs reassure them that it was. An example of this occurred several years ago when a large firm introduced a new analgesic which was available by prescription only. The drug had much the same properties as aspirin, and in only a small proportion of the cases would it have been preferable to aspirin. In spite of this, the drug enjoyed remarkable success. The firm discovered that physicians who had previously taken the "two aspirin and go to bed" approach with patients were now prescribing this drug. Patients felt that they were receiving better treatment. (This information was provided by an official of a major drug company in a private conversation.)

Market power and barriers to entry

Industry structure is determined by the interaction of economies of scale, by consumer attitudes toward product differentiation, and by resource control. Market power is conferred on some firms in the industry if these factors generate a structure significantly different from the market structure of perfect competition. Significant degrees of market power can persist for long periods of time if any one of these factors constitutes an effective barrier to the entry of new firms.

Economies of scale can constitute a barrier to entry if to enter profitably requires a plant of such size that the additional output from the plant would drive the rate of return on the potential entrant's investment below the level which would induce him to enter. Economies of scale may also give rise to a capital barrier; the plant of minimum optimum size may be so large that the potential entrant is unable to finance his entry in such a way that he could subsequently operate under cost conditions which would permit an acceptable rate of return.

Product differentiation constitutes a barrier to entry if the consumer's preferences for products of existing firms are so strongly established that a potential entrant would have to devote, over a long period of time, considerably more resources to attracting customers than the established firms would in retaining their existing accounts. Consumer preferences rest upon one of the following bases:

1) Non-transitive wants arising from intensive and repetitious advertising

2) Differences among products in quality, styling, or performance characteristics which the consumer can readily evaluate for himself

3) The inability of the consumer to evaluate significant technical aspects of the product, and his consequent reliance upon the reputation (and only established firms have "reputations") of the manufacturer

4) Provision of ancillary facilities such as service or credit.

Resource control constitutes a barrier to entry if the necessary materials are not so readily available to the potential entrant as they are to established members of the industry. In extreme cases, necessary inputs may be completely unavailable to the entrant; more usually, they are available only at a higher cost, either because the entrant must pay rents to the owners of these resources or because he must turn to inferior sources of supply. Patent protection can create significant resource control over production processes or over what is produced; the latter is of particular significance in the drug industry.

Entry is never "free" in the sense that there are no transitory disadvantages associated with being a newcomer. The entrant will encounter "start-up" costs which arise from his inexperience with production processes or with particular markets. These costs may be at least partly offset by the advantages which the entrant obtains from a new technology. Start-up costs constitute a barrier to entry only if they are predicted to exist for so long a time that the entrant will be deterred from entering.

Economies of scale in the drug industry: production

Since only sparse information exists about manufacturing costs in the drug industry, there is little, of a specific nature, that can be said about production economies. (The only comprehensive source of information concerning the industry—the various Congressional hearings—did not publish any significant cost data; but since the large firms argued that publication of cost data would damage their market position, it seems possible that the subcommittee staffs were in possession of some information of this kind.) Even in the absence of the necessary cost information, however, there are grounds for assuming that economies of scale in production are negligible. First, for many drugs, the production process involves fermentation. This process is performed in fermentation vessels which are, apparently, standard items in the chemical process industries. To expand its output, the firm typically adds more fermentation vessels of the standard size, rather than turning to larger vessels. This expansion process suggests that constant returns to scale may be achieved at a relatively low level of output.*

Even where technically more efficient continuous-flow processes could be used, there is reason to believe that the firm might prefer to use batch processes. The firm must be able to tell when and where a particular container of drugs was produced. Once a batch has reached the market, if a single container of drugs is found to be

* "Batch methods, which allow far less scope for economies of scale, are the rule, especially where fermentation is the key phase in the production process, as is the case in the production of antibiotics (except chloramphenicol) and synthetic corticosteroid hormones. These two categories of ethical drugs are the largest categories in terms of total sales volume. Fermentation vessels are 'amazingly standard.' Large antibiotic manufacturers usually employ 10 to 50 such vessels. Changes in output levels for such products may be accomplished by the employment of a differing number of individually identical fermentation vats, a circumstance conducive to constant returns to scale." Henry Steele, "Monopoly and Competition in the Ethical Drugs Market," *Journal of Law and Economics* 5 (Oct. 1962): 134.

substandard, the firm may have to withdraw the entire production run from the market. Using a continuous-flow procedure, the firm might have to withdraw a much larger quantity of the product than would be required if individual runs had been segregated. The larger the production run, the more difficult it would be to locate and recover individual shipments. The batch process may facilitate keeping track of the output once it has reached the market, and this may be an argument in favor of using what might otherwise be considered an inferior production process.

A second reason for considering economies of scale in production to be of negligible importance is the small physical quantities which are produced. Steele states that, for a given drug, "the physical volume of output of the active ingredients in drugs is typically very small, total national output being perhaps in the neighborhood of a ton per year."[5]

Finally, if there are potential economies of scale inherent in a particular production process, there is some reason to believe that the manufacturers are not likely to take full advantage of them. Since there is rapid change in the product mix of the firms, a given plant will outlast almost all the products which a firm produces at the time the plant is built. Presumably, plants are so designed as to be adaptable to the production of various drugs, and if this is the case, it would appear that flexibility is obtained at the expense of economic efficiency in the production of a particular product.

Economies of scale in the drug industry:
Research and development

Since the demand for pharmaceuticals is highly inelastic, and since the proportion of total costs accounted for by variable costs is quite low, "not only are competitive price declines likely to be large but also firms could easily be compelled to price below average total costs. As a result, there would be heavy pressures on profits if rivalry were allowed to take the form of price competition."[6] In fact, rivalry has been successfully diverted from price competition, and, instead, takes the form of "competitive product differentiation." The well-spring of these differentiated products is the research and development activity of the industry. Accordingly, if the vehicle of competition is research and development, one may ask to what extent small firms are at a disadvantage in the development of new products? Comanor found

> . . . some evidence that in the pharmaceutical industry there are substantial diseconomies of scale in R and D which are associated with large firm size; and that these disadvantages are encountered by even moderately sized firms.[7]

Even so, there are some diseconomies associated with very small size. Some minimum input of scientific personnel is required before output becomes positive; at least one chemist, one biologist, one pharmacologist, and one physician are required. A minimum quantity of laboratory equipment and some library facilities are necessary, and these will serve several scientists just as well as the minimum establishment. The stimulus of colleagues, and the desire of competent researchers to work with their colleagues, is well known; scientists who are professionally oriented, rather than firm oriented, are likely to see the very small laboratory as being of little benefit to the furthering of their professional careers and hence will be available to small firms only at higher salaries. The establishment and maintenance of programs of clinical testing are likely to be more difficult for the firm with limited contacts in the medical world—and one physician could surely provide no more than limited contacts.

In 1961, the average cost of employing a research-and-development scientist was $28,300 for those firms in the drug-and-medicines industry with total employment of less than 1,000 persons.[8] Such firms spent 3.8 percent of net sales upon research and development.[9] Taking four scientists as the minimum for an effective establishment, annual expenditures on research and development would be $113,200, and this would require net sales in the neighborhood of $3 million. Firms smaller than this would probably incur substantially higher average costs for research and development.

Economies of scale in the drug industry: Advertising

The selling efforts of the large firms constitute a large part of their total costs; in 1958, these activities accounted for 33.4 percent of the total costs of 22 large firms. (The proportion of total costs accounted for by selling efforts would be even higher if some costs, currently classified as research and development, were reclassified as advertising [see Chapter·IV].) The Subcommittee staff estimated that the industry spent $750 million on the promotion of drugs in 1958. Based on the experience of 20 large firms, the selling expenses can be allocated as follows: (*a*) Detailing, compensation and expenses of detailmen, and auxiliary material for visits accounted for 57 percent; (*b*) advertising, including advertising in medical journals, and direct mail accounted for 43 percent.

The large firms employ substantial numbers of sales representatives; the proportion of total employment of large firms accounted for by representatives runs from 12 percent to 20 percent. In 1958, the average total cost to the large firm employing a representative was approximately $15,000, and the cost of a single visit to a physician by a representative was estimated to be about $9 or $10.[10] There were approximately 42.8 million visits by representatives to physicians in 1958, and as there were approximately 200,000 physicians in the country at that time, each physician would have received, on the average, 216 visits per year, or almost one per working day. Hence, if $10 is taken as the cost of one visit, the cost to a drug firm of having someone visit each physician in the country once a year would be approximately $2,000,000.

The reason for this intensive selling activity is that much of what comes out of research laboratories does not represent any perceptible degree of medical progress. At best, much of what is introduced is merely "new" and thus can be sold only if the physician can be convinced that the "newest" is the "best."[11]

The ostensible purpose of advertising by the drug industry, therefore, is to inform the physician of new products and to advise him on their proper use. Small firms, doing no research, are at an immediate disadvantage. If they have any new products at all, they are likely to be minor modifications of existing products, and the physician may well feel that the representatives of these firms will have nothing useful to say to him. Detailmen from small firms will be less welcome than most.

Detailing and advertising in medical journals are probably strong complements. If the awareness or curiosity created by the journal advertisement is not reinforced by a visit from the detailman, the physician is probably less likely to prescribe the firm's product, and the value to the firm of reaching that particular physician through a journal advertisement is lost. Conversely, the willingness of the physician to see a detailman—particularly one unknown to him—is probably quite dependent upon what he thinks the detailman will have to say, and upon what questions the physician has about the firm's products. If an interest in the firm's products has not already been aroused by direct mail or by journal advertisements, the physician will be less willing to see the salesman.

Journal advertising is placed in journals with both national and regional circulations. The latter are largely the journals of the state medical associations. On the whole, these journals appear to be of indifferent quality and to be facing increasingly severe financial difficulties. On the former point, a survey of state medical association journals found 63 percent of the pages to be devoted to advertising (almost entirely by drug firms), 17 percent to announcements and miscellaneous items, and 20 percent to scientific articles on medicine. Forty percent of the articles had previously been presented at state or county medical association meetings, and slightly less than one quarter of the articles were written by authors with a medical school affiliation.[12] On the quality of the articles, the author stated:

> The most common type (fifty percent) of articles was the essay which reviews a clinical subject—usually a well-defined disease. These essays almost always approached the subject non-critically. They consisted of stylized discussion, drawing heavily on textbook references. The material was often repetitious, and sometimes outdated. Charts and diagrams were infrequently used. For those familiar with the subject, these essays failed to communicate anything new. For those who were not, they offered no real stimulus to further learning.
>
> • • • • •
>
> Of the two hundred and four articles, only nine could be considered in any way original; eight were in part original and only one was completely so.[13]

Beginning in 1956, state medical society journals as a group began to run deficits, and by the end of 1962 only two out of forty such journals surveyed were not running deficits.[14] Replacement of these journals by newsletters, or by state "inserts" in national general practitioners' journals, or by mergers of state journals to form regional journals (two have occurred) have been seriously considered as solutions to the problem. Raising advertising rates apparently provides no solution, and the long-run financial outlook for the journals is gloomy.

> If we raise rates, we encourage [drug] companies to seek alternative vehicles of advertising. The truth of this is apparent by looking at our balance sheets during the past 10 years. We have all raised rates. We have all lost advertisers and suffered deficits.
> . . . Every year the ratio of specialists in American medicine rises. Since advertisers must address themselves more and more to specialists, they are going to assign an ever increasing proportion of their budgets to national or specialized journals.[15]

No precise information is available concerning the way in which advertising expenditures are allocated among the various media. Advertising in medical journals and by direct mail has been estimated to account for 43 percent of the total promotional expenditures by large firms. A survey of the promotional activities surrounding the introduction of four new drugs showed that, of the advertising in journals and by direct mail, journal advertising accounted for 38 percent of the amount spent.[16] If this figure is representative, advertising in journals would account for 16.3 percent of all promotion expenditures, or for $122.6 million of the $750 million spent upon promotion in 1958. State medical societies allocate about $3 per member to the publication of the medical society journal, and this appropriation, together with revenues from drug-company advertising, accounts for virtually all the journals' incomes. Advertising accounts for between 76 and 100 percent of the revenues of these journals.[17] Suppose on the assumption that for all medical society journals, advertising accounts for 90 percent of the revenues, medical society appropriations would then account for the remaining 10 percent. If each of the nation's approximately 200,000 doctors belongs to one state medical society, then the total revenues for all state journals from society appropriations would be $600,000. Advertising income would therefore account for $5,400,000. Subtracting this amount from the total expenditures on all medical journal advertising leaves $117.2 million for expenditures on national journals, an expenditure that would account for 15.6 percent of all promotion expenditures.

The fact that much of the journal advertising is done on a na-

tional scale would appear to erect a substantial barrier to firms
wishing to operate on less than a national scale. To obtain a rough
idea of the order of magnitude of the problem, consider the position
of a firm of optimum size in all respects, except that it operates on
a regional, rather than on a national scale. Assume the following:

1) The firm employs a corps of detailmen who visit doctors in
the region just as assiduously as those employed by firms operating
on a national scale. The detailmen are supported by other promotional media used with the same intensity as that of the national
firms, and the detailmen enjoy the same success with physicians as
those representing national firms. The average cost per visit to a
physician is the same for this firm as it is for national firms.

2) Direct-mail advertising and regional journal advertising can
be restricted to doctors in the firm's regional market with no increase in the average cost per physician.

3) A physician will become a potential prescriber of the firm's
products only if he is first informed by journal advertising or by
direct mail and is then visited by the firm's salesmen. Since detailmen are confined to a particular region, journal advertising reaching physicians outside the region will generate no sales for the firm.

4) The firm allocates its promotional budget in the same manner
as national firms, so that the amount of promotional material
reaching a physician in the region is the same as those for national
firms. National journals give no discounts to advertisers with only
regional interests. The readership of national journals is directly
proportional to the number of physicians in the region.

On these assumptions, indices of the average selling cost per
physician can be constructed for regional firms of various sizes. The
scale of the firm is represented by a figure indicating what percent
of the national population of physicians practices in the region
served by the firm. Since promotional methods other than national
journal advertising account for 84.4 percent of the total selling
expenditures of large firms—which are taken to be national firms—
this figure is used as a base for the index number representing such
costs for smaller-scale firms. As constant returns to scale have been
assumed for these types of selling efforts, the index number is the
same for all scales. National journal advertising accounts for 15.6

percent of the promotional expenditures of national firms; this figure is used as the base of an index number representing the average cost per physician of national journal advertising. Since smaller firms have been assumed to advertise with the same intensity per physician, and since advertising in a national journal is assumed to be indivisible, regional firms probably have to purchase advertising in this medium at the same rates as large firms. The average cost per physician reached by this type of selling effort is obtained by dividing the base of the index by the scale of the firm. Adding together the two index numbers of selling costs gives an index number for the average total selling cost per physician, measured against a base of 100 (Table III–4).

III-4.   ESTIMATES OF SCALE ECONOMIES ARISING FROM SELLING

| Scale of Firm as Percent of National Market | Index Number of Cost per Physician of | | | Average Cost per Unit of Output: 66.6 + .334 x (3) Base: 100 |
	(1) National journal advertising Base: 15.6	(2) All other selling costs Base: 84.4	(3) All selling costs Base: 100	
5	312.0	84.4	396.4	199.0
10	156.0	84.4	240.4	146.9
25	62.4	84.4	146.8	115.6
44.8	44.8	84.4	119.2	106.4
50	31.2	84.4	115.6	105.2
80	19.5	84.4	103.9	101.3
100	15.6	84.4	100.0	100.0

For national firms, selling costs accounted for 33.4 percent of total costs. Nonselling costs, therefore, accounted for the remainder—66.6 percent. If this figure is used as the base of an index of nonselling costs, and if constant returns to scale for nonselling activities are assumed, the index will be the same irrespective of the scale of the firm. The index number obtained for all selling costs (e.g., 396.4) is multiplied by 0.334 and added to 66.6 to yield an index number, with a base of 100, for the average total cost per unit of output. The results are shown in Table III-4.

In 1958, the 22 large firms for which the subcommittee presented data earned on their drug operations a net profit of 13 percent per dollar of sales.[18] In the same year, much the same group of firms earned a net profit of 21.9 percent on net assets.[19] Thus a net profit of 1 percent on sales was equivalent to a net profit of 1.68 percent on net assets. In 1958, the rate of return on net assets for all manufacturing (as distinguished from drug manufacturing alone) was 9.8 percent. For a firm to earn this rate of return in the drug industry, a net profit of 5.83 percent on sales would have been required. In the above example, a firm operating in less than 44.8 percent of the national market would earn less than 5.83 percent on sales.[20] Thus, a potential entrant, contemplating entering the drug industry and competing with the large firms in a regional market smaller than 44.8 percent of the national market, could earn a greater rate of return in "all manufacturing."

Before estimating the optimum size of a hypothetical firm expecting to operate in 44.8 percent of the national market, we digress briefly to develop some necessary information on the intensity of detailing. The negligible use made of detailmen by small firms selling under generic names is disregarded. These firms accounted for 10.32 percent of industry sales, and large firms accounted for 80 percent. Assume, then, that large firms accounted for 89.2 percent, which is probably a conservative estimate of all visits by detailmen.[21] Then, of the 216 visits received per year by the average physician, representatives of the 33 large firms accounted for 193 visits. Dividing the number of visits by the number of large firms indicates that the average large firm called on the average doctor 5.83 times per year, or once every 8.6 weeks (50 weeks per year).

At the beginning of this example it was assumed that a regional firm would visit the doctors in its region with the same intensity as the average firm operating in the national market. Thus if the firm's representatives make 5.83 visits per year to each doctor in the region, the annual sales of a firm operating in 44.8 percent of the national market are estimated to be in the neighborhood of $33 million. The intermediate steps used in arriving at this figure are shown in Table III–5.

III-5.   COMPUTATION OF SALES OF HYPOTHETICAL FIRM OPERATING IN 44.8 PERCENT OF NATIONAL MARKET

44.8 percent of 200,000 physicians	89,600 physicians
5.83 visits per physician per year by firm's detailmen to 89,600 physicians	522,360 visits
Total cost of detailing at $10 per visit	$5.224 million
Detailing as a percent of all non-journal advertising: 57/84.4	67.53 percent
Total cost of all non-journal advertising: $5.224 million/0.6753	$7.735 million
Non-journal advertising as a percent of all selling costs: 84.4/119.2	70.81 per cent
Total selling costs: $7.735 million/0.7081	$10.924 million
Total selling costs as a percent of total costs: (119.2 x 0.334)/106.4	37.42 per cent
Total costs: $10.924 million/0.3742	$29.192 million
Gross profit	$3.853 million
Corporate income taxes at 50 percent	$1.927 million
Net income	$1.926 million
Total sales	$33.045 million
Net income as a percent of sales	5.83 percent
Net income as a percent of net assets	9.8 percent
Net assets	$19.653 million

The results in this example are derived from crude data and based upon several assumptions: indivisibility of national journal advertising,* fixed factor proportions in promotional activity, confinement of the firm's activity to a well-defined geographic region, and the production of a range of drugs similar to that of the national firms. These assumptions are not accurate descriptions of

* Because of the limited market for these journals there is only one edition rather than several regional editions.

the realities faced by a potential entrant, but even after the assumptions have been appropriately qualified the example retains some force.

Firms wishing to compete in the same manner as the large firms need not enter the market as "long-line houses"; instead, they can concentrate on therapeutic agents useful in one or more medical specialities. The firm can then advertise in national journals for medical specialists without incurring increased average costs per potential prescriber reached by this method. Some disadvantage in advertising in national journals addressed to the medical profession as a whole would still be incurred. (One diseconomy which could result from this type of specialization arises from the unexpectedness of some outcomes from research and development. The broader the scope and horizons of the firm, the more likely it is to recognize the usefulness of research which, in its immediate context, might appear to be a failure.)

Selling is not a process which requires rigid factor proportions. The smaller firm would have some latitude in adjusting its promotional mix. There is, however, some reason to believe that the latitude is not so great as it might appear. If regional journals are as weak, scientifically and financially, as—on the evidence given—they seem to be, the diversion of promotional resources to this medium may be of little value, since these journals probably command little attention from their recipients. Further, if the financial position of the state medical society journals does not improve, the option of advertising in them may cease to exist.

The scope for more intensive use of direct mail and detailing appears to be limited. The evidence suggests that the expenditures by large firms on these activities are already at the point where the marginal cost is at least equal to, if not greater than, the marginal benefits. If the typical large firm visits the physician once every 8.6 weeks, one suspects that an additional visit per year would generate less additional revenue for the firm than the visit would cost. The situation is similar for direct mail. One physician, who kept records of the amount of direct mail he received, reported that, during one month in 1959, the average number of pieces received per day was 10.5 and that the average weight of these pieces was 1.06 pounds.[22] As to the use made by physicians of this material, he reported:

In phone contacts with a hundred doctors' secretaries I found that 54 percent of them immediately dumped most of the circulars into the wastebasket, excepting only those which dealt with new drugs. They let only the first class mail go through to the doctors' desks, in this way avoiding repeated advertisements. The remaining 46 percent reported that the doctor sorted his own mail.

Doctors in two of the large medical clinics in town had an equally drastic policy. The mailroom clerk was instructed to throw out all circulars and store the samples in a separate room for the doctors' leisured perusal. One clinic tried to have the post office burn all their circulars before delivery to save wear and tear on the postman. This idea had to be shelved because "the mail must go through."

Hospital physicians often instruct their mail clerks to discard all circulars that are delivered. At one university hospital there are several huge wastepaper baskets at the foot of the mail slots for quick disposal of all third-class mail.[23]

Use of these media appears to be so intensive that the following hypothesis does not seem unrealistic. The short-run marginal benefits of detailing or direct mail (the additional revenue generated by an additional visit to the physician or by an additional piece of direct mail) are already below the marginal costs of these activities. In the long-run, however, intensive advertising is still profitable. Sustained use of detailing and direct mail impedes the access of possible competitors to the physician and thus serves to reduce their effectiveness as competitors. Large firms may inundate the physician with direct mail to the extent that direct mail becomes so irritating to him that he discards it all, unopened. In this case, the direct-mail activities of the large firms "jam" this line of communication between the physician and the small firm and ensure that he receives no information about their products. Alternatively, if the physician cannot look at every piece of mail, and is more likely to look first at the mail that comes to him from a firm that he knows, then the proper strategy for large firms is to send him so much direct mail that the pieces opened all come from large firms. Much the same tactic could be followed with detailmen. The fact that individual large firms do not equate short-run marginal benefits with marginal costs, and therefore do not diminish their use of these media, could be attributed to an oligopoly theory solution regarding the stability of advertising expenditures.[24]

Resource control: Patents

Resource control is a significant source of market power in the
industry. Monopolies of products and methods of production are
conferred by patents. One survey estimated that between two-thirds
and three-quarters of all prescriptions written in 1958 were for
patented drugs.[25] In Chapter VI it is estimated that approximately

III-6.   NATURE OF 970 PATENTS RELATING TO MEDICINES
ISSUED DURING FISCAL YEAR 1961[a]

	Percent	
New chemical compounds	65.4	
Animal and plant extracts (chemical structure unknown)	1.2	
Vaccines and serums	1.2	
Subtotal: Drugs as single entities		67.8
Mixtures of medicines including auxiliary ingredients, carriers, preservatives, etc.	7.2	
Processes for making or obtaining chemical compounds	20.4	
Processes involving the medicinal use only of a substance	0.7	
Vehicles, formulations, etc.	2.1	
Veterinary	1.8	
Total	100.0	

[a]U.S., Congress, Senate, Subcommittee on Antitrust and Monopoly of the
Committee on the Judiciary, *Hearings on Drug Industry Antitrust Act,* 87th
Cong., 2nd sess., 1962, pt. 3, p. 1261.

54 percent of the industry sales in 1961 were accounted for by
patented drugs which were produced by only one firm. Table III-6
shows the relative number of patents granted during the fiscal year
1961 according to the various classifications used by the Patent
Office. Patents on manufacturing processes are numerically less
important than patents on drugs, and still less important in creat-
ing monopolies than their numbers would indicate.

It happens that in drugs, as indeed in most chemical industries, process patents are a relatively weak form of protection because of the comparative ease with which, by a slight change in the process, the patent can be evaded. Probably more than any other industrial area, the chemical industries lend themselves to the manufacture of a given product by several, and often numerous alternative methods or processes; the result is that process patents in drugs are often commonly referred to in the trade as constituting only a "basis for litigation" or a "source of employment for patent attorneys."[26]

In the hands of a large firm, product patents are a much stronger form of protection than patents on manufacturing processes. They force a potential competitor to do one of the following: (a) remain out of the market; (b) seek a license from the holder to produce the drug; (c) produce the drug, without a license, under the threat of legal action. If the potential competitor is prepared to engage in research and development, he has the additional option of searching for a patentable product of his own with therapeutic properties sufficiently similar to those of the established drug that he can represent it to the medical profession as being at least no worse than the original drug.

Patents are clearly important in the explanation of monopoly in individual drug markets. On the assumption that drugs introduced prior to 1944 would, in 1961, no longer be covered by a patent, the drugs used in this study can be classified according to both the presumed existence of a patent and the existence of monopoly in individual markets. The results are presented in Table III-7. The application of a chi-square test for dependence shows the existence of a patent and the existence of monopoly to be highly related.

Patents not only confer monopoly power in and of themselves but may serve to augment existing sources of market power; large numbers of patents, in the possession of a few holders, may confer more market power than the sum of the parts would indicate. In view of the disparity in size between the large firms and the small firms in the drug industry, the following comment of Kaysen and Turner is particularly appropriate.

The costs and risks of patent litigation further enhance the oppressive effects of a large accumulation of patents. When a new firm or a new product appears on the market, the large holder will almost always find some patent among its many which the newcomer can be charged with infringing. Rather than undergo ordeal by trial, the newcomer may agree to take a license under restrictive conditions, or may decide to sell out and withdraw.[27]

III-7.   RELATIONSHIP OF PATENTS AND MONOPOLY IN 1961

		Drug Produced by Only One Firm		Drug Produced by More Than One Firm		Total
No effective patent in 1961	Observed	42	6.4%	147.0	22.4%	189
	Predicted	108.6	16.6%	80.4	12.3%	28.8%
Effective patent may exist in 1961	Observed	335	51.1%	132	20.1%	467
	Predicted	268.4	40.9%	198.6	30.3%	71.2%
Totals		377	57.5%	279	42.5%	656
						100.0%

Observed value of chi-square: 134.93
Theoretical value of chi-square at 0.005 level: 7.88

The large firm may patent everything in sight, thereby not only monopolizing the best products and processes for its own use, but also precluding the use of the second-best products and processes by potential competitors. There is some evidence that this occurs in the U.S. pharmaceutical industry. Thus, during the period 1950–60, the mean number of single chemical entities introduced per year was 41.8.[28] In 1961, of the 970 patents granted on medicines, 67.8 percent or 658 were granted on single entities—single chemical compounds, vaccines, serums, and extracts from plant and animal sources. While many of these patents were undoubtedly granted to individuals having no connection with the drug industry, such recipients must eventually look to the drug industry for profitable use of their products, and we may reasonably suppose that most of these patents were eventually assigned to large firms. Many of the patents would have been on products which subsequently proved to have little therapeutic value. Nevertheless, the fact that 15.7 times more patents were granted on single entities during a single year than were, in all likelihood, commercially introduced during the same year, provides some grounds for suspecting that patents are being used as a vehicle for excluding smaller firms from the second-best products and processes.

Companies with large patent holdings are the inevitable market for new patents. While there is almost no evidence to support this theory of behavior in the drug industry, we do observe that of the 30 single chemical entities that originated in the domestic, non-corporate sector (largely universities) during the period 1941–61 and that were in use in 1961, patents on 26 appear to have been held by large firms.[29]

Market power in the drug industry: Summary

Large firms operate principally in two different types of markets for individual drugs, and the basis of market power is different in each. The first type is that in which the large firm is the only seller, or one of very few sellers. Monopoly power in an individual market of this type is conferred by patent protection. Small firms are deterred from establishing such positions of monopoly for themselves partly by diseconomies associated with research and development, but more importantly by the scale of promotional activity which would be required if these firms were to try to influence physicians to prescribe their products.

In the second type of market the large firm is one of many sellers; usually this type of market contains one or more small firms selling the drug under its generic name. Here, the large firms owe their market power to the cumulative effects of intensive advertising, which has shaped the physician's preferences; to the anti-substitution laws, which confer monopoly power on brand names (or any other specification used by the manufacturer) by preventing the consumer from countermanding the physician's choice of firm; and to the inability of the small firms to engage in promotional activity on a scale that would be sufficient to overcome established preferences.

Position of small firms selling drugs under generic names

Small firms selling drugs under generic names appear to be firms with no market power; for the most part, the submarkets in

which this type of firm operates conform very closely to the
perfectly competitive market. There is a very large number of
potential buyers—chiefly, pharmacies and hospitals—and in each
market, for most drugs produced by this type of firm, there are substantial numbers of competing producers. Table III-8 shows the
distribution of the number of small firms selling a given drug under

III-8.   DISTRIBUTION OF NUMBER OF FIRMS SELLING THE MOST COMMON DOSAGE FORM OF A DRUG UNDER ITS GENERIC NAME[a]

Number of Small Firms Selling a Drug Under Its Generic Name	Markets Containing Two or More Types of Firm	Markets Containing Only Small Firms Selling Under Generic Name	Totals
	No. of drugs	No. of drugs	No. of drugs
1	28	15	43
2	24	7	31
3	10	4	14
4	9	4	13
5	8	1	9
6- 10	25	1	26
11- 20	18	0	18
21- 40	35	1	36
41- 60	14	0	14
61- 80	15	0	15
81-100	6	0	6
More than 100	2	0	2
Totals	194	33	227

[a]Note that the number of firms shown in this table has been determined
by counting the number of firms selling the most common dosage form of the
drug. There are other dosage forms, often resulting from a different tablet size,
that are produced by firms which may not sell the most common dosage form.
Thus, the number of firms in the market for a particular drug is almost invariably greater than the figures shown in the table. As a rough guide, the number
of firms in the market could be obtained by multiplying the total figures shown
by 1.5.

its generic name. Within their submarkets, the firms sell a homogeneous product and make no effort to differentiate it. Prices are published in a catalogue which is received by almost every potential buyer in the country; thus, buyers are well informed about prices. As the catalogue is readily available to manufacturers, they presumably have good information about the prices charged by their competitors.

The operating scale of these firms appears to be very small. Of the 379 firms which can be identified as small firms selling under generic name, the mean employment is estimated to be 19 persons. (See Chapter IV, p. 76.) Insofar as necessary resources (bulk drugs or raw materials) are available to these firms at all, they appear to be available without restriction.

There seem to be no barriers to the entry of such firms into the market as a whole, although many individual product markets are completely closed to them. The figures of the Census of Manufactures indicate no significant net exodus or entry into the field of pharmaceutical preparations; the Census report shows 1,123 firms in 1947; 1,128 in 1954; and 1,062 in 1958—an indication that small firms selling under generic names are able to earn a normal rate of return.

Measurement of market power

Existing measures of market power are theoretically inadequate and of little use in empirical work. All but one of the well-known measures identifies market power as a one-dimensional attribute, whereas, in fact, market power is complex and many-dimensioned. Thus, measures of industry concentration, insofar as they are used to identify market power, identify it by the relative size of firms. Three measures—cross-elasticity, Lerner's measure, and Rothschild's measure—require a knowledge of the industry's and the firms' demand curves, and base their evaluation of market power upon demand considerations only. Bain's measure, the most useful empirically, is based upon excess profit rates. The only measure which attempts to identify market power as a multi-dimensional variable—Papandreou's—requires information which economists are unlikely ever to possess.[30] Since the information required for the use of each of these measures is not available, none is empirically helpful in this study.

The mean price charged for a given drug by small firms selling the drug under its generic name is taken to represent the market price which would prevail in the absence of market power. To the extent that other (and predominantly larger) types of firm selling the same drug can charge a higher mean price than this, their ability to do so is attributed to the possession of market power. The degree of market power is measured as the ratio of the mean price charged by the other type of firm to the mean price charged by small firms selling the drug under its generic name. Such a measure yields values greater than or equal to one, with no conceptual upper limit. On occasions when values of less than one are obtained, the result can be attributed to reversals in the possession of market power by the various types of firm, to a lack of complete information about the market, or to transitory disequilibria in the structure of market prices at the time of the printing of the price catalogue.

CHAPTER FOUR

The Issue of Drug Quality

The discussion of market power in the previous chapter proceeded on the assumption that, for a given drug, the products of each type of firm could be regarded as therapeutically homogeneous, and hence, that price differentials observed between types of firm for the same drug could be attributed to differences in market power. In this chapter the assumption that the products of competing manufacturers are in fact therapeutically identical is examined. If the products of firms of various sizes do not have this property, then some or all of the price differentials may be attributable to differences in quality. Thus, unless the products of firms selling the same drug can be shown to be homogeneous, or very nearly so, market power cannot be immediately inferred from the existence of price differentials.

At the outset of this discussion it is necessary to distinguish between the issues of drug safety and drug quality. Drug safety refers to the undesirable side effects which may be caused by the basic properties of a drug. Safety must be judged against the severity of the disease and the alternative procedures which are available to treat the disease.

. . . No physician, no one who has ever been responsible for the welfare of individual patients will accept the idea that safety can be judged in the absence of a decision about efficacy. No drug is "safe" if it fails to cure a serious disease for which a cure is available. No drug is too dangerous to use if it will cure a fatal disease for which no other cure is available.[1]

As an issue of public policy, drug safety concerns the standards that the Food and Drug Administration should set for the introduction of new drugs and is not related to the question of homogeneity. Compounds that are therapeutically homogeneous or very nearly so may be homogeneously good or bad (safe or unsafe, effective or ineffective), but the goodness or badness of drugs does not account for differences in market power and may have little or nothing to do with the prices charged for them. On the other hand, the belief that differences in quality do exist can be exploited by drug manufacturers and used as a means of acquiring market power.

There are two related issues in a discussion of drug quality. The first is whether large firms produce drugs that actually are of superior quality to those produced by small firms, and in particular to those produced by small firms selling under generic names. The second is whether or not small firms, particularly those selling under generic names, produce drugs which are of a quality below the minimum acceptable standard.

Cost of quality control

Although the large firms take the position that effective quality control is very expensive, and constitutes a large part of the final cost of a drug, available evidence does not support this argument. The only small firm to submit information concerning its quality-control costs appeared to spend 2.7 percent of total costs on quality control. "The fact that this is adequate is evident from the fact that no Panray (the name of the firm submitting the data) products have been judged violative by Food and Drug Administration inspectors."[2] No information concerning the importance of quality control in the cost structure of the large firms is available for large firms operating in the United States. However, some relevant information on this point was uncovered in an investigation of the drug industry in Canada.[3]

In May, 1960, in the course of the investigation, a selected number of firms, operating in Canada, were asked to submit information on, among other things, their quality-control expenditures. Of the 27 firms requested to supply information, 13 had net sales in 1959 exceeding $4 million. Of these, one company (Frosst) was a Canadian firm, and two others (Ayerst and Horner) had been Canadian before their purchase by American firms. The manufacturing facilities of these three firms were located in Canada. The remaining 10 firms were branches or subsidiaries of American firms. Fourteen firms had sales in 1959 of less than $4 million but more than $1 million. Of these 14, two were Canadian, two were

IV-1.   DISTRIBUTION OF QUALITY-
CONTROL EXPENDITURES FOR SELECTED
CANADIAN FIRMS[a]

Quality-control expenditures as a percent of 1959 net sales	No. of firms
0.00–0.50	2
0.51–1.00	8
1.01–1.50	6
1.51–2.00	2
2.01–2.50	1
2.51–3.00	2

[a]Canada, Restrictive Trade Practices Commission, *Report Concerning the Manufacture, Distribution and Sale of Drugs* (Ottawa, 1963), pp. 106-110—hereafter cited as *Green Book*.

Swiss subsidiaries, two were British subsidiaries, and one was a French subsidiary; the other seven were American branches or subsidiaries. With the exception of the Canadian firms, the French firm, and one of the British firms, all the firms in this group operated as large firms in the U.S. market.

Six of the 27 reporting firms stated that they did not keep information in such a way that they could identify their quality-control expenditures—evidence in itself that quality control costs are not a major component of production expense.[4] For the remaining firms, the distribution of quality-control expenditures as a percentage of net sales is shown in Table IV-1. These firms reported net sales in 1959 of $93 million and quality-control expenditures of $1.125 million; the latter were 1.21 percent of net sales.

For all reporting firms, the "cost of goods sold" constituted 33.38 percent of net sales. If this figure is taken as the best estimate for the 21 firms for which quality-control data are available, the estimated cost-of-goods-sold would be $31.049 million, and quality-control expenditures would constitute 3.62 percent of cost-of-goods-sold.[5] This evidence does not support the contention of the large firms that small firms can sell at lower prices because they have inferior quality-control procedures.

The position of the large firms

For official drugs, standards of quality are given in the *United States Pharmacopeia* or the *National Formulary*. These specify, in accordance with accepted medical practice, the minimum and maximum values and tolerances for each therapeutically relevant aspect of a drug.[6] In the words of the *Pharmacopeia*:

> The minimum purity tolerances specified for pharmacopeial articles . . . are established with a view to the use of the articles as drugs. Such limits do not bar the use of lots of an article which more nearly approach 100% purity *nor do they constitute a basis for the claim that such lots "exceed" the pharmacopeial quality.*[7] [author's italics]

In the same vein, a professor of pharmacology, asked whether *U.S.P.* standards were not merely minimum standards which it was desirable to exceed, replied:

> Now there is no purpose in making medication purer than the standards set by the United States Pharmacopeia. The Pharmacopeia has certain tolerances, and it permits because this is a practical matter.
> Purification beyond these tolerances adds greatly to the expense and adds nothing to the efficacy of the medication. . . .
> If these so-called impurities were in any way deleterious, the United States Pharmacopeia standards would be elevated accordingly.[8,9]

An official drug is one which has received the recognition of either the *U.S. Pharmacopeia* or the *National Formulary*. The governing bodies of these publications set official standards of quality for recognized drugs, and manufacturers of such drugs are required

by the Food and Drug Administration to conform to these standards if they represent their products as being either *"U.S.P."* or
"N.F." Official recognition of drugs generally lags at least five
years behind the commercial introduction of the drug; hence official
drugs are typically not the newest drugs. Nonofficial drugs are
seldom sold by small firms using generic names.[10] The fact that
U.S.P. standards do not apply to the most recently introduced
drugs is, however, of little significance in a discussion of the relative
quality of drugs produced by firms of different size. The great
majority of drugs which are sold both by large firms and small firms
under generic name (i.e., drugs for which price comparisons can be
made), are older drugs for which official standards are defined.

In spite of the *U.S.P.* statement, and in spite of the fact that
U.S.P. standards are determined by periodic conventions of specialists drawn from medical schools, from the major drug companies,
and from other knowledgeable sources, the large drug firms—at
least publicly—view *U.S.P.* standards as merely minimum standards. This view is succinctly stated by the Chairman of American
Home Products Corp., Alvin G. Brush, and by Senators Dirksen
and Hruska in the following quotations:

The United States Pharmacopeia and the National Formulary contain good, but incomplete and general standards and tests for drugs
under their generic names. Our quality procedures impose more
stringent and additional standards and tests for constant purity, potency, and therapeutic efficacy. Many doctors prefer to prescribe drugs
under their trademarks rather than generic names simply because they
believe these extra qualities are desirable.[11]

. . . Every responsible manufacturer is concerned with extensive
clinical testing and quality control in order to meet standards that
exceed those of the U.S. Pharmacopeia. While it is perfectly true that
it would be legal for a firm to sell a product that met the minimum
standards, most established organizations attempt to manufacture their
product so that they surpass these qualifications by wide margins.[12]

Whether or not differences in quality exist in fact, it is clear that
if a firm can convince consumers and physicians that they do exist,
and that the products of its competitors are of inferior quality, the
firm benefits from the belief that is created. Such a strategy is not
new; drug companies have apparently taken this line since the
industry began. For example:

In the 1880s and for several decades thereafter, the drug industry was marked by exceedingly severe price competition. No firm could expect to meet all competitors on the basis of price and expect to survive. Upjohn accordingly determined to establish a reputation for quality from the very beginning—a fact reflected in the signs long posted throughout the plant: "Keep the quality up—W. E. Upjohn."[13]

In a rudimentary pattern of what in later years came to be the assigned task of specialized detail men, salesmen were urged to counsel physicians, "Always specify Abbott." And consistently and emphatically, by publication and by sales talk, the high quality of Abbott products was stressed, with warnings against shoddy competitors: "We expect, and do not object to, intelligent competition, . . . but the just-as-good and cheaper, price cutting, quality-destroying, non-creating-pirate-imitators, WE DESPISE! Dishonorable in one thing (in many things) he is dangerous in others. DO NOT TRUST HIM! Our goods are right; our prices are right; our service is unexcelled! Quality first, fair prices and prompt service is our platform! Do not let our imitators deceive you!"[14]

That this strategy continues in full force—with additional bows to the physician's omniscience on the subject of drugs—is seen in the following excerpts from the testimony of the president of the Pharmaceutical Manufacturers Association.

. . . Legitimate businessmen seem to have recognized the value to them of the Food and Drug Administration from the very beginning. These laws freed the majority of conscientious manufacturers from the unfair competition of the unscrupulous one who manufactures under unsanitary conditions, cheapens his product with low quality ingredients, and falsely labels his products as being better than it is, and at the same time offered added protection to the public from the unscrupulous.[15]

When the manufacturer, the reputable manufacturer, makes available his product, he wants it to be known in a way that identifies that product with his firm. He is willing to stake his reputation on it. So brand names in normal business practice become so important, and so far as the drug industry is concerned, become especially important as they provide a note of confidence for the physician and for the patient.

•   •   •   •   •

As physicians we have had experience in the United States with drugs that have been bought at what seemed a little cheaper price or for some other reason. But they did not do the job they were supposed to.[16]

By brand name prescription, too, the doctor orders for the patient a specific product *in which he has absolute knowledge of quality, purity, and any side effects that might have importance for a particular patient. . . .* (author's italics)

A system allowing pharmacists to substitute generic equivalents for brand name prescriptions is tantamount to restricting the physician's choice and authority, and transferring some of his decisions to the pharmacist. I scarcely think the American people would welcome this.

From the standpoint of the physician and pharmacist, the use of generic equivalents would in no way lessen, but might well increase their liability, because it could increase the chances for unfavorable reactions to the detriment of the patient. Under the American system of medical care, the physician alone arrives at the diagnosis and he alone should decide what drug is to be prescribed for his patient. This is a vital part of the physician's responsibility in medical care and it is his responsibility alone.[17]

As Steele observes:

There is probably no other industry in existence where the disparagement of the quality of lower priced products can so completely substitute for actual price competition.[18]

The view that differences do exist, and that they are therapeutically significant, is vigorously promulgated by the large firms. The principal manifestation of this view is to be seen in the activities of the National Pharmaceutical Council. The Council was formed in 1953 by the major firms in the industry, and now includes 22 of the large firms which sell under brand names; of the very largest firms, only Lilly and Parke-Davis do not belong. Its principal task has been to promote the passage of "anti-substitution" laws by state pharmacy regulatory boards. In a six-year period (1953–59) the Council secured the passage of such laws in forty-one states.[19] In most cases it provided state agencies with a model statute which the agencies then adopted as their own. With the success of this aspect of its program, the Council has turned its attention to retarding the growth of hospital formularies and to informing physicians, pharmacists, and consumers of the merits of prescribing by brand name.

Originally, "substitution" meant substituting a *different drug* for the one prescribed by the physician. Under the impetus of the Council, the term has taken on a quite different meaning; it now means the substitution of an unbranded variety or of another brand *of the same drug* for the brand prescribed by the doctor. The effect of the state laws, if the word substitution is interpreted in this way, is to guarantee to the firms which sell under brand names the fruits of their advertising to doctors. Presumably, this was the Council's purpose.

The Council's rationale for this activity is based upon the view that there are significant and therapeutically useful variations among the various brands of the large companies, and that there are significant and potentially harmful variations between the products of the large firms, on the one hand, and the products of the small firms, on the other hand. An archetypical statement of this position was given before the Subcommittee by an officer of the Council:

> The heart of the difficulty lies in the fact that drugs bearing the same generic name are not necessarily therapeutic equivalents. Significant variations can and do frequently occur and the results can be harmful to the patient.
>
> I do wish, however, to make clear that a physician, in prescribing a particular brand of drug for a patient may be doing so because that brand has characteristics which the physician wants his patient to have and which may not be present in other brands. The generic name does not indicate to the dispensing pharmacist what these characteristics are and he cannot necessarily tell from reading the prescription why the prescriber chose the brand he did. If the pharmacist is permitted to substitute the so-called generic equivalent, he very likely is not substituting a drug with equivalent characteristics and may be defeating the very purpose of the physician in selecting the brand of drug he chose.[20]

A similar statement comes from the president of a major drug company:

> While all pharmaceutical houses vary according to their size and integrity with respect to the efficiency of their quality control programs, it appears to be a common assumption among many physicians and pharmacists that between the larger more reputable houses there exists little difference in this respect. At least the assumption is made that products made by the leading houses and containing the same active drugs are, in fact, identical and hence may be ordered on a generic name basis.
>
> Nothing could be further from the truth. Subtle but important differences exist between Merck Sharp & Dohme products and those of its

best competitors. Gross differences are possible from unscrupulous or unknowing competitors.[21]

That there are significant and therapeutically useful variations among the brands of a given drug does not appear to be supported by other evidence. Medical professors report that it is impossible to cover all the common therapeutic agents in the time allotted to the usual therapeutics course given to medical students. Instead, the characteristics of the various families of drugs are discussed, and medical students are expected to understand the general principles of action of each class of drugs. Walter Modell, M.D., an associate professor of Pharmacology at the Cornell University Medical Center, spoke of the inadequate time allowed for instruction.

. . . With a large number of drugs that are now available in the teaching of the subject to students, we cannot teach about every single drug available. There are just too many of them and we have only a small part of the 4-year medical course.

So that in teaching we generally use what is called prototype teaching. For example, in the list of drugs related to sulfathiazole and that group we will teach about one or two drugs and explain the general principles that apply to drugs in that group, and expect the student to identify a new drug as belonging to the group, and to realize that the general principles of its use apply to the entire group, and that there are only slight differences between the new members.[22]

In view of this, it is unlikely that the medical student receives any formal instruction that would enable him to evaluate the variations which the large firms allege to exist among brands of a given drug.*

* The National Pharmaceutical Council claims that the following properties of a particular drug can yield significant variations: (a) potency; (b) compatability; (c) purity; (d) sustained release mechanisms; (e) enteric coating; (f) disintegration time; (g) solubility; (h) particle size; (i) vehicle or base; (j) quantity of active ingredient; (k) allergenic capabilities; (l) irritation; (m) pH; (n) tonicity; (o) caloric values; (p) melting point; (q) surface tension; (r) viscosity; (s) ease of application and removal; (t) flavor; (u) research and development effort, quality and manufacturing control; (v) packaging research; (w) storage; and (x) control numbers. See: National Pharmaceutical Council, *Twenty-four Reasons Why Prescription Brand Names Are Important to You;* reprinted in U.S., Congress, Senate, Subcommittee on Antitrust and Monopoly of the Committee on the Judiciary, *Hearings on Administered Prices in the Drug Industry,* 86th Cong., 1st sess., 1959 pt. 15, pp. 8637–44—hereafter cited as *1960 Hearings.*

The differences among brands do not appear to be advertised to physicians in the firm's direct-mail presentations, nor is any reference to these variations made in *Physician's Desk Reference,* the standard source of immediate information used by most physicians. (It is possible, however, that some of the drug firms advise the physician of these characteristics through visits by detailmen.) No reference to these characteristics appears to be made in the official sources of information on drugs—textbooks on pharmacology and therapeutics, journal articles, and *New and Nonofficial Drugs.* Accordingly, it would appear that the large firms do not expect the physician to choose their products on the basis of the therapeutically significant differences that are alleged to exist among brands of a given drug.

As for the supposed differences between products available under brand names and the same products that are available under generic names, it is to be noted that medical schools in teaching therapeutics use generic or official names.[23] Pharmacology textbooks, though they list the brand names of drugs (as a concession to reality) in addition to generic names, do not support the contention that there are significant differences between drugs sold under brand names and the same drugs sold under generic names. The same is true for *New and Nonofficial Drugs.* Articles in medical journals, reporting drugs, use the generic name of the drug.

With respect to the differences which are alleged to result from quality control, one professor of pharmacology stated that most of the quality control tests (which large firms represent as differentiating brand-name products from generic-name products) could be performed competently by a pharmacist in a drug store and that there would be no reason to believe that small firms could not perform the tests or control the characteristics which the tests are designed to evaluate.[24]

Nevertheless, the large firms have been highly successful in convincing doctors that they should prescribe by brand name. Their success in reaching medical students with this viewpoint is demonstrated by a report on an experimental course intended to teach medical students to evaluate claims made for new drugs. Solomon Garb, M.D. (Associate Professor of Pharmacology, Albany Medical College), describes the course, and its results:

During the first year of the project, the faculty urged the students to prescribe by official name only. Nevertheless, a single session with the detailmen apparently convinced half of the group to use brand name prescriptions. . . . It was clear that the detailmen's stories and descriptions of the inadequacies of official name drugs, manufactured by firms unknown to the doctor, convinced many students that brand name prescriptions were preferable. The detailmen seemed particularly skillful and well-trained in presenting this argument. Private talks with some of them indicated that they were accustomed to using the same arguments with equal success on practicing physicians. It seems probable that, throughout the country, detailmen are able to persuade physicians to use brand names by pointing out the "dangers" of drugs made by an unknown manufacturer.[25]

In his testimony before the Subcommittee, Garb pointed out that "the detailmen emphasized repeatedly the inability of the FDA to supervise adequately enough. . . ."[26] Of particular interest is the fact that "in all three years [of the project], it was found [by the medical students themselves] that the majority of the mailed ads [advertising brand-name products,] were unreliable, to the extent that a physician trusting them could be seriously misled."[27] Yet the detailmen, representing the companies whose ads the students evaluated, were able to convince half the students that it would be dangerous not to prescribe products by brand names.

There is evidence of widespread use of the products of small firms without any apparent ill effects upon the recipients. Approximately 60 percent of the nonprofit hospitals, having a capacity of 100 beds or more, use the formulary system for dispensing drugs. Under this system, members of the medical staff of the hospital agree to permit the hospital pharmacist to substitute any reliable generic equivalent for the brand specified in their prescriptions. The formulary system offers several advantages to the hospital. First, it permits the hospital to carry a lower inventory of drugs. In 1959, officials at the New York Hospital maintained an inventory of 359 drugs and estimated that, in the absence of the formulary system, approximately 2,500 different brands would have been required. Second, the hospital is able to purchase a particular drug from one manufacturer and may, therefore, qualify for quantity discounts or obtain competitive bids.

Since substitution of unbranded for branded drugs is permitted by the hospital, there are no restrictions on the choice of seller; if there are price differentials among sellers of the same drug, the hospital may select the seller offering the lowest price. At the New York Hospital where approximately $500,000 worth of drugs were purchased in 1959, it was estimated that, without the formulary system, the cost of these drugs would have been 50 percent greater.[28]

In 1959, the military services purchased approximately $40 million worth of drugs through the Military Medical Supply Agency. Drugs to be purchased are advertised by the Agency under their generic names, and the Agency receives bids from the large firms and from 50 to 100 small firms. The lowest bidder for the contract is visited by a representative of the Agency, and its facilities are inspected; if the firm meets the criteria for quality control, the firm is considered to be a qualified supplier and is awarded the contract. Thereafter, the firm is required to maintain quality-control records as specified by the contract and, if the Agency wishes, to permit surveillance of the production of the order.

It is significant that the Agency has not restricted its purchases to large firms. While a comprehensive record of the purchases of the Agency is not available, such evidence as was submitted at the hearings shows that contracts have been awarded to firms with an annual volume of business as small as $75,000 and that when the small firms submitted low bids, they were, typically, awarded the contract. The Agency has apparently found no evidence to support the contention of the large firms that small firms may produce an inferior product, nor has it found evidence that effective quality-control systems are peculiar to large firms.[29]

In summary, it appears to be a reasonable conclusion that whatever differences may exist among the brands of a given drug are of negligible therapeutic significance. If doctors know of these differences at all, it is most likely that their information has come from the large firms, which cannot be regarded as unbiased informants. Medical schools apparently view prescribing by generic name as a desirable procedure and they encourage their students to do so. If generic-name drugs are, in fact, inferior, then we are confronted with the following paradox:

. . . Drugs purchased competitively under generic names are used widely in the treatment of hospitalized patients in the country's major hospitals; here they are regarded as safe enough for patients suffering the most severe illnesses. The Veterans' Administration use these drugs throughout their hospitals. The drugs purchased in a similar manner by the Military Medical Supply Agency are used in the treatment of current military personnel of all ranks; indeed, these drugs are given to Members of Congress and high officials of the executive branch who are temporary residents at military hospitals. Now the AMA has recommended that generic name prescribing be used for welfare patients. If, as Senator Hart inquired, these classes of patients have been treated by drugs prescribed under generic name, what does this mean? Are they being given substandard drugs? Is there one standard for Congressmen and welfare patients, and another for the ordinary citizen?[30]

The physician's knowledge of drugs

The imposition of a generic name or a formulary system on the industry or profession could very well deprive physicians of full freedom of choice in the medications they think necessary for their patients. Simply stated, if the physician or patient wants what he thinks is best, he is entitled to it.[31]

The major firms place considerable emphasis upon the ability of physicians to make rational and accurate use of the arsenal of drugs available to them. One spokesman has credited physicians with absolute knowledge of the products they use. It will be instructive to consider, at this point, how well informed doctors are about drugs, and to find out what the source of their information is.

Peterson, *et al.,* made an intensive study of the practices of 88 general practitioners in North Carolina.[32] Each physician in the sample was observed by one of the authors (themselves physicians) for three to three and a half days. In general, the study concludes: "There [is] tremendous variation in the quality of medical care given. . . . At its very best the practice of medicine resembled that carried out in the medical school. . . . Other physicians' performances were antipodal."[33] Using a ranking scale of I to V, the authors placed 16 doctors in category I (lowest quality) and 7 in category V (highest quality). As a part of the study, the physician's ability to provide rational and specific therapy was observed; this included five general situations in which drugs were a part of the therapy. The comments of the investigators follow.[34]

Upper Respiratory Infections (87 physicians)

a) Antibiotics given indiscriminantly to all patients or to most patients   67%

b) Attempts made to separate viral and bacterial infections for the purpose of therapy   33%

Many physicians did not really understand the values and limitations of these drugs. For instance, the belief that antibiotics are effective in treating the common cold was found to be widespread. Other physicians used these drugs in treating colds on the assumption that they are harmless or might prevent complications. The demand by the patient or his family for a "shot of penicillin" obviously increased the pressure on the physician.

A common finding was the automatic association in the physician's mind between fever or a cold and penicillin. This was manifested by the immediate preparation of an injection of penicillin upon learning that the patient had a fever; this decision was frequently reached before the patient had been examined. . . .

Some physicians made an effort to differentiate between viral and bacterial respiratory infections. Although the efforts frequently involved the use of imperfect criteria, they were indicative of the physician's knowledge of the ineffectiveness of antibiotics against viral infections. The fact that some attempt was made is commendable.

Treatment of Anemia (72 physicians)

a) "Shot-gun" preparations always used   85%

b) Therapy related to type of anemia   15%

Treatment of anemia was rarely selective and definitive; that most frequently employed was one of several proprietary multi-vitamin and mineral compounds, containing in addition, various biologic anti-anemia principles. A few physicians indicated a preference for single iron compounds, vitamins alone or blood transfusions. The deluge of advertising matter undoubtedly influences the physician's choice of therapeutic agents; one pharmaceutical firm advances its product as being curative for all treatable anemias except those due to acute blood loss. This is certainly an attractive proposition to the busy practitioner. Use of many of these preparations is, of course, helpful in many situations, but it may aggravate others and frequently puts the patient to unnecessary expense.

Hypertension (82 physicians)

a) Assessment of hypertensive disease poor or limited to blood pressure determination only. Management not skilled; neglect of simple therapeutic procedures such as weight reduction, rest and salt restriction. Drugs poorly selected or administration unskilled   57%

b) Treatment of hypertension included assessment of arterial disease as evidenced by adequate examination of eye grounds, urine, blood pressure, heart and search for edema. Management included weight reduction, care in selection and supervision of treatment (sedatives, anti-hypertensive drugs, low salt diet, rest and reassurance)   43%

Treatment usually consisted of a single anti-hypertensive drug. Little attention was paid to ancillary measures such as weight reduction and restriction of sodium intake. This seemed to indicate a lack of understanding of hypertensive vascular disease as a whole. Physicians employing the newer anti-hypertensive drugs frequently did not exhibit a thorough knowledge of the values, limitations and proper methods of administration of these drugs.

Congestive Heart Failure (44 physicians)

a) Digitalis, quinidine, mercurials not used with proper indications; salt restriction not accompanied by adequate dietary explanation; management not skilled; no attention to weight reduction   39%

b) Intermediate skill   36%

c) Skilled use of digitalis in adequate amounts; skilled use of mercurial dieuretics, quinidine; use of low salt diet with adequate explanation thereof; management good   25%

Several physicians in treating heart failure appeared to place too much reliance on digitalis alone without individualizing the dose of this drug to fit the patient's needs and without giving sufficient thought and emphasis to other measures. Small doses of tincture of digitalis were occasionally prescribed as a "tonic" for "weak heart" or for the dyspneic patient. The values and limitations of the mercurial diuretics and the role of sodium restriction were poorly understood.

Careful Use of Potentially Dangerous Medications (67 physicians)

a) Doctor made no effort to avoid drug reactions
or complications.　　　　　　　　　　　　　　　　　　　46%

b) Doctor showed awareness of possible toxicity from a medication.
He inquired about previous penicillin injections. He provided proper
supervision and advice to patients receiving drugs such as Butazolidin,
propylthiouracil, ACTH, or cortisone.　　　　　　　　　　　54%

The increased number of potent and relatively specific medications
available today has placed an increased responsibility upon the physician to make a correct diagnosis so that these drugs may be employed
in the most efficaceous manner. The use of potentially dangerous medication is justified only in the case of a grave clinical situation involving
greater threat to life than does the medication. The use of such drugs
obviously depends upon making the correct diagnosis; otherwise their
use in the absence of a clear-cut need is indefensible.

The foregoing indicates that among general practitioners, at
least, many doctors have an imperfect knowledge of pharmacology
and that some physicians not only fail to select and administer
drugs effectively but, on occasion, use quite inappropriate agents.
Some of these errors are due to incomplete understanding of the
drugs themselves; some to inadequate knowledge of the diseases
which the physician is confronted with. That doctors are perfectly
knowledgeable about drugs is a stereotype fostered by the large
firms (among others) for public consumption. The manner in
which large firms promote their products to the doctor is evidence
that they are quite aware of his inadequacies and that they use
these inadequacies to facilitate their marketing programs.

Accordingly, there is some reason to ask how well prepared
doctors are to understand and evaluate new drugs and—once they
have left medical school—where they get their information about
drugs. A study of the quality of medical care in general practice,
prepared for the College of General Practice of Canada, is helpful
in answering the first question.[35] This study, which is largely a
replicate of the North Carolina study, examined the practices of 86
general practitioners in Ontario and Nova Scotia. As a part of the
study, each physician was asked: "Were your medical school
courses in each of the following subjects satisfactory or unsatisfactory *for the purposes of general practice?*" Pharmacology was

regarded as unsatisfactory by 40.9 percent of the Ontario physicians and 29.3 percent of the Nova Scotia physicians.[36]

Pharmacology . . . was described by a number of doctors in both provinces as "antiquated," "archaic," or "outdated." It was said that too much time was spent on "pill-rolling" or "old-fashioned pharmacy" and not enough on the mechanism of the action of the new drugs.[37]

The following lengthy quotation from the study provides an indication of how the typical general practitioner feels about his training in respect to the evaluation of new drugs.

Because new drugs have appeared in overwhelming numbers in recent years and physicians have been beseiged by detail men and bombarded with advertisements and samples, the doctors were asked, "How well did your medical training prepare you to evaluate the claims made for new drugs? Very well? Fairly well? Or not very well?" In Ontario, 57 percent replied "Very well," 9 percent "Fairly well," 32 percent "Not very well," and one doctor did not answer. The corresponding percentages in Nova Scotia were 26 percent, 33 percent, and 40 percent, respectively. When the doctors were grouped according to age, the groups did not differ significantly in their answers, in either province. Thus there is no indication that the evaluation of new drugs is less of a problem to the younger doctors, who might be expected to be better prepared in this respect, than to the older doctors, whose training preceded the modern therapeutic avalanche.

Those who told us that they had been adequately prepared in this respect told us that they had been encouraged to develop a critical attitude. A number of doctors who chose to specify where this attitude had been fostered made it plain that it was not in the department of pharmacology, but in the department of medicine. These comments were intended by the doctors as a criticism of the teaching of pharmacology. Though such criticism may be justified, it is also possible that practical advice was given in the pharmacology course but that, because its applicability was not immediately evident, it fell on deaf ears. In fact, one doctor, one of the younger men, said that the pharmacology course comes too early in the course [medical school curriculum] so that, by the time of graduation, a student has forgotten the fundamentals of pharmacology and is familiar with proprietary preparations.

These doctors who regarded their preparation as inadequate said that they had not developed scientific scepticism and that they were "vulnerable" or "wide open" to drug travellers. One doctor, a fairly recent graduate, said: "We were not prepared for general practice therapeutics. The best drugs, the cost of drugs, and what to look for in dealing with drug travellers were not covered." Several doctors, though aware of their own inability to evaluate the claims made for new drugs, did not recognize even the necessity that they be able to do so, as is shown by one doctor's comment, "It didn't matter really that the pharmacology course at _____ was no good because you learn all the new stuff from the travellers," and by another doctor's statement that he thought the time devoted to teaching medical students to evaluate new drugs would not be well spent "as you use the drug house products anyway." In this connection, we quote from a recent letter written by a member of the College of General Practice of Canada to the Executive Director of the College, "I heard some drugs representatives the other day detailing Aldactone. Out of curiosity I asked them how many general practitioners they talked to even knew what aldosterone [the generic name of Aldactone] was. Their answer was: 'Not very many.' "38

The physician has two general sources of information about drugs—the profession and the industry. In the former groups are the journal articles that he sees, *New and Nonofficial Drugs, The Medical Letter on Drugs and Therapeutics,* and textbooks on therapeutics; hospital staff meetings, medical conventions, and conversations with colleagues; formal education; and rather exotic sources such as "Mediphone." In the latter group:

Besides advertisements in medical journals, two other, more direct, approaches are made to physicians. Daily, the postman brings a flood of advertising material of all shapes and sizes—letters extolling one or another product, magnificent brochures, and boxes containing samples of drugs; and at regular intervals, the practitioner is visited by the companies' local representatives, sometimes by several of these "detail men" in a single afternoon, who take from five to fifteen or twenty minutes to describe their companies' products and usually leave more samples.

How much of a physician's day, on the average, is taken up with detail men and advertisement, we do not know. We do know that all the printed material that arrives in many offices could not be read critically in less than several hours, but much of it is not read at all. Some finds its way, along with samples, straight into the waste-paper basket; some, tossed unlooked-at into a drawer or cupboard, must rest there for weeks or months before rejoining the flow of waste material to the garbage pit; some grows into mountains that threaten to force the physicians from their very desks; and some items, especially certain samples, they find useful.[39]

A measure of the relative importance of the two sources is provided by a study "sponsored and financed by the American Medical Association as the second in its series of basic studies in pharmaceutical marketing undertaken as a service to the pharmaceutical industry."[40]

Table IV–2 identifies the 55 physicians in the study according to the mean number of prescriptions written per week, the mean number of detailmen seen per week, and the most important source of information. Slightly over half of the doctors named the drug industry as the most important source of information. There is a strong association between large numbers of prescriptions written per week, large numbers of visits by detailmen per week, and the proportion of doctors naming the industry as the most important source.

Doctors are clearly influenced by these selling efforts. The authors of the North Carolina study commented:

It was apparent from observation and statements from physicians that their practices in regard to medications and therapy are influenced significantly by the information and products supplied by the drug salesman. This would appear to indicate that the practitioner's habits are not immutable or so rutted that they cannot be directed.[41]

A much blunter statement is the following:

Drug companies have learned that doctors respond to the same kinds of emotional appeals as laymen—i.e., they are influenced by the same advertising techniques that are used in mass consumer advertising. They accept new drugs with amazing rapidity—in part, it would appear, because the physician's own "market position" is strongly influenced by his reputation for using the "latest drug."[42]

Lederle introduced Achromycin—its brand of tetracycline— in November, 1953. The next year, the firm made 105 mailings of advertising material to every physician in the country. "Achromycin ads were run in a long list of publications, at high frequency, and for month after month. The idea was to 'sell' the Achromycin name."[43]

Pfizer is reported to have

. . . run golf tournaments throughout the country, giving out free golf balls bearing the company seal. Greens fees have been paid, and

IV-2. PHYSICIANS' MOST IMPORTANT SOURCES OF INFORMATION ABOUT NEW DRUGS[a]

Number of Prescriptions Written per Week	Number of Physicians	Mean Number of Detail Men Seen per Week	Sources of Information about New Drugs						
			Industry source					Professional source	
			Detailing	Journal Advertisements	Direct Mail Advertisements	Total Industry Source			
None	9	2.33	3	1	0	4	44.4%	5	55.5%
1- 10	10	2.80	3	0	1	4	40.0%	6	60.0%
11- 30	9	3.44	2	1	0	3	33.3%	6	66.7%
31- 50	12	3.42	3	1	2	6	50.0%	6	50.0%
51-100	8	4.13	4	1	1	6	75.0%	2	25.0%
101-150	4	4.00	3	0	0	3	75.0%	1	25.0%
Over 150	3	8.00	2	1	0	3	100.0%	0	0.0%
Totals	55	3.53	20	5	4	29	52.7%	26	47.3%

[a]Ben Gaffin and Associates, "Fond du Lac Study, A Basic Marketing Study Made for the American Medical Association" (Chicago, 1956); reprinted in U.S., Congress, Senate, Subcommittee on Antitrust and Monopoly of the Committee on the Judiciary, *Hearings on Drug Industry Antitrust Act*, 87th Cong., 1st sess., 1961, pt. 2, pp. 739-40.

free golf lessons provided. Fishing contests, bowling tournaments, skeet shoots have been held for non-golfers. The company once rented 3,000 acres of marshland to entertain 700 physicians who enjoyed duck shooting. In Alabama, 460 doctors were treated to a fishing trip and barbecue, with the company supplying fishing equipment and boats and practically hooking the fish.[44]

In contrast to the above is the "soft-sell." In November, 1960, William S. Merrell Co. established 762 "Kevadon Hospital Clinic Programs" involving 29,413 patients.[45] The purpose of these studies was "to observe the effects of the oral administration of Kevadon [thalidomide] in the treatment of insomnia at a dosage of 100 mg. per day." In obtaining physicians to serve as clinical investigators in the program, salesmen were cautioned:

> Bear in mind that these are not *basic* clinical research studies. We have firmly established the safety, dosage and usefulness of Kevadon by both foreign and U.S. laboratory and clinical studies. This program is designed to gain widespread *confirmation* of its usefulness in a variety of hospitalized patients. If your work yields case reports, personal communications or published work, all well and good. But the main purpose is to establish local studies whose results will be spread among hospital staff members. You can assure your doctors that they need not report results if they don't want to but that we, naturally, would like to know of their results. . . . Don't get involved in selling a basic clinical research program instead of Kevadon. *Appeal to the doctor's ego —we think he is important enough to be selected as one of the first to use Kevadon in that section of the country.*[46] [italics in original]

The role of the Food and Drug Administration

The hypothesis that there are significant differences in quality between the drugs produced by large firms and the drugs produced by small firms is not supported by the regulatory behavior of the Food and Drug Administration. The FDA submitted to the Senate hearings the record of legal actions initiated during a ten-year period (January, 1950, to June, 1960) because of composition (control) violations.[47] Actions were begun against 236 firms. Of these, 5 firms are large firms within the definition of this study. Although the remaining firms are not large, it is by no means clear that they are genuine members of the drug industry. (By our procedure, only 44 of the firms can be identified as "small firms selling ethical drugs under their generic names." Undoubtedly, some of the other firms fall into this classification, but they cannot be identified.) No quantitative estimate is provided of the sales of 37 firms; instead, their sales are referred to as "small" or "unknown," or the firms are referred to as being "dormant," "defunct," or "out of business" in 1960. Of those firms for which quantitative estimates are provided, many are very small: 6 firms have annual sales of less than $1,000; 6 have sales between $1,000 and $5,000; and 4 have sales between $5,000 and $10,000. Some of the "firms" are individuals—including one person with the title "Doctor." Some, at least, of the firms must produce proprietary preparations; some, judging from their names, are veterinary medicine firms; still others appear not to be drug companies at all (for example, the Marblehead Lime Co. of Hannibal, Missouri).

For all pharmaceutical preparations firms (*S.I.C.* group 2834), the 1958 Census of Manufacturers indicates that the value of shipments per employee was $31,600. For firms with less than 4 employees, the shipments per employee were $15,200. Thus, firms with sales of $50,000 or less would have three or fewer employees. The Census identifies 503 such firms, and 49 appear in the record of regulatory actions.[48] Are these firms truly members of the industry that we are talking about? In particular, are they "small firms selling under generic name"? This group of firms was estimated to have mean sales of $585,000, and, using the industry figure for shipments per employee, average employment of 19 persons.

Table IV–3 shows the legal actions initiated according to the size of firm. While there is a very pronounced inverse relationship between the number of legal actions initiated and the size of firm, it is impossible to determine which of the small firms are genuine members of the industry, and which are not.

A further difficulty in interpreting this evidence arises from the sampling procedures of the FDA. During the period covered, the FDA apparently sampled the small firms much more intensively than the large ones. The agency selected 8,376 samples from 30 large firms and based four legal actions upon these samples. Using the FDA's estimates of the sales of this group of firms, the number of samples selected was 4.23 per million dollars of 1959 sales.

IV-3. LEGAL ACTIONS INITIATED BY F.D.A. ACCORDING TO SIZE OF FIRM[a]

Size of Firm in terms of 1959 Sales ($ millions)	No. of Firms Engaged in Legal Actions	Total No. of Legal Actions	Mean No. of Legal Actions per Firm Engaged in Legal Action	No. of Firms Engaged in More than One Legal Action	Total No. of Legal Actions for Firms Engaged in More than One Action	Mean No. of Legal Actions per Firm for Firms Engaged in More than One Legal Action	Mean No. of Legal Actions per $ Million of 1959 Sales for All Firms Engaged in Legal Actions	Approx. No. of Firms in Category of Size	No. of Legal Actions per Firm
Less than 0.1	61	94	1.54	17	50	2.94	54.7	503	0.187
0.1-0.2	39	84	2.15	22	67	3.05	17.1	156	0.538
0.2-0.3	23	44	1.91	11	32	2.91	8.5	137	0.591
0.3-0.4	14	37	2.64	8	31	3.86	8.1	140	0.430
0.4-0.6	16	38	2.38	8	30	3.75	5.0		
0.6-1.0	11	22	2.00	7	18	2.57	3.1	59	0.780
1.0-2.0	16	46	2.88	9	39	4.33	2.3	61	0.560
2.0-6.0	10	34	3.40	6	30	5.00	1.2	58	0.310
More than 6.0	10	18	1.80	2	10	5.00	0.06		
Totals	200	417		90	307			1,114	

[a] 1960 Hearings, 2nd sess., pt. 22, pp. 12137-65.

77

Over the same period, 8,621 samples were selected from the remaining firms in the industry. (The FDA estimates that there are 1,200 other firms, but it did not select samples from all of them.) On the basis of these samples, 484 legal actions were begun.* The number of samples selected per million dollars of 1959 sales is 29.13.† On the basis of the number of samples selected, it would seem that small firms were inspected 6.89 times more intensively than were large firms.

The record of samples selected from individual firms is available only for the large firms and for the 17 small firms which had appeared before the Subcommittee prior to the time of the Commissioner's testimony. The contrast between these two groups is even more marked. From the FDA's estimate, these 17 firms had sales in 1959 of $20.9 million, or 7.1 percent of the sales of all small firms; but the FDA took 2,479 samples from them, or 28.8 percent of the samples selected from all non-large firms. On the basis of these samples, the FDA initiated 42 legal actions, or 8.7 percent of the legal actions were brought against the entire group of 17 small firms. The rate of sampling from this group was 118.6 samples per million dollars of sales in 1959. These firms were, therefore, sampled at a rate approximately 29 times greater than the rate for large firms.

Further, there are substantial variations in sampling rates within the two groups of firms, and these do not appear to be systematically related to the number of legal actions initiated. Thus, one firm within the group of 17 small firms had sales in 1959 of $200,000 and was sampled at the rate of 590 samples per million dollars of sales; one legal action was brought. Another firm, in the same group, had sales of $190,000, but no samples were selected during the ten-year period.

Among the large firms, Bristol, with sales in 1959 of $21 million, was sampled at the rate of 17.48 samples per million dollars of

---

* Table 3 in *1960 Hearings* (2nd sess., 22, pp. 12141–44) shows that only 412 "non-large" firms were involved in litigation. The additional legal actions —72—are noted in a summary table (No. 7 in *1960 Hearings,* 2nd sess., 22, p. 12147), but no explanation of the discrepancy is given. It would appear that the FDA did not submit the complete record.

† This figure and the others on the following pages (??, ??) were arrived at by using the FDA's estimates of sales for the group of firms in question.

sales, the highest rate for the large firms. No legal actions were initiated. Wallace Laboratories, a firm of much the same size—$23 million of sales in 1959—was sampled at the rate of 2.3 samples per million dollars of sales. One legal action was initiated. For the large firms, the lowest sampling rate was 0.6 samples per million dollars of sales.

If these figures can be interpreted at their face value, it would appear that the FDA does not allocate its sampling resources to areas where their marginal benefits would be the greatest. Extensive sampling is done on the products of firms with small outputs, and only a very few violations are discovered. On the other hand, sampling is less intensive—relatively and sometimes absolutely— for large firms even though a higher rate of violations relative to sales is discovered. That the agency does not allocate its total resources in a manner consistent with the hypothesis that there are significant differences in quality— and, in fact, *does not feel that increased resources are necessary*—is suggested by the following excerpt from the views of the majority of the members of the Subcommittee.

Nor can the Food and Drug Administration have recourse to the in-adequate funds defense. During the period 1952–60 appropriations for the agency were increased by 60 percent. What is more relevant here, the Congress has usually appropriated substantially the amount re-quested, *or more*. . . . Moreover, the manner in which the agency apportioned its appropriation on work involving ethical drugs as con-trasted to other and perhaps less important types of activities is open to question. This would particularly be the case if the problem of in-ferior quality of products offered by small firms is as serious as the large firms profess it to be.[49]

The evidence of drug "recalls" suggests that when violations are uncovered, the FDA treats large firms differently from small firms. Thus:

During the same period [January 1950 to June 1960], 84 incidents of irregularities developed in connection with drugs made by large firms, 79 of which were handled by the "drug recall" procedure and five of which led to legal actions. For small firms, 690 such irregulari-ties developed, 206 of which led to legal actions. The ratio of legal actions is almost 100 to one, while the ratio of drug recalls is only five to two. Clearly, those irregularities involving large firms are much more frequently negotiated than those involving small firms.*

Such differences in the treatment of large and small firms are partly, at least, the result of the aging process to which all regulatory agencies eventually succumb. Wilcox, in describing this phenomenon, might very well have been writing of the Food and Drug Administration:

. . . In time, however, the agency matures. The force that gave it impetus is spent. The quality of its personnel declines. It loses its taste for conflict. Divorced from other sources of support, it turns for strength to the industry it regulates. Through constant contact, it comes to accept the industry's standpoint as its own. . . .

In its old age, the commission loses all contact with the public interest. It envisages its function as that of protecting the health and welfare of the regulated industry and maintaining its own status as the industry's protector. It ceases to adapt its thinking to external change. Its policies are encrusted with tradition; its procedures hardened into routine. It comes to be institutionalized, embodying vested interests and seeming to have values in itself. Its members become more concerned with preserving its existence than with forwarding its purposes.[50]

In 1963 the FDA employed an average of 2,696 persons during the year, of whom approximately 1,150 were medical, scientific, and technical personnel. In a five-year period (January 1, 1959 to December 31, 1963) 813 employees in these classifications left the FDA. Of those resigning, 83 accepted employment with firms in industries regulated by the FDA; of this latter group, the major drug companies hired 20.[51] Concerning this matter a further quotation from Wilcox is apt: ". . . Serving for low salaries for limited terms, they see well-paid lifetime jobs awaiting them in the regulated industries. And they may let these factors influence the decisions that they make."[52]

That the agency has tended to accept the industry's (or the large firms') viewpoints as its own is exemplified by the different levels of authority required to accept or reject a new drug application.

* Henry Steele, "Monopoly and Competition in the Ethical Drugs Market," *Journal of Law and Economics* 5 (Oct. 1962): 144–45. He adds: "It must not be assumed that irregularities involving legal action were more serious, on the average, than those settled by drug recall. If anything, the reverse is true" p. 145.

A medical officer in the New Drug Branch has the power to release any new drug on his own initiative, without review by any of his colleagues. To refuse to release a new drug, however, he must have the unanimous support of the Chief of the New Drug Branch, the Director of the Bureau of Medicine, the Commissioner, and usually also the Director of the Bureau of Enforcement and the General Counsel's office.[53]

The experience of one medical officer in examining new drug applications is instructive on this point.

. . . When a drug firm submits a new drug application for an important new drug, it is common for their representatives to call the Chief of the New Drug Branch a few days later and inquire which medical officer is handling the application. It is promptly supplied.

The medical officer then receives a call to the effect that the firm wishes to send representatives to discuss the application, and he is expected to make such an appointment promptly. If he does not do so, perhaps for the very valid reason that he has not yet studied the application, he is reprimanded by his Chief as uncooperative, and the appointment is made anyway by a clerk.

A day rarely passes without several such conferences in the New Drug Branch. If the firm anticipates no difficulties, they send a single representative. If the medical officer has suggested over the phone that the new drug application may not be completely satisfactory, four or five men appear in his office to argue the case. He may also be invited to attend a medical meeting sponsored by the firm at which the drug in question will be discussed by the clinical investigators.

Frequently, at such meetings, the investigators who have been lukewarm or cold about the merits of the drug are not invited to participate.

If the medical officer is still not satisfied with the evidence of safety, the Company will frequently make an appointment with the Medical Director, who has not seen the data on the new drug application, to present their side of the story to him. I have known such conferences to be followed by an order to the medical officer to make the new drug application effective, with the statement that the company in question has been evaluating drugs much longer than the medical officer and should, therefore, be in a much better position to judge their safety.[54]

The foregoing discussion concerns the FDA's regulation of new drugs; documentation of the same sort is not available concerning the surveillance of drugs already on the market. However, if liberality of this sort is permitted with new drugs, the following hypothesis about the regulatory process for established drugs as it existed at the time of the hearings would not seem unduly cynical. Violations by large firms give rise to expressions of mutual good will and are handled by "gentleman's agreements between law-yers,"[55] with the result that no record—and no legal action—is found. Violations by small firms are dealt with severely—in part, so that the agency will have a record to show that it has moved with full vigor against those who would endanger the public health. Furthermore, cases against small firms are probably easier and less expensive to win.

The majority of the Subcommittee concluded that the large firms, with the assistance of the FDA, had been successful in persuading doctors of the imprudence of prescribing by generic name.

. . . The hard fact is that the drug companies have been largely suc-cessful in persuading physicians to write their prescriptions in terms of trade names; this is attested to by the very small proportion of com-mercial sales made of generically prescribed drugs. This successful campaign of persuasion by the large firms has been achieved in the face of two obstacles which make the accomplishment all the more remark-able. The first is the existence of Government inspection, coupled with enforcement powers, designed to assure acceptable quality of all drug products, whether sold by large or small companies. In this industry governmental intervention in the economic process to assure that prod-ucts of all companies meet similar quality standards is and has long been a reality, dictated by the necessity of protecting the public health. To overcome whatever inclination the physician might have to pre-scribe generically because of this reality, the drug companies have sought to create the impression that the governmental body involved, the Food and Drug Administration, has regrettably been derelict in its duty. The Agency, it is stressed, simply cannot get around to policing all the companies which make up the industry, and therefore, it is held, the wise physician should rely on those companies whose products he can be sure of. It is a considerable understatement to say that this cam-paign has in no way been hindered by the Food and Drug Adminis-tration.[56]

As an example of the last point, the former Medical Director of the Food and Drug Administration, Dr. Albert H. Holland, is quoted by the president of Merck as saying:

The naive belief that if the product is not good the FDA would prohibit its sales is just not realistic. FDA labors long and diligently to protect the public but the fact of the matter is that it is completely impossible for the FDA to check every batch of every product by every manufacturer that is marketed. Hence the integrity and reputation of the manufacturer assumes unusual significance where drugs and health products are concerned.*

In summary, the record of the Food and Drug Administration does not provide conclusive evidence that the public is any more secure with large manufacturers than with small. If small firms appear to be less reliable than large firms, the answer probably is that the two classes of firm are differently treated by the FDA.

The "reputation" of firms

The large firms represent themselves to be scrupulously honest, professing that medical and scientific considerations always outweigh commercial considerations, and contend that the small firms have exactly the opposite hierarchy of values. The large firms argue that their unimpeachable standards of integrity will be reflected in quality control. There is no evidence, however, that in this respect large firms enjoy any preponderance of virtue over small firms.

If professions of integrity are to be convincing, adequate standards must prevail throughout all phases of the firm's operations where medical and commercial considerations could conflict. In the case of the large firms, taken as a group, aberrations from standards appear to be not infrequent. This observation is suggested by the kind of information which these firms disseminate to the medical profession about the properties and usefulness of individual drugs.

In most industries, the criticism that scientific and medical con-

* John T. Connor, *1960 Hearings,* 1st sess., pt. 14, p. 8198. The unfortunate Dr. Holland is also cited in the following note: "This time I went directly to Dr. Holland, suggesting that we should insist on a strong warning to this effect. [The medical officer had been advised Public Health Service physicians had observed physical withdrawal symptoms, including convulsions, associated with meprobamate.] I was ordered to do nothing about it because 'I will not have my policy of friendliness with the industry interfered with.' " Barbara Moulton, *1960 Hearings,* 2nd sess., pt. 22, p. 12032.

siderations are not paramount in the preparation of advertising material would be trivial. Though the seller may repeat his claims *ad nauseam,* no one seriously believes that consumption of a particular brand of cigarette will confer sexual prowess or that the use of a particular brand of deodorant will bring lasting happiness. Advertising of consumer goods is largely the incessant and banal repetition of nonsense which the consumer is free to succumb to or not. For most products, the maxim of *caveat emptor* is adequate. Producer goods are bought mostly by knowledgeable buyers who have both the incentive and the competence to be critical of the seller's claims.

Ethical drugs, however, do not fall into either category. The very fact that such drugs require a physician's authority for their purchase, i.e., that the patient is required to consult with a professional "purchasing agent," is evidence that *caveat emptor* provides insufficient protection. As we have seen, doctors are unable to evaluate the claims which are made for many drugs. Recognizing this, the large firms represent their promotional activities as constituting the physician's "post-graduate education" and assume the posture of disinterested consultants.[57] Unlike other industries, the pharmaceutical industry represents its selling efforts as being consistent with the canons of scientific impartiality. Doctors are expected to believe what is said about the advertising, and hence to believe the advertising itself. They can be seriously misled, however, for much of the advertising is flagrantly unconforming to the standards of science.

Numerous instances of unprofessional behavior can be cited. One firm falsified the results of its research and was convicted.[58] Another knew for several years that one of its products had serious side effects but did not so inform the medical profession; and still another either suppressed the evidence or denied the fact. "Research" is sometimes no more than an attempt to get testimonials from doctors. A number of journals that derive their revenue from the sale of reprints to pharmaceutical companies exist to publish articles favorable to the products of the companies that back these journals.[59] Some firms "promote" their prescription drugs to the general public by having a public relations organization plant stories of "medical progress" in the lay press.[60] A senior official of the Food and Drug Administration was forced to resign after the discovery that he had been writing what amounted to testimonials for a drug company, and in some firms the judgment of the medical directors is overridden by the decisions of the marketing department. In fact, it is not too much to say that all the means available to make evidence appear to say what it does not are used in the advertising of drugs.

One of the most serious charges against the drug industry is that it withholds or suppresses information regarding undesirable side effects of new drugs. In one such case Pfizer had data from 1,922 cases in which Diabinese (chlorpropamide) had been used. Of these, 27 percent of the patients showed one or more side effects, and 9 percent showed liver damage. The majority view expressed in the *Report* was:

Despite the substantial information known to Pfizer with respect to side effects as early as the summer of 1958, the company made no attempt to supply this essential material to physicians in its advertising. For example, a typical ad dated May 1959, . . . contained these words: "Diabinese is 'well tolerated with minimum side effects in the therapeutic range of 100 to 500 mg.' Its striking effectiveness and 'almost complete absence of unfavorable side effects' have led to the prediction that 'Diabinese will eventually prove to be the drug of choice in the sulfonylurea field.' "[61] One doctor commented: ". . . the incidence of 1 percent or one-half of 1 percent of jaundice should deter any physician from prescribing this agent when there is insulin or tolbutamide available, both of which never cause liver damage."[62]

In another case Parke-Davis ignored the advice of the National Research Council and, in fact, made statements directly contradicting the findings of the FDA. Beginning in 1950, reports of aplastic anemia associated with the use of chloramphenicol began to appear. In June, 1952, the Food and Drug Administration asked the National Research Council to make recommendations for the future use of the drug. In August, 1952, the Council's *ad hoc* committee of physicians presented its conclusions, which are summarized below:

1. Certain cases of serious blood dyscrasias [have] been associated with chloramphenicol (brand name: Chloromycetin).

2. Although this complication [has] thus far been uncommon, it [is] considered sufficiently important to warrant a warning on the label of the packages of the drug and in advertisements of the drug and the recommendation that chloramphenicol not be used indiscriminately or for minor infections.

3. When prolonged or intermittent administration is required, adequate blood studies should be made.

4. Further studies of serious reactions to chloramphenicol and other drugs should be made.[63]

At the FDA's request, Parke-Davis agreed to the labelling changes recommended by the Council. On August 12, 1952, the president of the firm advised detailmen that Chloromycetin had been "officially cleared by the FDA and the National Research Council with *no restrictions* on the number or range of diseases for which Chloromycetin may be administered."[64] A month later, the firm wrote to detailmen saying "the recent decision reached by the Food and Drug Administration with the assistance of the National Research Council and a board of nationally known medical experts was undoubtedly the highest compliment ever tendered the medical staff of our Company."[65] In November, detailmen were "instructed to memorize and repeat verbatim to the physician: '. . . intensive investigation by the Food and Drug Administration, carried on with the assistance of a special committee of eminent specialists appointed by the National Research Council, resulted in the unqualified sanction of continued use of Chloromycetin for all conditions in which it has previously been used.' "[66]

One physician, formerly the acting medical director of the Roerig Division of Pfizer, described the promotion of brand name drugs:

In reference to promotion, it should be mentioned that a great many clinical studies are carried out and extensively supported financially for the sole purpose of producing allegedly scientific articles at regular intervals. These articles are published and actively keep the name of the drug before the medical profession. Reprints of such articles are considered invaluable for detailing the product to physicians.[67]

The former medical director of Squibb, Dr. A. Dale Console, also commented on drug promotion:

Testimonials are used not only to give apparent substance to the promotion and advertising of relatively worthless products, but also to extend the indications of effective drugs beyond the range of their real utility. They appear either as complete reprints or as priceless quotations in advertisements or brochures. They convince too many physicians that they should prescribe the drug.

Now, the true nature of these testimonials is well known to the industry and its own contempt for them is shown by its vernacular for sources from which they are easily obtained. These are called stables. Still it is an important function, usually of the medical division, to send representatives with generous expense accounts to all parts of the country searching out these sources. The burlesque is compounded by calling the drug trials "scientific studies" and by supporting them with grants which are charged to research cost.[68]

In view of the large firms' claim to scientific rectitude, it is interesting to note the position of company medical officers in relation to the financial administrators. A former medical director commented:

In some companies the medical director is more or less a screen, and by that I mean a smokescreen. . . . He merely throws a cloak of respectability over what are really business decisions. In other companies on some products he has the final word. Usually, if the investment in a product has been large, and if it has great potential for sales, and particularly if the underground indicates that another company is going to market it, the medical director will be overruled. He has one vote.[69]

The former medical director of the Roering division of Pfizer said, "My decision to leave Pfizer's employ was long-standing because I had come to realize that the managerial policies in the marketing division were incompatible with both the ethics of my profession and my sense of morality."[70]

Many of the ruses used in advertising commercial health aids (toothpaste, sugarless chewing gum, and proprietary drugs) are also used to promote the sales of ethical drugs.

Implied endorsements by vague illusion to the use of the product by "many" physicians or hospitals is expected to be convincing, as are the results of inadequate surveys showing "9 out of 10" answering a mail questionnaire favored the product although it was not mentioned that only a small percentage of those questioned bothered to answer.

The appeal to the eye is seldom neglected, but the mind may not be taxed at all with useful information as to the contraindications, side effects, toxicity, etc. Least of all can one hope to find any discouraging data on actual or comparative cost of "new" preparations versus established forms of a drug.[71]

The main reason for all this frenetic and questionable activity in the promotion of drugs is that drug companies manufacture many new products that are useless or less valuable than existing drugs. "Even in a decade of furious research activity, only a handful of pharmaceutical world-beaters can be expected to appear, and the introduction of three or four *thousand* compounds over the same period of time means that advertising agencies are being asked to palm sows' ears off on the medical profession for silk purses"[72] (italics in original).

Doctors are impressed by new drugs and take them up quickly. Following Console, these new drugs may be classified as follows:

1) effective drugs to be prescribed only to patients who need them;

2) effective drugs to be prescribed to patients who do not need them;

3) drugs from which patients derive no more benefit than would be derived from less expensive drugs;

4) drugs from which patients derive no benefit; and

5) drugs which have more potential for harm than good.[73]

Introduction of new products is the vehicle of competition in the industry. The firm which finds that its research efforts have yielded a drug with a low sales potential must compensate for this competitive disadvantage by endowing the drug with properties which it does not have.

. . . The problem arises out of the fact that they market so many of their failures.

•   •   •   •   •

I doubt that there are many other industries in which research is so free of risks. Most must depend on selling only their successes. If an automobile does not have a motor no amount of advertising can make it appear to have one. On the other hand, with a little luck, proper timing, and a good promotion program a bag of asafetida with a unique chemical side chain can be made to look like a wonder drug. The illusion may not last, but it frequently lasts long enough. By the time the doctor learns what the company knew in the beginning, it has two products to take the place of the old one.[74]

CONCLUSIONS

The evidence presented in this chapter appears to support the following conclusions:

1) The standards of quality of the *U.S. Pharmacopeia* appear to be acceptable to medical schools, large hospitals, and government agencies. Support for standards "higher" than those of the *U.S.P.* however, comes only from the large drug firms. It does not appear that these allegedly better standards confer any significant therapeutic benefits.

2) Quality control is not a particularly difficult or expensive process. Small firms would gain no perceptible cost advantage by resorting to procedures that were inferior in respect to quality control.

3) There is no evidence, other than what appears in promotional or other statements from the large firms, that the variations existing among brands of a given drug permit the physician to prefer, on medical grounds, one brand of a given drug to another.

4) Physicians are not in possession of complete knowledge concerning the appropriate use of even the long-established drugs, much less the newer drugs. They sometimes use drugs inappropriately, and they have no special training which equips them to evaluate the claims made by the large firms for newer drugs.

5) The record of legal actions initiated by the Food and Drug Administration, while showing the large firms to have fewer legal actions per million dollars of sales, does not demonstrate that small firms selling under generic name have inferior quality-control procedures. The agency, which sometimes identifies itself with the large firms, has not denied their claim that they have superior quality-control procedures; but the marginal regulatory actions of the Food and Drug Administration do not indicate that the alleged differences in quality have any significance for public health.

6) A large proportion of the nation's physicians rely heavily upon the industry for their information about new drugs. The industry has found that procedures other than the objective dissemination of information are effective in promoting the sale of its products. The claims made by the large firms for the integrity of their quality-control processes must be judged against the some-

times dubious advice given to doctors by these same firms on the appropriate use of drugs.

7) In general, it seems that brand names neither permit the physician to discriminate in a therapeutically useful way among the products of several competing large firms selling the same drug, nor provide "protection" against the allegedly inferior products of the small firms. The physician appears to have no reason *consistent with the welfare of his patients* to prefer the products of the large firms. It would also appear that no harm would come to the patient if the physician used only the generic name of a drug in writing his prescription, thereby allowing the patient to take advantage of whatever price competition might exist.

A thorough review of the procedures and actions of the Food and Drug Administration is not feasible within the limits of the present study, but it is worth noting that the criticisms of existing inspection procedures would be fairly met by subjecting all drugs to batch inspection. Serums are now so inspected by the Public Health Service, and—given the practice among nearly all drug manufacturers of producing drugs in batches—there is no reason to doubt that uniformly adequate batch-inspection procedures, administered by a fully empowered federal agency, would deprive the large firms of their claim to superiority in respect to quality control. As we have seen, this claim is questionable. Large firms use it in denying that drugs in any given category may be therapeutically homogeneous (e.g., homogeneously unsatisfactory or satisfactory) and in impugning the procedures and standards of small firms. Evidently, a policy or a combination of policies that insured absolute homogeneity in respect to quality control would both guarantee the safety of drugs and enable doctors to prescribe and patients to buy on the basis of price.

CHAPTER FIVE

Price Relationships

In this chapter the relationships among the prices charged by the different types of drug firm are examined and, as well, the methods of making price comparisons. The resulting data are then presented in Tables V–1 and V–2. Finally, some hypotheses about the nature and degree of market power are investigated in order to see whether price differences lend support to the hypotheses proposed.

The following hypothetical example will illustrate the method used in setting up ratios for the comparison of prices charged by the four types of firm. Suppose that a consumer is given the opportunity to purchase a specified drug at the price which the manufacturer charges the pharmacist. From among all the types of firm which produce the drug, two types are selected: call them Type A and Type B. Without any knowledge of the prices, the consumer selects a firm at random and pays the price charged by that firm. If the consumer chooses a firm from among Type A firms, the expected value of the price that he will pay, designated as $E(A)$, is the arithmetic mean of the prices charged by Type A firms. Similarly, if the consumer chooses a firm from among Type B firms, the expected price will be $E(B)$. If the mean of prices charged by Type B firms is greater than that charged by Type A firms, then by always selecting a firm at random from among Type A firms the consumer will have an expected saving equal to the difference between $E(B)$ and $E(A)$. This is an acceptable method for representing the saving on an individual drug, but it does not permit the comparison of several drugs because the amount of the saving depends upon the quantity of the drug and the units which measure quantity are not comparable from one drug to another. This problem can be circumvented by measuring the expected saving as a ratio: $E(A)/E(B)$. Thus, suppose a value of 0.753 is obtained for the ratio. This can be stated as $E(A) = 0.753 \times E(B)$, which in turn says that if the consumer selects a firm randomly from among Type A manufacturers, he would expect to pay 75.3 percent of the expected price charged by Type B firms.*

This example uses only two types of firm. The ratios that can be computed for a particular drug will depend upon how many types of firm produce the drug. If a drug is produced by only one type of firm, as 429 of the drugs are, there will be no ratios for that drug.† If the drug is produced by two types of firm, one ratio will exist; correspondingly, three types of firm will generate three ratios and four types of firm, six ratios. Since 227 drugs are produced by more than one type of firm, these drugs will have at least one ratio. The ratios, their definitions, and the notation used in referring to them are listed in Table V–1.

As an example, consider the ratio SG/LB. If a drug is found

* In using a ratio as the measure of benefit for a single drug, which type of firm is put in the numerator of the ratio and which in the denominator is arbitrary. Thus, the measure of benefit could just as well have been represented by $E(B)/E(A)$, since $E(B)/E(A) = 1/[E(A)/E(B)] = 1/0.753 = 1.328$.

If the consumer chooses from among Type B firms, he expects to pay 132.8 percent of the price that he would expect to pay if he chose from among Type A firms. Obviously both ratios say the same thing.

† The fact that there are 429 drugs for which it is not possible to construct a price ratio is in no way a limitation of the study. The implication is that a policy of eliminating brand names in the prescribing of drugs would have no effect upon the prices of these 429 drugs, but it should be noted that the prices of 354 of the 429 would be affected by the removal of patents (see pp. 105–106) and that a total of 581 would be affected by the simultaneous removal of brand names and patents. (This figure is determined by adding the difference between 656—all drugs—and 429—those for which there are no ratios—to 354.)

to be produced both by small firms selling under generic names and large firms selling under brand names, the ratio is computed by dividing the mean price charged by small firms selling under generic names by the mean price charged by large firms selling under brand names. There are 102 drugs which are produced by both of these types of firm and hence 102 observations of $E(SG)/E(LB)$. This procedure is repeated for each ratio. A frequency distribution of the observations of each of the six principal ratios is presented in Table V–2.

V-1. DEFINITIONS OF PRICE RATIOS

Definition of Price Ratio	Type of Firm in Numerator of Price Ratio	Type of Firm in Denominator of Price Ratio	Symbolic Notation for Price Ratio
$E(SG)/E(SB)$	Small firm using generic name	Small firm using brand name	SG/SB
$E(SG)/E(LG)$	Small firm using generic name	Large firm using generic name	SG/LG
$E(SG)/E(LB)$	Small firm using generic name	Large firm using brand name	SG/LB
$E(SB)/E(LG)$	Small firm using brand name	Large firm using generic name	SB/LG
$E(SB)/E(LB)$	Small firm using brand name	Large firm using brand name	SB/LB
$E(LG)/E(LB)$	Large firm using generic name	Large firm using brand name	LG/LB
$E(S)/E(L)$	Small firm	Large firm	S/L
$E(G)/E(B)$	Firm using generic name	Firm using brand name	G/B
$E(SG)/E(L)$	Small firm using generic name	Large firm	SG/L
$E(SB)/E(L)$	Small firm using brand name	Large firm	SB/L

It is useful to have some summary measures of the frequency distributions, and these are presented in Table V–3. As the observations are ratios in which the selection of the numerator and the

FREQUENCY DISTRIBUTIONS OF EACH PRICE RATIO[a]

Type of Price Ratio

Value of E(A)/E(B)	SG/SB	SG/LG	SG/LB	SB/LG	SB/LB	LG/LB
0.0-0.1			1			
0.1-0.2	3		9		2	
0.2-0.3	5	9	16		4	1
0.3-0.4	13	8	8		3	1
0.4-0.5	10	11	16	1	3	1
0.5-0.6	11	11	13	3	12	0
0.6-0.7	6	9	11	2	7	2
0.7-0.8	3	10	6	2	4	2
0.8-0.9	8	14	11	2	5	4
0.9-1.0	6	18	3	3	8	7
1.0-1.1	3	9	2	1	11	11
1.1-1.2	0	3	1	4	5	4
1.2-1.3	0	1	2	2	3	2
1.3-1.4	2	0	0	1	3	2
1.4-1.5	2	1	1	0	2	1
1.5-1.6	1	1	1	0	0	1
1.6-1.7	0	0	0	1	2	0
1.7-1.8	0	0	0	0	0	0
1.8-1.9	0	0	0	0	1	1
1.9-2.0	0	1	1	1	0	
2.0-2.1	0			0	0	
2.1-2.2	0			1	1	
2.2-2.3	0			0		
2.3-2.4	1			0		
2.4-2.5	0			1		
2.5-2.6	0					
2.6-2.7	1					
Totals	75	106	102	25	76	40
Number of observations less than 1.0	65	90	94	13	48	18

[a]The figures in the body of the table indicate the number of drugs for which the value of the ratio is between the limits shown in the left-hand column. For example, there are 13 drugs produced by both SG and LB types of firm for which the price ratio is between 0.5 and 0.6, i.e., for which the SG firms charge between 50 and 60 percent of the price charged by LB firms.

V-3.   DESCRIPTIVE STATISTICS SHOWING THE DISTRIBUTIONS
OF PRICE RATIOS

	SG/SB	SG/LG	SG/LB	SB/LG	SB/LB	LG/LB
No. of observations	75	106	102	25	76	40
Geometric mean	.5748	.6623	.4666	.9662	.7462	.9457
Arithmetic mean	.6783	.7302	.5589	1.0734	.8490	1.0020
Median	.5808	.7450	.5024	.9142	.8518	1.0000

denominator is arbitrary, the arithmetic mean of the ratios will
give ambiguous results. The geometric mean of the observations
yields unambiguous results, and is used in place of the arithmetic
mean.*

* The geometric mean may be defined as the nth root of the product of N
observations. Thus, the geometric mean of 2 and 8 is the square root of their
product—i.e., 4—and the geometric mean of three numbers would be the
cube root of their product. For the purpose of calculating the geometric mean
of the observations used in this study, the observations were converted into
logarithms; the arithmetic average of the logarithms was taken; and the antilog
of that average, computed.

The ambiguity that arises when the arithmetic mean is used is illustrated
by the following example:

Drug	Price charged by Mfgr. A	Price charged by Mfgr. B	Ratio of price A to price B	Ratio of price B to price A
1	$1.00	$4.00	.25	4
2	2.00	4.00	.5	2
3	1.00	3.00	.33	3
Arithmetic mean of ratios:			.36	3

The arithmetic mean of the ratios in Col. 4 is .36 and of those in Col. 5 is 3;
hence, on the arithmetic mean, Manufacturer A charges 36 percent of what
Manufacturer B charges, or Manufacturer B charges 3 times what Manufacturer A charges. The ambiguity appears in the discrepancy between the
reciprocal of .36, which is 2.85, and the arithmetic mean in Col. 5, which is 3.
This discrepancy will occur whenever the arithmetic mean of the price ratios
for several different drugs is used.

Unambiguous results can be obtained by using geometric rather than arithmetic means; thus, in the hypothetical example, the geometric mean of the
values in Col. 4 is .3467 and of those in Col. 5 is 2.884, the reciprocal of
.3467.

Tests of hypotheses concerning the direction of market power

We expect market power to be related to the size of the firm and to the use of brand names. Within a given market, small firms would be expected to have less market power than large firms and less power than firms selling under brand names. *A priori,* the following set of hypotheses is specified:

1)	Small firm Generic name	Has less market power than	Small firm Brand name
2)	Small firm Generic name	Has less market power than	Large firm Generic name
3)	Small firm Generic name	Has less market power than	Large firm Brand name
4)	Small firm Brand name	Unspecified	Large firm Generic name
5)	Small firm Brand name	Has less market power than	Large firm Brand name
6)	Large firm Generic name	Has less market power than	Large firm Brand name

These relationships are further considered in Appendix A (pp. 161–68). The existence of market-power relationships can be investigated by using tests to determine whether a firm with less market power charges significantly lower prices than a firm classified as having greater market power. With the exception of (6), the tests used in Appendix A support all the relationships specified above. The results of the test show that the degrees of market power possessed by small firms selling under brand names and large firms selling under generic names are about equal, and there seems to be no significant difference (in a statistical sense) between the market power possessed by large firms selling under generic names and large firms selling under brand names.

Relationship between drug age and the value of the price ratio

Assume that for a given drug the products of all manufacturers reveal no systematic, objectively testable differences in quality.

Suppose, however, that physicians believe that there are such differences and therefore prescribe the drug by specifying the seller of the drug irrespective of the price charged by that firm. We hypothesize that this belief would be strongest when the drug was first introduced but that as physicians received additional information about the drug, they would come to regard it as therapeutically homogeneous (irrespective of manufacturer), and thereafter would be willing to specify a manufacturer on the basis of price, or at least to permit the consumer to select the seller. In time, an increasing number of doctors would stop specifying brand names in their prescriptions and would start to prescribe by price alone. As this process continued, firms which had benefited from the belief in the existence of quality differentials would find their market positions deteriorating and would reduce their prices to reverse this erosion. With each reduction in the prices charged by such firms, there would be an increase in the value of the appropriate price ratio, indicating a decline in the benefit to the consumer of choosing the type of firm shown in the numerator of the ratio.*

To test this hypothesis, price information for each drug in each year since its introduction would be required. With such information, a time series for the price ratios could be constructed for each drug. This information is not available, but one can determine whether the age of a drug is significant in an explanation of the values of particular price ratios. The question is, do older drugs exhibit higher price ratios than newer drugs? If they do, we can assume that market power is less for the older drugs than for the newer drugs and that this difference is attributable to the gradual acceptance of the idea that drugs in any given category are therapeutically homogeneous regardless of what firm manufactures them. If, on the other hand, age and price ratio appear to be independent, then we conclude that belief in the existence of quality differentials has a permanent effect on price ratios.

The procedures used in analyzing this hypothesis are explained

---

* An increase in the value of a ratio (expressed as a quotient) would be accompanied by a corresponding decrease in the value of the denominator of the ratio. Hence, the advantage to the consumer of choosing a firm symbolized in the numerator would decline as the value of the ratio approached unity and would disappear as soon as the value exceeded unity. Some representative values are shown in Table V-3 (p. 95).

in Appendix A (pp. 161–68). The results of the analysis indicate that age is in fact irrelevant in explaining variations in price ratios and that relative market power is not affected by the passage of time.

Relationships between method of administration and price ratio

The method by which a drug is administered indicates something about the purchaser of the drug. If the drug is administered orally, the patient typically receives a prescription from the physician and takes it to a pharmacist to have it filled. If the physician has specified the selling firm, the patient faces a monopolist; he may buy the product of the specified firm or he may make no purchase. In the case of injectibles, the physician purchases the drug in dosage form for resale to the patient. In purchasing the drug, the physician is not restricted to one firm, unless there is only one firm making the drug. If there is more than one firm, the physician may choose the firm that offers the lowest price. The patient does not have this choice with oral drugs. The two types of markets have different potentials for price competition.

We expect that market power will be greater in markets for orally administered drugs or, in general, for drugs that the patient himself purchases, than in markets for parenterally administered drugs or, in general, for drugs that the physician purchases himself and then administers to the patient. This hypothesis is examined in Appendix A (pp. 161–68). The results of the analysis support the conclusion that physicians when purchasing drugs that they will administer to the patient are more likely to select a firm on the basis of price than they are when prescribing a drug for the patient that the patient will himself purchase at a pharmacy.

The other two methods of administration (serums and bulk drugs) are of minor importance. It is worth noting, however, that immunological serums are subject to the inspection of the Public Health Service rather than the Food and Drug Administration and that the Public Health Service, unlike the FDA, inspects each batch of serum before it goes on the market. In fact, it is precisely the lack of complete coverage by the FDA, which inspects the physical facilities of the producers at widely separated times and samples only a small proportion of drug shipments entering interstate commerce, that is exploited by the large firms in their representations to the physician. Their contention is that in the absence of adequate coverage, the physician should, if he wishes to have some assurance of the quality of drugs, prescribe the products of firms that he knows by reputation—i.e., the large firms. This argument, of course, makes no reference to the possibility of subjecting all drugs to inspection procedures of the kind used by the Public Health Service. In this way, the physician—assured by a regulatory agency that drugs were of uniformly high quality—would be less inclined to rely on the claims of the large firms, and their market power would be correspondingly reduced.

When a bulk drug is prescribed, the pharmacist must prepare the dosage form (as he did for all drugs until thirty years ago), and it is the pharmacist, in this case, who selects the manufacturer. Since the market power of large firms *vis a vis* small firms is least in this category, we infer that the pharmacist is less likely than the physician to accept the claims that large firms make about the higher quality of their products and that he feels freer to select a firm on the basis of price.[1]

We have, then, considered a method of comparing drug prices by type of firm and concluded from the resulting comparisons that large firms, particularly those selling under brand names, charge much higher prices than small firms selling the same drugs under generic names. We have also seen that these price differentials appear to be unrelated to the age of the drug and that the market power possessed by the larger firms does not diminish with the passage of time. Finally, we have noted that in those markets where the immediate purchaser of a drug is likely to be the physician, the price ratios are higher than those observed in markets where the patient is the immediate purchaser.

Policies to Diminish Market Power

The principal sources of market power in the drug industry are patents and the legal power of the physician to specify the manufacturer. If several companies produce a drug, the physician can select one either by referring to the brand name used by that firm or by identifying the desired firm by name. In many markets, however, there is only one manufacturer, and the drugs sold in them are assumed to be protected by patents. In most of these markets, the firm assigns a brand name to its product and encourages the physician to prescribe the drug under its brand name. In such cases, it is not the existence of the brand name that confers market power but rather the existence of a patent. Until such time as there is more than one firm in the market, the seller is uniquely identified by the generic name of the drug. Of course, the use of a brand name in such circumstances is undoubtedly a good investment in future market power, for the patent will eventually expire and other firms will consider entering the market. In a static examination, however, we would expect that, if there is only one firm in the market, the firm's decision to use or not to use a brand name would not make a substantial difference in the degree of market power possessed by that firm in the particular drug market. The power

100

given to the physician to select a particular drug manufacturer is significant in the determination of market power only when there are several companies producing that drug.

There appear to be three obvious policies which could be used to remove market power based upon the above sources; these are:

1) Removal of the authority of the physician to specify the manufacturing firm, but retention of patent protection.

2) Removal of patent protection, but retention of the authority of the physician to specify the manufacturer.

3) The simultaneous removal of both the authority of the physician to specify the manufacturer and patent protection.

It is convenient to refer to the removal of the authority of the physician to select the manufacturer as the "removal of brand names" since this is the mechanism by which the physician currently identifies the seller in almost all cases. It should be clearly understood, however, that what is being eliminated by the policy of removing brand names is the authority and inclination of the physician to specify individual firms.

The object of this chapter is to estimate the effects upon the industry, and upon the four types of firm* under consideration, of each of these three policies. The statistical methods used in determining what these effects would be are described in detail in Appendix D, pp. 193–207. The general procedure has been to estimate the total sales in 1961 of the 656 ethical drugs produced by the industry and then to estimate what the sales of each drug by each type of firm would have been under each of the three policies.†

---

* These are SG (small firm selling a drug under its generic name), SB (small firm selling a drug under a brand name), LG (large firm selling a drug under its generic name), and LB (large firm selling a drug under a brand name).

† In the absence of any information about the dollar volume of the sales of individual drugs, values showing the proportion of total sales accounted for by drugs introduced in each year from 1950–1961 were combined. If more than one drug of a particular type was introduced in a given year, it was assumed that the two or more drugs had an equal proportion of the sales. This assumption can be expected to produce underestimates of the sales of a few drugs and moderate overestimates of the sales of the remaining drugs, but since we are concerned with the total sales of all drugs, the assumption is less significant than it first appears.

I. EFFECT UPON EXPENDITURES OF
THE REMOVAL OF BRAND NAMES

If brand names alone were removed, the physician would, of course, continue to prescribe drugs, but, as we have seen, he would no longer effectively specify the producer of the drug. This could occur if the existing laws on "substitution" were revoked, and if consumers, regarding the products of competing producers of the same drug as homogeneous, selected a seller on the basis of price. Consumers would be expected to select the firm offering the lowest price; and, to remain in the market, other firms would have to offer prices which were not significantly different from this price. Since there appear to be no significant economies of scale in production, the expected effect of the removal of brand names would be to reduce the prices charged by the various firms in the market to the level charged by the firm offering the lowest price. Also, under the assumption of perfect inelasticity of demand in relation to price, no increase in purchases would be expected to result from this price reduction.

In order to determine the effect on sales revenue of removing brand names, a ratio was established between the sales of the industry in 1961 and the sales that would be expected after introduction of the policy. For this purpose, the mean prices charged by each of the four types of firm were used rather than the prices charged by individual firms.* From the resulting estimate, it appears that removal of brand names would reduce the total sales of the industry from $2,188 million to $1,960 million, or to 89.6 percent of the level of sales under brand names. The sales of drugs affected by the policy would be expected to fall from $883 million to $656 million, or to 74.2 percent of the old level. The effect of the change would be felt mainly by the large firms, whose sales account for $184.3 million (80.6 percent) of the reduction ($227.5 million). It is estimated that brand-name drugs sold by large firms would experience a decline in sales to two-thirds of their former level, whereas small firms selling under generic names would be relatively unaffected by the policy, as theirs is almost always the

* It was expected that mean prices would better represent the probable hypothetical prices in a state of market equilibrium.

lowest mean price in the market. This is not true of small firms selling under brand names (these firms would suffer a greater reduction in the sales of all their drugs than the large firms), but in the sale of only those drugs affected by the removal of brand names the reduction (to 71.5 percent of the former level) would be approximately the same as the reduction in drugs sold under generic names by large firms. Other relationships are shown in Table VI–1, which summarizes the effects of the policy upon the various types of firm. In summary, only 227 drugs out of 656 would be affected by the policy; the remaining 429 would not be affected.

II. EFFECT UPON EXPENDITURES
OF THE REMOVAL OF PATENTS

Under the policy of patent removal, previously monopolized markets would be transformed into markets in which market power would be conferred by brand names. Price differences, similar to those observed in markets already covered by brand names, would continue to exist. It is assumed that after the removal of patents sales would be divided among the four types of firm according to the share that each type had obtained in markets protected by brand names. In other words, for each type of firm the share of the market (as measured by a quantity index of output) would approximately equal the average physical share obtained in markets in which the firm had previously competed with at least one other type of firm. The rationale for this assumption is that whenever physicians have the option of choosing from among different types of firm in a given drug market, their use of this option has determined how much of the market each of the different types of firm obtains and, if the option is extended to other drug markets, continues to have much the same effect. Hence, it is not expected that the market shares obtained by the different types of firm would be significantly different from one market to another if the physician's option were extended to additional markets. It should be remembered here that under the policy of removing patents—but not brand names—the physician would continue to be free to prefer one firm over another—for reasons which might not be related to his patients' welfare—and that the existence of product homogeneity would probably not be taken into consideration.

VI-1. EFFECT OF REMOVAL OF BRAND NAMES UPON SALES OF THE INDUSTRY ($ millions)

Type of Firm	Total Sales before Removal of Brand Names: All Drugs	Total Sales after Removal of Brand Names: All Drugs	Sales after Removal as Percent of Sales before Removal: All Drugs	Total Sales before Removal of Brand Names: Affected Drugs	Total Sales after Removal of Brand Names: Affected Drugs	Sales after Removal as Percent of Sales before Removal: Affected Drugs	Change in Sales Attributable to Removal of Brand Names
Small Firm Generic Name	234.0	227.89	97.93%	200.39	194.29	96.95%	– 6.11
Small Firm Brand Name	204.0	166.98	81.86%	130.00	92.98	71.53%	– 37.01
Large Firm Generic Name	304.51	237.49	77.99%	246.51	179.50	72.82%	– 67.01
Large Firm Brand Name	1,445.31	1,327.95	91.88%	306.18	188.82	61.67%	–117.37
Subtotal Large Firms[a]	1,750.0	1,565.44	89.45%	552.69	368.32	66.64%	–184.34
Totals	2,188.0	1,960.22	89.60%	883.04	655.56	74.24%	–227.48

[a]Figures printed in italic are not included in column totals.

A drug market is most likely to be affected by the removal of patent protection if the drug was (1) introduced in 1944 or later, (2) produced by only one type of firm, and (3) not produced by a small firm selling under a generic name. Of the total of 656 drugs produced, 467 were introduced in 1944 or later, and of these, 368 are produced by only one type of firm; of the latter group, 14 drugs are produced by small firms selling under generic names. Thus, there are 354 drugs (produced by LB, LG or SB) which could be affected by the removal of patent protection.

In the absence of information about the time lags between patent applications and the granting of patents, it is assumed that patents are granted in the same year as the commercial introduction of the drug. Since the life of a patent grant is seventeen years, drugs introduced prior to 1944 are assumed to be no longer protected.

If a drug introduced after 1943 is produced by only one firm and if that firm is not a small firm selling under generic names, the inference is that the resulting market structure exists because there is a patent on the drug and that the patent holder is using the patent to exclude all other firms from the market. If a drug introduced during this period is produced by more than one firm, it is concluded that the patent holder has licensing agreements with other manufacturers or that there is no patent. The procedure adopted is to assume that if the several firms producing a drug are all the same type, then a patent exists and that if the several firms are of different types, there is no patent.

Drugs that are produced by two or more firms of the same type would probably be affected by the removal of brand-name protection, but, unfortunately, the procedure used to estimate the effects of the removal of brand names is not applicable to drugs in this category. Here it was assumed that after the removal of brand names, the prices in the market would fall to the lowest mean price charged by any type of firm in the market before the policy went into effect.* As there is only one mean price for this group of drugs,

---

* In the case of a drug produced by two or more different types of firm, it was possible to determine the difference in the mean prices charged by the types of firm and to specify an equilibrium price which might be established if brand names were removed. Hence, for the purpose of studying the effects of the policy of removing brand names, drugs produced by two or more different types of firm were the ones considered.

any change in price after the removal of brand names would not be observable by means of this procedure.

It is also true, however, that in the category of drugs produced by only one type of firm—with the exception of small firms selling under generic names*—there are relatively few manufacturers in each market. Of 396 drugs, only 34 are produced by two or more firms. This distribution supports the position that the structure of these markets is attributable to patent protection (i.e., it appears that the originating firm decided to license one or two other firms— of the same type—to produce the drug). Twenty-eight of the thirty-four drugs were introduced in 1944 or after, and are included in the estimates of the effects of removing patents. The other six drugs do not figure in the present examination of the policy of removing patents.

Since patents in the drug industry are generated by the research and development activities of the firms, and since small firms selling under generic names do not engage in this type of activity, it is assumed that the latter hold no patents. Drugs introduced in 1944 or later that are produced only by small firms selling under generic names are therefore assumed not to owe their market structure to patent protection. The absence of other types of firm from these markets is attributed to the fact that they chose not to enter.[1]

There are substantial differences between the proportion of original sales of each type of firm which would be affected by the removal of patents and by the removal of brand names. Of the sales of large firms, 63.5 percent would be affected by the removal of patents, but only 29.9 percent by the removal of brand names. Of the drugs sold by large firms, 12.5 percent of the sales of those sold under generic names would be affected by patent removal, but 81.0 percent by the removal of brand names; for the sales of drugs sold under brand names, the corresponding figures are 74.3 percent and 21.2 percent. For small firms selling under brand names, 63.7 percent of sales would be involved in a removal of brand names and 32.4 percent in a removal of patents. Since drugs sold by small

---

* The thirty-three drugs produced only by small firms selling under generic names are not considered under either policy (brand-name removal or patent removal), nor under the policy of removing both brand names and patents. Since these firms typically offer the lowest price on the market, this omission is not relevant to consumer benefits nor does it affect the estimates regarding the outcomes of the policies.

firms selling under generic names are excluded, the removal of patents would have no effect upon the original sales of this type of firm; but 85.6 percent of the sales of such firms would be affected by a policy which removed brand names.

The estimated total reduction in industry sales owing to the removal of patent protection is $274 million. The results show that this net reduction would be obtained entirely at the expense of drugs sold by large firms under brand names. The sales of drugs sold under generic names by large firms and the sales of the two kinds of small firms would be increased by the policy. Notice that these changes are not gross changes. For a given drug, the type of firm originally in the market loses sales to the entering firms, which, since their sales of the drug were originally zero, gain sales. The only type of firm that would not lose sales on a gross basis would be the small firm selling under generic names, as none of their original products would be affected by the policy.

Table VI–2 summarizes the effects of patent removal upon the sales of the industry. The decrease of $274 million for the industry reduces overall sales to 87.5 percent of their previous level and decreases the sales of drugs affected by the policy to 76.8 percent of their previous level. (The corresponding reductions for the removal of brand names are 89.6 percent and 74.2 percent.) The largest percentage gain in the sales of all drugs, 176.8 percent, is made by small firms selling under generic names. The only type of firm to lose sales is the large firm selling under brand names; the total sales of this type of firm are reduced to 51.8 percent of the former level, whereas the sales of drugs by large firms using generic names increase to 152.2 percent of the old level.* For large firms as a group, sales of affected drugs are reduced to 51.5 percent of the level existing under patents.

III. REMOVAL OF BOTH BRAND NAMES AND PATENTS

The simultaneous removal of brand names and patent protection is predicted to have an effect greater than the sum of the effects of

---

* Note, however, that the sales of drugs that are sold under brand names by large firms and that are affected by the removal of patents are reduced to 35.0 percent of previous levels.

VI-2. EFFECT OF REMOVAL OF PATENTS UPON SALES OF THE INDUSTRY ($ millions)

Type of Firm	Total Sales before Removal of Patents: All Drugs	Total Sales after Removal of Patents: All Drugs	Sales after Removal as Percent of Sales before Removal: All Drugs	Total Sales before Removal of Patents: Affected Drugs	Sales after Removal of Patents: Affected Drugs	Sales after Removal as Percent of Sales before Removal: Affected Drugs	Change in Sales Attributable to Removal of Patents
Small firm Generic name	234.0	413.66	176.78%	0.0	179.67	undefined	179.67
Small firm Brand name	204.0	289.12	141.73%	66.12	151.25	228.75%	85.13
Large firm Generic name	304.51	463.31	152.15%	97.97	196.80	518.36%	158.83
Large firm Brand name	1,445.31	747.91	51.75%	1,073.10	375.73	35.01%	−697.37
Subtotal Large firms[a]	*1,750.0*	*1,211.22*	*69.21%*	*1,111.07*	*572.53*	*51.53%*	*−538.54*
Totals	2,188.0	1,913.96	87.49%	1,177.16	903.41	76.75%	−273.75

[a]Figures printed in italic are not included in column totals.

108

the two policies considered separately. It is hypothesized that drugs which are potentially affected by the removal of brand names will behave as they did when brand names alone were removed, but the hypothesis is not applicable to drugs that are covered by patent protection. For the latter, it was assumed that patent removal alone would induce entry by all four types of firm and that those firms which sold under brand names would thereby gain a considerable degree of oligopolistic power in a market where price differences would exist. Under a policy which removed both brand names and patent protection, this type of behavior would not be observed. For the drugs affected, the results of this policy can be viewed as occurring in two steps. First, the removal of patents permits entry and the entering firms behave as though market power were conferred by brand names alone. Second, the removal of brand names causes all prices to become equal to the lowest mean price charged by any type of firm in the market after the removal of patents. The drugs considered to be affected by the policy of removing both brand names and patents are those assumed to be affected by either one of the two previous policies. There are 581 such drugs; the remaining 75 (656 less 581) are assumed to be not affected.

The effects of the removal of both brand names and patents are summarized in Table VI–3, and the procedures used in deriving them are explained in Appendix G (pp. 224–27). The removal of brand names and patents together is estimated to reduce industry sales by $617 million—from $2,188 million to $1,571 million, or to 71.9 percent of the original total. Each type of small firm (SG and SB) would have a net gain in sales as a result of the introduction of the policy. The policy would have little effect upon the sales of large firms selling under generic names, but large firms selling under brand names would be severely affected, since their sales after the introduction of the policy would be only 29.2 percent of the original. On balance, the sales of all drugs by large firms would be reduced from $1,750 million to approximately $732 million.

IV. GENERAL EFFECTS OF THE POLICIES

Effects of the policies according to type of firm

The assumptions underlying a policy to remove brand names alone were such that in no case did any of the four types of firm

VI-3. EFFECTS OF REMOVAL OF BRAND NAMES AND PATENTS UPON THE INDUSTRY
($ millions)

Type of Firm	Total Sales before Removal of Brand Names and Patents: All Drugs	Total Sales after Removal of Brand Names and Patents: All Drugs	Sales after Removal as Percent of Sales before Removal: All Drugs	Total Sales before Removal of Brand Names and Patents: Affected Drugs	Total Sales after Removal of Brand Names and Patents: Affected Drugs	Sales after Removal as Percent of Sales before Removal: Affected Drugs	Change in Sales Attributable to Removal of Brand Names and Patents
Small Firm Generic Name	234.0	620.29	265.09%	200.39	586.71	292.78%	+ 386.30
Small Firm Brand Name	204.0	218.21	106.97%	196.11	210.33	107.25%	+ 14.21
Large Firm Generic Name	304.51	310.18	101.86%	284.48	290.15	102.00%	+ 5.67
Large Firm Brand Name	1,445.31	421.71	29.19%	1,379.23	355.62	25.78%	–1,023.60
Subtotal Large Firms[a]	1,750.0	731.89	41.82%	1,663.71	645.78	37.61%	–1,017.93
Totals	2,188.0	1,570.33	71.87%	2,060.15	1,442.76	70.03%	– 617.38

[a]Figures printed in italic are not included in column totals.

obtain an increase in the value of its sales of a given drug as a result. In all cases the value of sales remained the same or declined. Reductions in sales, both absolutely and relatively, are greatest for drugs sold under brand names by large firms, and least for small firms selling under generic names.

Under the policy of brand-name removal large firms selling under brand names experience a fairly heavy loss ($117.5 million); and the sales of large firms using generic names are reduced by $67.0 million. As we should expect, the gains of small firms selling under generic names are substantial under both of the other policies,* and the losses that occur under the removal of brand names are relatively insignificant. For small firms selling under brand names and for large firms selling under generic names, substantial gains result from the removal of patents, but only small gains from the removal of both patents and brand names.

Table VI–4 summarizes the effects of each of the policies upon the market shares held by the four kinds of drug firm. The table shows the estimated sales of each type of firm, the share of the market held, and the increase or decrease in the latter after the introduction of any of the policies. For example, small firms selling under brand names—with sales of $204 million, or 9.32 percent of the total market of $2,188 million—experience a decline in sales to $167 million, and their market share is reduced to 8.52 percent of the new total sales of $1,960 million, or 91 percent of the original. The effects of the same policy upon the other three types of firm are also comparatively insignificant, but the shifts in market shares resulting from the removal of patents or of brand names and patents are, as noted, considerable. The market shares of small firms selling under generic names are more than doubled under both policies; the market shares of small firms selling under brand names and of large firms selling under generic names are increased by nearly 50 percent under both policies, whereas the market share for drugs sold under brand names by large firms is reduced to nearly half of its former level (from 66% to 39%) by the removal of patents and to less than half of its previous level by the removal of both brand names and patents (from 66% to 27%). Overall, the share of large firms is unaffected by the removal of brand

* The removal of patents and the simultaneous removal of patents and brand names.

VI-4. SHARE OF INDUSTRY SALES HELD BY TYPE OF FIRM

Type of Firm	Before Policy	After Introduction of Policy to Remove		
		Brand names	Patents	Brand names and patents
Small firm	(a) 234.0	227.9	413.7	620.3
Generic name	(b) 10.78%	11.63%	21.61%	39.50%
	(c)	1.10	2.05	3.75
Small firm	(a) 204.0	167.0	289.1	218.2
Brand name	(b) 9.32%	8.52%	15.11%	15.90%
	(c)	0.91	1.62	1.71
Large firm	(a) 304.5	237.5	463.3	310.2
Generic name	(b) 13.92%	12.12%	24.21%	19.76%
	(c)	0.87	1.74	1.42
Large firm	(a) 1,445.5	1,328.0	747.9	421.7
Brand name	(b) 66.07%	67.74%	39.08%	26.85%
	(c)	1.03	0.59	0.41
Subtotal	(a) 1,750.0	1,565.4	1,211.2	731.9
Large Firms*	(b) 80.00%	79.86%	63.28%	46.61%
	(c)	1.00	0.79	0.58
Totals	(a) 2,188.0	1,960.2	1,914.0	1,570.3

(a) Estimated sales (S millions) (b) Market share of type of firm (c) Ratio of market share under policy to market share before policy

*Figures printed in italic are not included in column totals.

names, but is reduced to nearly four-fifths of its former level (from 80% to 63%) by the removal of patents and to nearly half of its former level by the removal of both brand names and patents (from 80% to 47%).

The effect of the policies upon sales according to the method of administration of drugs

In Chapter V it was pointed out that classifying drugs according to the method of administration used gives some indication of who the actual purchaser is. It was suggested that, in the case of orally administered drugs, the consumer—receiving a prescription from his physician and having it filled at a pharmacy—is usually the actual purchaser. This was not true, however, of parenterally administered drugs, which the physician himself purchases and then administers to the patient. It was then hypothesized and the hypothesis was confirmed by the results of the analysis, that the market power of large firms is much less in markets for parenterally administered drugs because of the responsiveness of physicians— when they themselves are the purchasers—to prices.

Table VI–5 provides a summary of the effect of removing brand names, patents, and both brand names and patents on the sale of orally administered drugs, parenterally administered drugs, and bulk drugs and serums. From the table we see that of total sales of $2,188 million approximately $1,505 million were accounted for by orally administered drugs, $563 million by parenterally administered drugs, and $120 million by bulk drugs and serums. In other words, the sales of orally administered drugs account for 69 percent of total sales; the sales of parenterally administered drugs, for 26 percent; and the sales of bulk drugs and serums, for 5 percent.

The reduction in total sales attributable to each of the three policies is not distributed proportionately according to the method of administration. The reduction in sales of orally administered is greater, as we should expect, than for parenterally administered drugs. Thus, referring again to Table VI–5, we see that if brand names are removed, the sale of orally administered drugs will fall to approximately 88.6 percent of their former sales, while the sales of parenterally administered drugs will be reduced to 91.0 percent of previous sales. The removal of brand names leads to a reduction in industry sales of $227 million, and of this total, orally administered drugs account for $172 million or 75.4 percent of the total reduction, and parenterally administered drugs for $51 million or 22.2 percent. The reduction in sales is, of course, much more pronounced with the removal of patents and with the removal of both brand names and patents.

In this chapter, then, we have estimated the effects upon industry sales of policies that removed one or both of the sources of market power in the drug industry. These estimates have been determined

VI-5. EFFECTS OF POLICIES ACCORDING TO METHOD OF ADMINISTRATION OF DRUG

Policy Variable and Method of Administration	Total Sales before Removal of Variable: All Drugs	Total Sales after Removal of Variable: All Drugs	Sales after as Percent of Sales before Removal of Variable: All Drugs	Total Sales before Removal of Variable: Drugs Affected	Total Sales after Removal of Variable: Drugs Affected	Sales after as Percent of Sales before Removal of Variable: Drugs Affected	Change in Sales Attributable to Removal of Variable	Percent of Change in Sales Accounted for by Drugs of Given Method of Administration
Brand names								
Oral	1,504.7	1,333.1	88.60%	544.6	373.0	68.50%	−171.6[a]	75.42%[a]
Parenteral	562.8	512.3	91.03%	234.6	184.1	78.48%	− 50.5	22.19%
Bulk and serums	120.4	114.9	95.48%	103.9	98.5	94.76%	− 5.4	2.39%
Total	2,188.0	1,960.2	89.60%	883.0	655.6	74.24%	−227.5	100%
Patents								
Oral	1,504.7	1,266.2	84.15%	893.5	655.0	73.31%	−238.5	87.11%
Parenteral	562.8	532.2	94.56%	276.7	246.1	88.94%	− 30.6	11.18%
Bulk and serums	120.4	115.7	96.11%	7.0	2.3	33.68%	− 4.7	1.71%
Total	2,188.0	1,914.0	87.49%	1,177.2	903.4	76.75%	−273.8	100%
Brand names and patents								
Oral	1,504.7	1,013.2	67.34%	1,438.0	946.5	65.82%	−491.5	79.61%
Parenteral	562.8	447.1	79.44%	511.3	395.5	77.36%	−115.7	18.75%
Bulk and serums	120.4	110.2	91.59%	111.0	100.9	90.88%	− 10.1	1.64%
Total	2,188.0	1,570.3	71.78%	2,060.2	1,442.8	70.03%	−617.4	100%

[a]The projected loss in sales for oral drugs is −171.6, and this figure is 75.42 percent of the total loss (−227.5) for oral drugs, parenterals, and bulk drugs and serums.

for each of the four types of firm and are based upon assumptions about the reactions of the firms to the removal of brand names alone, patents alone, or brand names and patents together. If brand names were removed and if physicians were assured that all manufacturers produced a therapeutically homogeneous chemical entity, physicians would have no reason consistent with the welfare of their patients to specify the manufacturer of a drug. The choice could then be left to the patient, who would be expected to select the firm that charged the lowest price. The introduction of price competition into these markets would cause prices to fall to an equilibrium level, and we have assumed that for any given drug this would equal the lowest mean price charged by any of the types of firm that produced it. If patents were removed but brand names remained, and if physicians did not have the assurance of uniform quality in drugs, we would expect that a market in which patent protection had previously existed would become similar to markets in which brand names were the basis of power. New firms—formerly excluded by patents—would enter the market, and would set prices related to the prices that would be charged in a market where brand names existed. With the removal of both brand names and patents, new firms would enter individual drug markets, and the prices charged by all firms would reach an equilibrium determined by competition.

The estimated effects of the three policies have been summarized in Table VI–1 (for the removal of brand names), in Table VI–2 (for the removal of patents), and in Table VI–3 (for the removal of brand names and patents). As we have seen, the removal of both brand names and patents has the greatest effect. Under this policy, the same quantity of drugs would become available for $1,571 million, which represents a decline in sales income of $617 million. For each of the other two policies, the reduction is less than half this amount. If brand names alone are removed, total sales income is reduced by $227 million, and if patents alone are removed, sales income declines by approximately $274 million.

These reductions may be regarded as gross benefits resulting from the introduction of each of the three policies. The net, as distinguished from the "gross," benefits can be computed only after the costs associated with the introduction of each policy have been determined. These costs we take to be exclusively the effect of each policy on the willingness of the large firms to conduct research and development; hence, the choice of an appropriate policy will depend upon the size of the net benefits. In the remaining three chapters, the costs of the three policies are estimated, and the ability of the large firms to survive each policy is examined.

CHAPTER SEVEN

The Effect of the Policies on Consumers and Large Firms

In this chapter some of the implications of the policies* for improving the performance of the drug industry are examined. First, the effect of these policies upon consumer expenditures for drugs is considered. Then the degree of monopoly power conferred upon large firms by the use of brand names and patents is estimated by calculating the loss of sales that would be experienced under the removal of these policies. The possible reactions of the large firms and the anticipated effects upon the dynamic allocation of resources are discussed in Chapters VIII and IX.

The static benefits to the consumer

To study the effects of the three policies upon the public, it is necessary to consider first the possible reactions of the retail pharmacist, the normal intermediary between the manufacturer and the public, to the policies.[1] Pharmacists usually determine their retail prices by adding a standard markup to the cost of the goods. This markup is regularly in the neighborhood of 50 percent; or, alter-

---

* Removal of brand names, removal of patents, or a combination of the two.

natively, the cost-of-goods-sold constitutes two-thirds of the retail price. Since we are assuming manufacturers' sales to be equal to the pharmacists' cost-of-goods-sold, a reduced level of manufacturers' sales would result in a smaller absolute gross margin for the pharmacist under the application of the same standard percentage markup, and the gross revenues of the pharmacist would decline.

The removal of brand names, either alone or in combination with the removal of patents, would relieve the pharmacist of the necessity of carrying all the brands of each drug. On the other hand, the removal of patents alone would increase the number of brands he would have to stock. In the first case, the inventory costs of the pharmacist would decrease, while in the second case they would increase. There appear to be no other reasons why the pharmacist's operating costs might decrease. It is reasonably certain, however, that in either case the loss in revenue would greatly outweigh the reduction in costs.

If the past behavior of retail pharmacists is any guide, it can be safely predicted that pharmacists could and would successfully resist any reduction in their incomes. The considerable power of the National Association of Retail Druggists over Congress, state legislatures, manufacturers, state boards of pharmacy, and individual pharmacists who have shown leanings toward price competition has been demonstrated on many occasions.*

One estimate of the benefits to the consumer could be obtained under the assumption that pharmacists would react to the introduction of policies that threatened them with a reduction in income by adding a new standard markup to the cost-of-goods-sold and thus maintaining their overall gross incomes.

In general, let the original standard markup be represented by

---

* The point is noted by Clair Wilcox in the following: "The statutes legalizing resale price maintenance were whipped through the legislature at breakneck speed. There is no record of hearings having been held in forty states. There is no transcript of hearings available in any state. . . . The care with which the laws were considered is indicated by the fact that [an identical version of the statute] was passed by the House and the Senate and signed by the governor, not only in California, but also in Arizona, Iowa, Louisiana, New Jersey, New York, Pennsylvania, and Tennessee. The N.A.R.D. held the hoop and cracked the whip. The legislatures and the executives obediently jumped." *Public Policies Toward Business,* 3rd ed. (Homewood, Ill., 1966), p. 381.

"k," and the original level of manufacturers' sales (which is the pharmacists' cost-of-goods-sold), by "TS." Then the original expenditures by the public, TE, are:

$$TE = TS + (k \times TS)$$

Using this markup, the pharmacist derives a "gross income" of $k \times TS$. If, after the introduction of one or all of the policies, manufacturers' sales declined to TS′, the original "gross income" could be sustained by using a new markup, k′. Total public expenditures after the introduction of the policy would be:

$$TE' = TS' + (k \times TS) = TS' + (k' \times TS')$$

in which "$k \times TS$" equals "$k' + TS'''$" so that the "gross income" of pharmacists would be unchanged. The benefit to the public of the policy would be the reduction in expenditures for therapeutically identical ethical drugs. Thus

$$TE - TE' = (TS + [k \times TS]) - (TS' + [k' \times TS']) = TS - TS'$$

A completely successful "defensive" action by the pharmacists would therefore mean that the gross benefit of a policy to the public would be equal to the reduction in manufacturers' sales.*

After the introduction of the policy, the new markup needed to generate the original margin of gross profits would be $k' = (k \times TS)/TS'$. In 1961, sales of the industry are estimated to have been $2,188 million. Taking the standard markup to be 50 percent ($k = 0.5$), the "gross income" of pharmacists is estimated to have been $1,094 million, and total public expenditures to have been $3,282 million. To generate $1,094 million after the reduction in manufacturers' sales which would result from the introduction of the policy would require new markups as shown in Table VII–1.

It has been assumed that the compensatory tactics of the pharmacists would have the effect of equalizing the overall social benefit to consumers and the reduction in industry sales, but since there are two groups of drugs that would not become less expensive, not all consumers would be better off as a result of the adoption of a particular policy. Drugs in the first group would be unaffected by the policy; for these, the cost-of-goods-sold to the pharmacist would

---

* This situation would occur if the reduction in manufacturers' sales were 50 percent and the pharmacists' second markup (k′) were 100 percent.

remain unchanged, and the increased markup applied to them would raise their prices to the consumer. The ratios of these prices before and after adoption of the policy are shown in Table VII–2. For the drugs in the second group, the reduction in manufacturers' sales would be so small that after adoption of the policy the retail prices of these drugs would also be increased. Table VII–2 gives the **maximum** ratios—before and after introduction of the policy— that would be required for a decline in the retail prices of these drugs.

VII-1.   PUBLIC EXPENDITURE AND MARK-UP UNDER EACH POLICY

Policy	Reduced Public Expenditure (TE')	New Mark-up (k')	TE'/TE[a]
Removal of			
Brand names	$3,054	0.558	93.06%
Patents	$3,009	0.572	91.65%
Brand names			
and patents	$2,665	0.697	81.18%

[a]TE'/TE represents the ratio of expenditures by the public before and after introduction of the policy.

Table VII–3 summarizes the distributive features of each policy at the retail level. The table divides the drugs into two groups: those for which public expenditures would increase as a result of the policy, and those for which public expenditures would decrease. The number of drugs, the expenditures before and after the adoption of the policy, and the relevant percentage changes are shown for each group. The increase in public expenditures for those drugs unaffected or slightly affected by the three policies are as follows: Under the policy to remove brand names, consumer costs increase by $82 million; under the policy to remove patents, by $74 million; under the policy to remove both brand names and patents, by $64 million. The average increase in total expenditures resulting from each of the policies is 3.8 percent for the removal of brand names, 4.8 percent for the removal of patents, and 10.4 percent for the removal of both brand names and patents.

For drugs for which public expenditures decrease as the result of the introduction of each policy, the reductions are $310 million for the removal of brand names, $347 million for the removal of patents, and $681 million for the removal of both brand names and patents.

If there were no gross increase in public expenditures as the result of the policy adopted, then every consumer would be, at least, no worse off as a result of the adoption of the policy. Once a gross increase is introduced, however, balancing the welfare loss that this represents to some consumers with the welfare gain that the gross decrease represents to other consumers becomes difficult "in practice" and impossible under the rules of strict welfare economics. The higher the ratio of the gross increase to the gross decrease, the more widely dispersed are the net benefits, and the more difficult it is "in practice" to say that a given net reduction represents a net social welfare gain. Table VII-3 presents the ratio

VII-2.   PROPORTIONATE CHANGES IN CONSUMER EXPENDITURES: DRUGS NOT AFFECTED BY THE POLICIES AND DRUGS ONLY SLIGHTLY AFFECTED

	Brand Names	Patents	Brand Names and Patents
Ratio of expenditures under policy to expenditures before policy (unaffected drugs)	103.9%	104.8%	113.1%
Maximum ratio of industry sales under policy to sales before policy if total public expenditures are to decrease (slightly affected drugs)	96.3%	95.4%	88.4%

of gross increases to gross decreases for each policy. The removal of brand names is seen to have the highest value, and the removal of both brand names and patents to have the lowest value.

Table VII-4 summarizes the effects of the policies at the retail level according to the way in which the drugs are administered. The table shows the ratio of public expenditures after the introduction of each policy to the public expenditures before the policy. Taken as a group, only bulk drugs and serums show an increase in expenditures as the result of the adoption of any policy.

The foregoing estimates of the benefits to consumers were, as

VII-3.   DISTRIBUTIVE EFFECTS OF THE THREE POLICIES
(\$ millions)

	Policy to remove		
	Brand names	Patents	Brand names and patents
Drugs for which public expenditures are increased			
Number of drugs	467	318	150
Public expenditures before policy	\$2,169	\$1,544	\$616
Public expenditures after policy	\$2,251	\$1,618	\$680
Gross increase	\$ 82	\$ 74	\$ 64
Ratio of expenditures after policy to expenditures before	1.038	1.048	1.104
Drugs for which public expenditures are decreased			
Number of drugs	189	338	506
Public expenditures before policy	\$1,113	\$1,738	\$2,666
Public expenditures after policy	\$ 803	\$1,391	\$1,985
Gross decrease	\$ 310	\$ 447	\$ 681
Ratio of expenditures after policy to expenditures before	0.725	0.800	0.745
Net change as result of policy	\$ −227	\$ −273	\$ −617
Ratio of gross increase to gross decrease	0.265	0.213	0.094

has been said, obtained under the assumption that pharmacists would react in such a way as to maintain their gross incomes in the face of any of the policies. Clearly, other reactions are possible. The pharmacists might be unable to effect any increase in the standard markup (or otherwise increase the price for their services), with the result that their gross incomes would decline in proportion to the reduction in manufacturers' sales. Consumers would thus benefit by one and a half times the reduction in manufacturers' sales. This outcome would drive the marginal pharmacies from the retail drug industry and might, in the long run, lead to a significant rationalization of the retail distribution of drugs. On the other hand, with their powerful and well-organized trade association, the pharmacists might be able to appropriate the whole of the reduction in the cost-of-goods-sold. It is most probable, however, that although they would be able to effect an increase in the standard markup, or gain widespread adherence to the use of a

VII-4.   DISTRIBUTIVE EFFECTS BY METHOD OF ADMINISTRATION

	Brand Names	Patents	Brand Names and Patents
Orally administered drugs	92.03%	88.17%	76.16%
Parenterally administered drugs	94.57%	99.07%	89.85%
Bulk drugs and serums	99.18%	100.70%	103.60%

"compounding fee" as the method of pricing, their revenues would nevertheless decline. In this case, the estimates of consumer benefit, obtained by assuming no decrease in the gross incomes of pharmacists, are probably conservative.

The value of brand names and patents

What is the value—in terms of the additional value of sales—of brand-name protection and patent protection to the large firms? The power of the physician to specify manufacturers, and the success of the large firms in convincing him that he should do so, enables these firms to charge prices which are higher than those which would exist if consumers were free to choose drugs on the basis of price. If, for those drugs for which brand-name protection is significant, this protection were removed, then, assuming no reallocation of the physical output among types of firms, the value of the sales of these products by large firms would decline by $184 million.

If patents alone were removed, so that physicians could still specify sellers and firms would still use brand names, then, assuming that the physical quantities sold in markets previously covered by patents were reallocated among other types of firms according to the physical shares obtained in markets covered by brand-name protection, the sales of large firms would be reduced by $539 million.

If both brand names and patents were removed, the sales of

large firms would be reduced by $1,018 million. Of this, $184 million is attributable to a decline in the value of the sales of drugs originally protected by brand names. The loss of patent protection on drugs previously covered by patents accounts for another $539 million. The remaining amount, $295 million, is attributable to the loss of market power which large firms would have had if patents, but not brand names, had been removed from drugs previously covered by patents.

If brand-name protection were removed, the loss to the large firms would be valued at $184 million. If patent protection were subsequently removed, the sales of large firms would decline by an additional $834 million. Alternatively, if patents were removed, the loss to large firms would be valued at $539 million. If, subsequently, brand-name protection were removed, the sales of large firms would decline by $479 million. The value of patents and of brand names can be summarized as follows:

Value to large firms of patent protection if:

Brand names exist	Brand names do not exist
$539 million	$834 million

Value to large firms of brand-name protection if:

Patents exist	Patents do not exist
$184 million	$479 million

These figures do not represent the value of the two sources of market power to the industry as a whole. The value of brand names is greater than $184 million because the small firms derive some benefit from them. The value of patents is less than $539 million because the small firms would benefit from the removal of patents, since they would obtain a share of the markets previously protected by patents. The net value of brand names and of patents to the industry can be obtained by following the argument used to determine the value for large firms. The results are as follows:

Value to the industry of patent protection if:

Brand names exist	Brand names do not exist
$274 million	$390 million

Value to the industry of brand names if:

Patents exist	Patents do not exist
$227 million	$343 million

The net value to the industry of the existence of both brand names and patents is therefore estimated to be $617 million (the sum of their two separate values: $390 million and $227 million).

The foregoing estimates were obtained under a restrictive set of assumptions made necessary by the lack of data. One of these was that the demand for drugs was perfectly inelastic. If the demand for drugs is highly inelastic, but not perfectly so, then the effect of each of the policies upon the revenues of the firms will be less than the above estimates indicate. A price reduction would cause some increase in the quantity demanded, and revenues would not fall by as much as predicted.

CHAPTER EIGHT

Research and Development in the Drug Industry

The estimated benefits of alternative policies to reduce the degree of market power in the industry must be judged against whatever costs might arise from the policies. One major "cost" could be the retarding or cessation of progress in the industry. As progress in the drug industry takes the form of improved drugs, which in turn are the result of the research-and-development efforts of the firms, it is appropriate at this point to discuss the research-and-development activities of the drug industry. Consideration of the effects of the three policies on these activities is deferred to the following chapter.

Magnitude of research and development in the drug industry and its relation to the total industrial effort

The National Science Foundation estimates that, in 1961, $10.872 billion was spent in the U.S. on industrial research and development.[1] The pharmaceutical preparations industry (S.I.C. group 283) spent $196 million—1.80 percent of the total industrial effort. Of the total expenditures for research and development, industrial firms financed $4.631 billion, or 42.6 percent, while other sources—largely the federal government—financed the remaining 57.4 percent. The relative importance of these sources of support for commercial drug research and development was quite different. Drug firms financed $192 million, or 98.0 percent, while other sources contributed 2.0 percent. The drug industry was the highest ranking in terms of the proportion of total research financed by industry. The drug industry paid for 4.15 percent of all research and development which was financed by industry and received 0.06 percent of all federal funds allocated to the performance of industrial research and development. The drug industry performed 1.67 percent of the research and development performed by industry. A comparison of the absolute amounts spent on research and development is presented in Table VIII–1.

VIII-1.   PERFORMANCE AND FINANCING OF INDUSTRY
RESEARCH AND DEVELOPMENT IN 1961[a] ($ millions)

Source of Financing	Performer		
	Industry-performed	Contracted to non-industrial sector	Total
All Industry			
Industry financed	4,522	109	4,631
Other sources (Federal Government)	6,241		6,241
Total	10,763	109	10,872
Drug Industry (SIC #283)			
Industry financed	176	16	192
Other sources (Federal Government)	4		4
Total	180	16	196

[a]National Science Foundation, *Research and Development.*

In January, 1962, all industry employed the equivalent of 319,800 full-time professionals in research and development; the drug industry, employing the equivalent of 6,600 full-time professionals, accounted for 2.07 percent of total professional employment in industrial research and development. For industry as a whole, the performance cost of research and development per professional was $34,700, and the corresponding figure in the drug industry was $28,100, or 81.0 percent of the all-industry figure. Considering all employees, industry financed research and development at the rate of $410 per employee. The drug industry financed research and development at the rate of $1,520 per employee, making it much the highest ranking industry in respect to this variable.

Industrial firms contracted $151 million of industrial research and development to other performers; $42 million was contracted to other industrial firms and the remainder, $109 million, was contracted to performers outside the industrial sector. Thus, of the research and development financed by industry, 2.35 percent was contracted to the nonindustrial sector. Of the research and development financed by the drug industry, $16 million, or 8.33 percent, was contracted to nonindustrial performers, and approximately one half of this amount went to hospitals and universities. Thus the drug industry accounted for 14.7 percent of the work contracted to the nonindustrial sector and was second—behind nonmanufacturing industries—in the proportion of industry-financed research and development contracted to other performers.

The four largest drug firms accounted for 40 percent of the research and development performed by the industry, the eight largest firms accounted for 63 percent, and the twenty largest firms accounted for 95 percent. These figures indicate that the concentration of research and development among the top drug firms is not significantly different from the typical industry.

In industry generally, 3.7 percent of the funds was allocated to basic research, 18.0 percent to applied research, and 78.3 percent to development. The corresponding allocation of funds in the drug industry is strikingly different. Basic research accounted for 16.7 percent of the funds, applied research for 52.8 percent, and development for 30.5 percent. The drug industry was the highest ranking industry in the proportion of funds allocated to basic research and in the proportion allocated to applied research; hence, it was the lowest ranking industry in the proportion devoted to development.

The ratio of funds expended for research and development to

net sales was 4.4 percent for all industry and 4.7 percent for the drug industry, which ranks eighth out of twenty-one industries; but for the ratio of industry-financed research and development to net sales the drug industry has much the highest ranking: The drug industry figure is 5.1 percent, compared to 1.9 percent for all industry. (The apparent paradox by which a component of total expenditures is greater than total expenditures is accounted for by the fact that contracted research is not included in the figure for industry-performed research and development but is included in industry-financed research and development. The percentages in question are 4.7 and 5.1.)

*Expenditures on research and development
in the drug industry: 1941–61*

During the period 1949–61, current dollar expenditures on research and development in the drug industry increased at the average annual rate of 17.14 percent or more than six-fold over the twelve-year period.* Much of this increase was probably due to increases in the prices of research and development inputs. There is no index-number series for the cost of research and development inputs, and consequently no means of converting these expenditures from current into constant dollars; nor is there any readily available series, such as the annual salaries of professional chemists, which could be used as a proxy for the desirable index-number series. Hence, conversion of research and development expenditures must be accomplished by cruder methods.

In the period from 1950 to 1960, the number of professional personnel employed for research and development by 26 large

* Raw data for the computation from: Pharmaceutical Manufacturers Association, *Prescription Drug Industry Fact Book* (Washington, D.C., 1962), pt. 2, p. 5—hereafter cited as *Fact Book*. Much of the information in this source does not conform to the estimates made by the National Science Foundation; but the *Fact Book* is the only source that provides time-series data for research. Hence, in discussing changes over a period of time in research and development in the industry, the P.M.A. data are used; in discussing research-and-development expenditures in 1961 in a static context —as for example, in estimating the subsidy required to the industry to offset the loss of incentive to perform research and development—N.S.F. data are used.

VIII-2. MEASURES OF INPUT AND OUTPUT FOR RESEARCH AND DEVELOPMENT IN THE DRUG INDUSTRY: 1949-61
($ millions)

	Research and Development Expenditures: Current Dollars	Price Deflator for Research and Development Inputs	Research and Development Expenditures: Constant Dollars 1961 = 100	New Single Chemical Entities Introduced during Year	Average Cost per New Single Chemical Entity Introduced during Year: Current Dollars	Average Cost per New Single Chemical Entity Introduced during Year: Constant Dollars: 1961 = 100
1949	34	49.7	68.4			
1950	39	52.7	74.0	28	1.39	2.64
1951	50	55.8	89.5	35	1.43	2.56
1952	63	59.2	106.4	35	1.80	3.04
1953	67	62.7	106.7	48	1.40	2.22
1954	78	66.5	117.3	38	2.05	3.09
1955	91	70.5	129.1	31	2.94	4.16
1956	105	74.7	140.5	42	2.50	3.35
1957	127	79.2	160.3	51	2.49	3.14
1958	170	84.0	202.4	44	3.86	4.60
1959	197	89.0	221.3	63	3.13	3.51
1960	206	94.3	218.4	45	4.58	4.85
1961	227	100.0	227.0	41	5.54	5.54
Average Growth Rate	17.1%	6.0%	10.5%	3.5%	12.1	6.95%

firms increased from 1,985 in 1950 to 4,306 in 1960, or 117 percent.[2] During the same period, expenditures on research and development in the industry increased from $39 million in 1950 to $206 million in 1960, or 428 percent. If the wages of research-and-development personnel represent all research-and-development inputs, then the increase in costs over the period is approximately 140 percent. This probably overstates the cost of factor inputs because the large firms appear to have used their capital more intensively in research-and-development procedures—particularly in routine chemical analysis—and, at the end of the period, to have employed a greater number of supporting technical personnel per professional than they did at the beginning of the period. To be conservative in the estimate, we say that research-and-development costs approximately doubled between 1949 and 1961, or, specifically, that they grew at the annual rate of 6 percent.

Table VIII–2 shows the series of research-and-development expenditures (input) from 1949 to 1961 and the corresponding series (output) for the same period. Values are shown in current dollars and constant dollars with 1961 as the base year. Thus, for 1950, input costs (research and development) came to $39 million in current (1950) dollars and to $74 million in constant (1961) dollars; correspondingly, the average cost per new single chemical entity introduced during 1950 was $1.39 million in current (1950) dollars and $2.64 million in constant (1961) dollars. Measured in 1961 dollars, the average annual rate of growth for research and development in the drug industry for 1949–61 was 10.5 percent.

The marketable outputs of a firm's research-and-development inputs take the form of: (a) new single chemical entities; (b) single chemical entities which are duplicates of existing products, but which are new to the firm;[3] (c) products which are combinations of existing single chemical entities; and (d) new dosage forms of existing single chemical entities. The number of introductions in each of these categories in each year in the period 1950–60 is shown in Table VIII–3.

Since the entry of additional firms into the market does not cause price competition, the social benefit of research and development on duplicate single chemical entities is probably negligible. Large firms are the ones that are likely to engage in such research,

VIII-3. OUTPUT OF NEW PRODUCTS IN THE DRUG INDUSTRY: 1950-60[a]

	New Single Chemical Entities Introduced during Year	New Single Chemical Entities Introduced during Year: Base Year: 1960 = 100[b]	Duplicate Single Products Introduced during Year	Duplicate Single Products Introduced during Year Base: 1960 = 100[b]	Compounded Products Introduced during Year	Compounded Products Introduced during Year Base: 1960 = 100[b]	New Dosage Forms Introduced during Year	New Dosage Forms Introduced during Year: Base Year: 1960 = 100[b]
1950	28	62.2	100	156.3	198	98.0	118	120.4
1951	35	77.8	74	115.6	212	104.9	120	122.4
1952	35	77.8	77	120.3	202	100.0	170	173.5
1953	48	106.7	79	123.4	226	111.9	97	99.0
1954	38	87.4	87	135.9	255	126.2	108	110.2
1955	31	68.9	90	140.6	282	139.6	96	98.0
1956	42	93.3	79	123.4	280	138.6	66	67.3
1957	51	113.3	88	137.5	261	129.2	96	98.0
1958	44	97.8	73	114.1	255	126.2	109	111.2
1959	63	140.8	49	76.6	203	100.5	104	106.1
1960	45	100.0	64	100.0	202	100.0	98	100.0
Totals	460		860		2,574		1,182	
Annual Growth Rate	3.5%		-4.4%		0.2%		-1.8%	

[a]Paul de Haen, *New Product Surveys: 1950-59*—cited in U.S. Congress, Senate, Subcommittee on Antitrust and Monopoly of the Committee on the Judiciary, *Hearings on Drug Industry Antitrust Act*, 87th Cong., 2nd sess., 1961, pt. 3, p. 1156. W. S. Comanor, "The Economics of Research and Development in the Pharmaceutical Industry" (Ph.D. diss., Harvard University, 1963).
[b]The values shown in these four columns are index numbers.

and the price they set for duplicate products is identical (or very nearly so) with the price of the original product. The benefits to the firm can be considerable, for this type of research and development permits the firm to enter a (possibly very lucrative) market which was previously closed to it. Research-and-development expenditures which yield combinations of existing drugs are probably very small and of negligible social value. Expenditures yielding new dosage forms of existing drugs may, on occasion, be of considerable social benefit; such cases are usually those that involve the introduction of an injectible form of a drug which is poorly absorbed when administered orally. It seems probable that almost all the industry's research-and-development expenditures are associated in some way with the search for, or development of, new single chemical entities. In the discussion which follows, it is supposed that *all* research and development costs can be attributed to new single chemical entities. As the social benefits of drug research are nearly all due to new single chemical entities, it is not inappropriate to attribute research-and-development costs to them alone.

Over the period 1950–60, the mean number of new single chemical entities introduced per year was 41.8; the number grew at the average annual rate of 3.5 percent. If research-and-development expenditures for a given year, measured in constant dollars, are divided by the number of new single chemical entities introduced in that year, a measure of the average cost of a single chemical entity is obtained. This average cost, measured in terms of constant dollars, grew at the average annual rate of about 7 percent per year, although the trend is subject to substantial variations.

The benefits of drug research and development: "Medical"

In the past three decades, extraordinary progress has been made in the practice of medicine; some, but by no means all, of this advance can be attributed to the development of new drugs. While the relative importance of drugs in medical progress in this period can never be precisely stated, it will, nevertheless, be instructive to see whether some crude indication of their role can be obtained.

The Commission on the Cost of Medical Care asked twenty

VIII-4.   IMPORTANCE OF DRUGS ACCORDING TO SPECIALITY[a]

Medical Speciality	Number of Advances Listed in Speciality	Number of Advances Which Were Pharmaceutical	Total Points Obtained by Drugs in List	Proportion of Total Points Obtained by Drugs[b]
Anesthesiology	12	3	26	0.333
Dermatology	12	7	53	0.679
Diseases of the chest	13	4	34	0.374
Gastroenterology and proctology	12	3	25	0.321
General practice	14	11	84	0.800
Internal medicine	20	13	132	0.629
Neurological surgery	18	3	19	0.111
Nuclear medicine	9	0	0	0.000
Obstetrics and gynecology	16	7	54	0.397
Ophthalmology	16	4	43	0.316
Orthopedic surgery	18	4	53	0.310
Pathology	13	0	0	0.000
Pediatrics	13	4	32	0.352
Physical medicine and rehabilitation	13	4	20	0.220
Plastic surgery	13	2	16	0.176
Preventive medicine	17	2	22	0.144
Psychiatry and neurology	16	5	47	0.346
Radiology	12	0	0	0.000
Surgery	10	2	12	0.218
Thoracic surgery	17	2	30	0.175
Urology	10	1	8	0.145
Median ratio (excluding nuclear medicine, pathology and radiology)				0.316

[a]American Medical Association, *Report of the Commission on the Cost of Medical Care,* 4 vols. (Chicago, 1964), 1: 111-19.

[b]Total points in a list are obtained as $n(n + 1)/2$.

doctors in each of twenty-three medical specialties to list the ten advances in their field, for the period 1935–60, "which medical practitioners would least like to do without in their own practice of medicine."[4] Advances that were listed by more than 16 percent of the respondents in a given specialty were included in the final list for that specialty.

The Commission presented the results for each specialty in the form of a list of advances, beginning with the most often mentioned and ending with the least often mentioned. No numerical ranks were assigned to the entries, and some entries were undoubtedly tied. We have assigned points on the basis of how many different advances were included in the list for the specialty; thus, if there were n advances in a list, the first mentioned advance received n points, the second received $n-1$, and so on. The points assigned to advances which are clearly identifiable as drugs were added up, and divided by the total number of points available in the list. The ratios obtained for each specialty are shown in Table VIII–4.

Three specialties—nuclear medicine, pathology, and radiology—did not include any drugs in their list of advances. This is not surprising, since these specialties are concerned almost entirely with the diagnosis of illness, rather than the treatment. In the remaining specialties, drugs received from 11 to 80 percent of the total points. The median percentage was 31.6.

These figures provide an indication of how the physician views drugs as they assist him in his particular specialty. To obtain a crude idea of how these advances are distributed among patients, the twenty-three specialties were reduced to seven—six specialties plus a residual. The proportion of points received by drugs in each specialty was weighted by the proportion of physicians in the specialty, and a mean proportion of points received by drugs was computed. The value obtained, 0.52, suggests that *roughly* one-half of the progress in the treatment of patients during the period 1935–60 could be attributed to progress in therapeutics. The procedure for obtaining this computation is shown in Table VIII–5.

The benefits of drug research and development: "Economic"

The valuation of the social benefits brought about by research is clearly a difficult task. The effect of drugs ranges from the temporary relief of minor discomforts to the saving of life. To the extent that the people enjoying these effects are members of the labor force, drugs contribute to present and future productivity.

VIII-5.   PROGRESS ATTRIBUTABLE TO DRUGS WEIGHTED BY NUMBER OF PHYSICIANS IN THE SPECIALTY[a]

Medical Specialty	Number in Private Practice	Proportion of all Physicians in Private Practice	Progress in Specialty Due to Drugs
General practice	67,499	0.386	0.800
General surgery	16,688	0.096	0.218
Internal medicine	21,066	0.121	0.629
Obstetrics and gynecology	11,750	0.067	0.397
Pediatrics	9,093	0.052	0.352
Psychiatry	7,434	0.043	0.346
All Others	41,155	0.236	0.220[a][b]
Total	174,685	1.000	
Weighted mean			0.517

[a]American Medical Association, *Distribution of Physicians in the United States* (Chicago, 1965). Data as of April, 1964.
[b]Median of remaining specialities, excluding nuclear medicine, pathology, and radiology.

Drugs reduce the duration of illnesses, thereby (usually) reducing the cost of illness. Benefits such as these are at least conceptually measurable—but drugs also reduce death rates and relieve pain among infants and the aged. Here considerations of productivity are negligible: Reduced death rates among the aged increase the probability that these people will outlive their economic resources; reduced death rates among infants can lead to explosive population growth.

The best that can be done to evaluate the economic desirability of drug research is to compare the discounted flow of expenditures with the discounted flow of measurable benefits for a given period of time. If the discounted measurable social benefits from drug research are greater than the discounted research expenditures, it can be concluded that the level of investment in drug research produces a net social gain. If the discounted research expenditures exceed the discounted measurable social benefits of the expenditures, then the question of whether or not these expenditures have a net social worth depends upon the discounted value placed upon nonmeasurable benefits.

Estimates of the benefits of drug research are both few and crude. The only conceptually adequate estimates of which the author is aware are those made by Arthur D. Little, Inc. In a study prepared for the Pharmaceutical Manufacturers Association, the analysts concluded that "approximately 4,400,000 working age people are survivors [in 1960] from all of the possible causes of death, had the 1935 death rates persisted."[5] Not all these "survivors" owe their good fortune to the introduction of new drugs. But, "there are more than 2 million working age survivors alive today [1960] who, if the 1935 death rate had continued, would have been a victim of tuberculosis, syphilis, influenza, or pneumonia."[6] These are diseases which have proven to be particularly susceptible to drug therapy, and much of the "survival" from these causes may reasonably be attributed to advances in therapeutics. Using the average wage rates prevailing in 1960 for all employed persons, the Little study estimated that the employed "survivors" from these four diseases added $4.90 billion to the 1960 gross national product and that the employed "survivors" from all causes of death added an estimated $10.42 billion. Further, in 1959, approximately 240 million working days were lost because of acute illnesses alone, and it is estimated that, if the 1943 morbidity rates for these illnesses had prevailed in 1959, an additional 162 million working days would have been lost. If these additional days are evaluated at the rate of $15.44 per day—the mean earnings per day prevailing in 1959—then the net economic gain due to the reduction in morbidity rates from acute conditions can be valued (in 1960 dollars) at 2.6 billion.

From the foregoing analysis, three estimates of additions to the GNP from 1960 can be derived:

(1) Employed "survivors" from the four diseases noted in the Little study add $4.90 billion.

(2) Employed "survivors" from all causes of death add $10.42 billion.

(3) The net economic gain owing to the reduction in morbidity rates from acute conditions and the corresponding gain in working days add $2.5 billion.

Suppose that the only benefits of research-and-development expenditures during 1949–60 are those added to the GNP by "1." Suppose further that these benefits are considered to start at the beginning of 1961 and to continue in perpetuity.* As we have seen, they have been estimated at $4.9 billion and are here considered to be net of any costs to the recipient of new drugs, on the grounds that in the absence of effective drugs, sufferers from these four diseases would have spent at least the same amount on other medicines. Taking the estimated figure—$4.9 billion—for 1960 as a continuing flow of benefits, we then capitalize it at a discount rate of 10 percent and get $49 billion as a capitalized (lump-sum) estimate of the benefits of research and development over a very long period of time.† This figure represents the total social return on funds invested in research and development over the period 1949–60. For the purpose of obtaining a comparative measure of this return, we hypothesize that the same amount of money (equivalent to that which was spent on research and development in 1949–60) was invested in some other way in the same period of time, and determine what rate of interest would have been needed to increase the investment to the capitalized value—$49 billion—of the estimated return from research and development in 1961. The resulting estimate—65.1 percent—is considerably higher than the rate of interest prevailing elsewhere in the economy.‡

* Any benefits accruing prior to 1961 will be attributed to research done during the period 1935–48.

† Since the stream of benefits is considered to continue in perpetuity, the capitalized value of the benefits has been determined as the sum of an infinite series. This procedure is equivalent to dividing 4.9 by .1.

‡ The reader is referred again to Table VIII-2 for an analysis of research-and-development expenditures over the period 1949–60.

These computations can be repeated with alternative social discount rates and with alternative values for the annual benefits. Table VIII–6 shows the results of using discount rates of 20 percent, 10 percent, 6 percent, and 4 percent with four alternative levels of benefit that might be attributed to the results of research and development during the period 1949–60. Also shown are the rates of interest at which investments in drug research over the period 1949–60 would have had to appreciate in order to equal the capitalized value of the annual benefits. Thus, if $4.9 billion is capitalized at 20 percent, investments in drug research in 1949–60 would have had to earn 53.4 percent in order to reach the capitalized value—$24.5 billion—of an annual benefit of $4.9 billion.

It is also possible to determine the interest rate, "i," which, when applied as a growth rate to the research expenditures and as a discount rate to the stream of benefits, yields the same capital sum at the end of 1960. Thus, in the following equation "i" may be regarded as the rate of social return on capital investments which would have had to prevail over the period 1949–60 in order that the benefits from drug research taken as a whole might be regarded as no better than alternative marginal investment projects.*

$$\text{Annual Benefits}/i = \sum_{t=1949}^{t=1960} (\text{R\&D Expend.})_t \times (1 + i)^{1961-t}$$

While, in general, average rates of return imply nothing about the corresponding marginal rates of return, in cases where the *a priori* productivity of alternative investment projects depends upon highly uncertain outcomes—and the ranking of the projects is at best very imperfect—it may not be inappropriate to regard the observed average rate of return on a group of projects as an approximation of the long-run marginal rate of return.

Even for conservative estimates of the annual measurable bene-

* This is a single equation with one unknown, "i," the rate of interest. "t" stands for the year in question, and 1961, in the exponent, represents the terminal year. The equation states that "i" has the property that: annual benefits of research and development discounted at the rate of "i" percent (the left-hand side of the equation) are equal to the value of research-and-development expenditures during the period 1949–60 capitalized at "i" percent in 1961 (the right-hand side of the equation).

VIII-6. ESTIMATES OF THE ANNUAL SOCIAL RATE OF RETURN FROM DRUG RESEARCH EXPENDITURES: 1949-60

Nature of Annual Benefits	Annual Value of Benefits	Annual Benefits Are Capitalized at the Rate of:				
		1%	20%	10%	6%	4%
Expenditures on drug research and development during the period 1949-60 are assumed to account for all of:		Annual rate of interest over the period 1949-60 on drug-research expenditures during these years required to generate the necessary capital investment by the end of 1960				
(a) Addition to GNP in 1961 by "survivors" from four diseases as a result of the reduction in death rates from these diseases during 1935-60	$4.9 billion	41.3%	53.4%[a]	65.1%	73.9%	81.1%
(b) Benefits included in (a) and addition to GNP in 1961 resulting from the reduction in morbidity rates of acute illnesses during the period 1943-59	$7.4 billion	46.4%	60.5%	72.3%	81.3%	88.6%
(c) Addition to GNP in 1961 by "survivors" from all causes of death as a result of the reduction in death rates during 1935-60 and addition to GNP in 1961 resulting from reduction in morbidity rates of acute illnesses	$12.9 billion	53.3%	69.9%	82.1%	91.4%	98.9%
(d) One half of the above benefits in (c)	$6.5	44.7%	58.1%	69.9%	78.9%	86.1%

[a]The necessary capital investment in this case would have been $24.5 billion. This and the other capitalized values can be determined by dividing the annual value of benefits by the discount rate (for example, $6.5 billion by .04). Inclusion of these values would have unduly complicated the presentation, so they have been omitted.

fits from drug research and development, the rate of social return on these expenditures appears to be considerably higher than the rates of return generally used as criteria for the undertaking of public investment projects. An estimate of $6.5 billion (entry "d" in Table VIII–6) for annual net measurable benefits attributable to research-and-development expenditures in the industry during 1949–60 is probably an understatement; even so, if the social discount rate is taken as 10 percent, then the annual social rate of return on drug research expenditures is approximately 70 percent. If nonmeasurable benefits could somehow be added, the rate of return would be higher still.[7]

Investment by the industry in research and development is substantial and, on the whole, socially productive. If policies to reduce market power in the drug industry were introduced, it would be important to ensure that most of this research-and-development activity were maintained. Thus, if a policy were predicted to impair the willingness or ability of the industry to continue to finance research and development, then the costs of financing this activity by some other method should be charged against whatever benefits arise from the introduction of the policy.

The Net Effects of Policies
to Reduce Market Power

In Chapter VI it was predicted that the removal of the principal sources of market power in the drug industry would, under given assumptions, have particular effects upon the sales of the various types of firm in the industry. These effects, which, for the convenience of the reader, are resummarized in Table IX–1, may be regarded as the gross benefits of the policies. To determine the net benefits, it is necessary to consider the ways in which the industry could react to the policies and the extent to which the alternative reactions would give rise to social costs.

Throughout this study, the figure $1,750 million has been used as the estimate of domestic sales of ethical drugs (in final dosage form) in 1961 by the 33 large firms. The corresponding estimate for the whole industry is $2,188 million. The staff of the Senate Subcommittee estimated that in 1958 expenditures on research and development by 22 large firms were equivalent to 6.3 percent of sales.[1] If this percentage is applied to $1,750 million, the resulting estimate of expenditures on research and development in 1961 falls far short of estimates obtained from other sources. The reason for this discrepancy is that the staff of the Subcommittee took a percentage of the total domestic and foreign sales of both human and veterinary ethical drugs in final dosage and bulk form. In 1961,

these total sales of the member firms of the Pharmaceutical Manufacturers Association are estimated to have been $2,992 million.[2]
Taking 6.3 percent of this figure gives an estimated $188.5 million
for research-and-development expenditures in 1961; this figure
corresponds very closely with the National Science Foundation
estimate of $192 million for the same year.

U.S. drug firms perform almost all their research and development in the United States.[3] If the N.S.F. estimate of $192 million
is taken as the amount spent by the drug industry on research and
development in 1961, it is assumed that: (a) this constitutes the
total amount of research and development financed by the industry;
(b) that it was performed entirely in the United States; (c) that 98
percent of this amount was financed by the 33 largest firms (recall
that the top 20 firms financed about 95 percent); and (d) that
the entire cost of research and development can be attributed to
domestic production of ethical drugs (for human consumption) in
final dosage form. The last assumption is made in order to obtain
a severe statement of the possible effects of the proposed policies
upon the capacity and willingness of the firms to finance research
and development, and hence to obtain a conservative estimate of
the net benefits of the policies.

The staff of the Subcommittee estimated that the total costs for
22 large firms in 1958 could be accounted for as follows:

Cost of goods sold	32.1 percent	
General and administrative	10.9	
Selling	24.8	
Research and development	6.3	
Total costs		74.1
Gross income		25.9
Corporate income taxes	13.0	
Net income	12.9	
Total revenues		100.0

In 1961 the largest firms earned a net profit of 10.5 percent of
sales.[4] If we assume a corporate income tax of 50 percent, gross
income in 1961 would have been twice the net income (two times
10.5), or 21 percent, and total costs would have equalled the

difference between total revenues—100 percent—and gross income, or 79 percent. Since the Subcommittee staff's estimate of research and development—6.3 percent of total sales—was found to be well below estimates obtained from other sources, a larger percentage, 10.7, has been used instead. Taking 10.7 percent of $1,750 million (our estimate of the total domestic sales of ethical drugs, in final dosage form, in 1961), we obtain $187.3 million as the total for research and development; then, subtracting 10.7 percent from 79 percent, we find that the remaining costs come to 68.3 percent of the total. These are allocated below (Table IX–1) among three categories: Cost of Goods Sold, General and Administrative, and Selling. The figures used are prorated estimates based upon the values shown for 1958 (p. 6).

IX-1.   ALLOCATION OF REVENUES USED TO DETERMINE THE ADJUSTMENT OF LARGE FIRMS TO THE VARIOUS POLICIES

Components of Total Revenue	Percentage	Amount
Cost of goods sold	32.3	$565.2 million
General and administrative	11.0	192.5
Selling	25.0	437.5
Research and development	10.7	187.3
Total costs	79.0	1,382.5
Corporate income taxes	10.5	183.8
Net income	10.5	183.7
Gross income	21.0	367.5
Total revenues	100.0	$1,750.0

The largest firms earned a net profit on net assets in 1961 of 18.4 percent.[5] Since profits in that year on domestic sales of ethical drugs in final dosage form amounted to about $183.7 million (Table IX–1), net assets employed in earning these profits would have been approximately $1 billion.

The adjustment by large firms to the removal of brand names

Suppose that a public policy which removed the power and the inclination of the physician to specify one of two or more sellers of a given drug were introduced, so that consumers would be at liberty to choose the drug on the basis of price. Prices of drugs affected by such a policy are assumed to fall to the lowest mean price charged by any type of firm in the particular drug market. It has previously been estimated that such a policy would affect drugs sold by large firms in such a way that original sales of $552.7 million would be reduced to $368.4 million for the same quantity. (The relevant figures are presented in Table IX–2.) The effect of this policy upon the large firms in the very short run (i.e., within a period of time too brief to allow them to adjust any of their costs) would be that the original costs* associated with the production of these drugs would continue to be incurred and that the large firms would therefore suffer losses at an annual rate of $68.3 million on this segment of their business. (Net annual income on these drugs before introduction of the policy is estimated to be $58.0 million.) The very short-run effect upon the overall operations of the large firms would be to reduce net income from an estimated $183.7 million to $95.0 million and to lower the net rate of return on invested capital from approximately 18.4 percent to approximately 9.5 percent.

As large firms would be incurring losses on the production of drugs affected by the policy, a long-run adjustment might be to abandon the production of these drugs. Immediately after a shutdown of this phase of their operations, the large firms would be free of "cost of goods sold" and selling expenses, but would continue to incur "general and administrative" costs. Hence, if the firms continued to perform research and development at the same rate as they did before the introduction of the policy, they would continue to suffer a loss during this short-run period. Their net income would be approximately $65.7 million (as against $95.0 million), and their net rate of return on invested capital would be approximately 6.6 percent. In the long run, however, fixed costs associated with the production of these drugs—"general and administrative" costs—would no longer be incurred, and the net income of the large firms would increase to an estimated $96.1 million, equivalent to a rate of return on original net assets of

---

* These are determined by taking a percentage of total sales—$552.7 million—of drugs that would be affected by the removal of brand names. Thus, if original costs are estimated to be 79 percent of total sales, we obtain $436.6 million (79 percent of $552.7 million) as the value for original costs.

IX-2. ADJUSTMENT OF LARGE FIRMS TO THE REMOVAL OF BRAND NAMES

| | Situation before Removal of Brand Names | | | Alternative Adjustments to the Removal of Brand Names | | | | | | | |
| | | | | (1) No change in cost to firms | | (2) No selling cost incurred on affected drugs | | (3) Short-run shut down: cost of goods sold and selling costs are variable | | (4) Long-run shut down: research is the only fixed cost | |
	Total	Un-affected	Affected	Affected	Total	Affected	Total	Affected	Total	Affected	Total
Revenues	1,750.0	1,197.3	552.7	368.3	1,565.5	368.3	1,565.5	0.0	1,197.2	0.0	1,197.2
Costs											
Goods sold	565.2	386.7	178.5	178.5	545.2	178.5	565.2	0.0	386.7	0.0	386.7
Gen. & admin.	192.5	131.7	60.8	60.8	192.5	60.8	192.5	60.8	192.5	0.0	131.7
Selling	437.5	299.3	138.2	138.2	437.5	0.0	299.3	0.0	299.3	0.0	299.3
Research	187.3	128.1	59.1	59.1	187.3	59.1	187.3	59.1	187.3	59.1	187.3
Total costs	1,382.5	945.9	436.6	436.6	1,382.5	298.4	1,244.3	119.9	1,065.8	59.1	1,005.0
Income											
Gross	367.5	251.4	116.1	−68.3	190.0	69.9	320.9	−119.9	131.5	−59.1	192.3
Corp. tax	183.8	125.7	58.1	0.0	95.0	35.0	160.5	0.0	65.8	0.0	96.2
Net	183.7	125.7	58.0	−68.3	95.0	34.9	160.4	−119.9	65.7	−59.1	96.1
Rate of return on net assets	18.4				9.5		16.4		6.6		9.6

approximately 9.6 percent. Eventually, with the withdrawal of capital used in the production of these goods, the net rate of return on actual net assets used in the production of the remaining drugs would presumably rise above 9.6 percent.

The average rate of return on net assets for all manufacturing in 1961 was 9.9 percent.[6] It might be concluded, therefore, that the large firms in the drug industry could make a long-run adjustment to the removal of brand names by abandoning, to other types of firms, the production of the drugs which would be affected by such a policy. (The assumption that large firms would lose all the sales of drugs which are covered by brand names is made in order to obtain an estimate which can be referred to as an upper limit on the possible effects of the policy upon large firms.) If the large firms continued to finance research and development at the same level as they did in 1961, this long-run adjustment would permit the large firms as a group to earn approximately the normal rate of return on invested capital.

There is, however, an alternative reaction to the removal of brand names. The prices of drugs affected by the policy are assumed to fall to the levels charged by other types of firms in the individual drug markets. This outcome is assumed because both physicians and consumers are expected to regard the products of competing sellers as homogeneous, and hence to have no basis for preferring one seller to another on any ground but price. Moreover, if consumers and purchasing agents do not develop preferences for the product of a particular seller, it is reasonable to hypothesize that sellers will no longer make any effort to influence preferences in these markets and that their promotional expenditures on these drugs will cease.

If selling expenditures for drugs in this group fall to zero (if the drugs are, in effect, sold under their generic names), then the total costs associated with them are reduced from $436.6 million to $298.4 million. In this case, large firms would earn a net profit on these drugs of $34.9 million. The overall net income of the large firms would be $160.4 million, and the net rate of return would be about 16.4 percent.

An adjustment of this general nature would appear to be much the most profitable reaction to the policy. The high level of profits which the industry would still be able to maintain, together with the continued protection afforded by patents, suggests that the incentive and the financial capability of the large firms to perform research and development would not be significantly impaired under the policy of removing brand names.

The adjustment by large firms to the removal of patents

The removal of patents is assumed to transform drug markets affected by the policy into markets in which there would be only the protection afforded by brand names. In this case, competition would take the form of selling effort. Previously excluded types of firms would enter these markets, with the result that the quantity share held by the large firms would decline; and the estimated quantities sold by the large firms would be 52.9 percent of the pre-policy levels. The prices charged by the large firms in these newly transformed markets would bear the same relation to the prices charged by other types of firms as that observed in markets which were originally protected only by brand names.

The income of large firms from the sale of drugs affected by the removal of patents would be expected to decline from $1,111.2 million to $572.5 million. (The relevant figures are presented in Table IX–3.) In the very short-run period following the introduction of the policy, large firms would continue to incur the original costs of $877.8 million associated with the production of drugs affected and would therefore experience losses on these drugs at an annual rate of $305.3 million. The total sales of large firms would be reduced to $1,211.2 million, but costs would remain at the original level of $1,382.5 million, so that, on all drugs, the firms would incur losses at an annual rate of $171.3 million.

As the production of drugs affected by the removal of patents is estimated to decline to 52.9 percent of the original levels, an expected short-run adjustment to the introduction of the policy would be the reduction of some costs. Since, with the removal of patents, the markets would be characterized by product differentiation and selling efforts, it is assumed that large firms would not significantly alter their selling expenditures on the drugs affected. However, the "cost of goods sold" could be reduced, and it is assumed that for affected drugs, this would decline to 52.9 percent of the original

IX-3.   ADJUSTMENT OF LARGE FIRMS TO THE REMOVAL OF PATENT PROTECTION

| | Before Removal of Patents | | | Alternative Adjustments to the Removal of Patents | | | | | | | | |
| | | | | (1) No change in costs to firms | | (2) Cost of goods sold reduced to 52.9% of original level to reflect reduced quantity sold | | (3) General and admin. reduced to 52.9% of original level | | (4) No research expenditures | |
	Total	Un-affected	Affected	Affected	Total	Affected	Total	Affected	Total	Affected	Total
Revenues	1,750.0	639.8	1,111.2	572.5	1,211.2	572.5	1,211.2	572.5	1,211.2	572.5	1,211.2
Costs											
Goods sold	565.2	206.7	358.9	358.9	565.2	189.9	396.6	189.9	396.6	189.9	396.6
Gen. & admin.	192.5	70.4	122.2	122.2	192.5	122.2	192.5	64.6	135.0	64.6	135.0
Selling	437.5	160.0	277.8	277.8	437.5	277.8	437.5	277.8	437.5	277.8	437.5
Research	187.3	68.4	118.9	118.9	187.3	118.9	187.3	118.9	187.3	0.0	0.0
Total costs	1,382.5	505.4	877.8	877.8	1,382.5	708.8	1,213.9	651.2	1,156.4	532.5	969.1
Income											
Gross	367.5	134.4	233.4	−305.3	−171.3	−136.3	−2.7	−78.7	54.8	40.0	242.1
Corp. tax	183.8	67.2	166.7	0.0	0.0	0.0	0.0	0.0	27.4	20.0	121.1
Net	183.7	67.2	166.7	−305.3	−171.3	−136.3	−2.7	−78.7	27.4	20.0	121.0
Rate of return on net assets	18.4				−17.1%		−0.3%		2.7%		12.1%

149

level. Hence, losses on drugs affected by the policy would be reduced to an annual rate of $136.3 million, and losses on all drugs to an annual rate of $2.7 million.

Over a longer period of time, the "general and administrative" costs associated with the drugs affected could also be reduced. If, for affected drugs, these costs fell to 52.9 percent of their original levels, then losses on the same drugs would be reduced to an annual rate of $78.7 million, and a net profit on all drugs of approximately $27.4 million would be earned—equivalent to an annual net rate of return of approximately 2.7 percent.

Such adjustments would leave the large firms earning a rate of return much below normal. If selling costs are assumed to remain unchanged, the only other component of costs which could be reduced would be research-and-development costs. As profit rates would be substantially below the normal rate, and as patent protection would have been removed, it is probable that the large firms would be unwilling to finance significant amounts of research and development, with the result that the industry would produce a relatively static mix of drugs. In this case—with the cessation of research and development—the costs associated with drugs affected by the policy would decline to $532.5 million. The net annual profit on these drugs would then be $20.0 million, and the annual net profit on all drugs would be $121.0 million—equivalent to a rate of return on invested capital of approximately 12.1 percent.

If the large firms reacted to the abolition of patent protection on both present and future goods by reducing the fixed and variable costs associated with the drugs affected (in other words, by reducing production of them) and if all research and development expenditures stopped, then it would appear that these firms would be able to earn approximately the normal rate of return on investment after the introduction of the policy. Clearly, not *all* research and development expenditures would cease. Even in the absence of patent protection, some projects which promised a sufficiently high rate of return (and whose results competitors would find sufficiently difficult to imitate) would continue to be undertaken. Such projects would probably be comparatively rare, however, and the assumption of no expenditures on research and development is a reasonable approximation of what might be expected if patent protection were abolished. Thus, a significant social cost attribut-

IX-4. ADJUSTMENT OF LARGE FIRMS TO REMOVAL OF BOTH BRAND NAMES AND PATENTS

Alternative Adjustments to the Removal of Brand Names and Patent Protection

	Before Removal of Patents			No change in costs to firms (1)		Cost of goods sold reduced to reflect reduced quantity sold (2)		No selling costs (3)		Reduction in general and admin. costs to reflect decrease in quantity (4)		No research expenditures (5)	
	Total	Unaf- fected	Af- fected	Af- fected	Total	Af- fected	Total	Af- fected	Total	Af- fected	Total	Af- fected	Total
Revenues	1,750.0	86.3	1,663.7	645.8	731.9	645.8	731.9	645.8	731.9	645.8	731.9	645.8	731.9
Costs													
Goods sold	565.2	27.9	537.4	537.4	565.2	368.4	396.3	368.4	396.3	368.4	396.3	368.4	396.3
Gen. & adm.	192.5	9.5	183.0	183.0	192.5	183.0	192.5	183.0	192.5	125.4	134.9	125.4	134.9
Selling	437.5	21.6	415.9	415.9	437.5	415.9	437.5	0.0	0.0	0.0	0.0	0.0	0.0
Research	187.3	9.2	178.0	178.0	187.3	178.0	187.3	178.0	187.3	178.0	187.3	0.0	0.0
Total costs	1,382.5	68.2	1,314.3	1,314.3	1,382.5	1,145.3	1,210.6	729.4	776.1	671.8	718.5	493.8	531.2
Income													
Gross	367.5	18.1	349.4	−668.5	−650.6	−499.5	−478.7	−83.6	−44.2	−26.0	13.4	152.0	200.7
Corp. tax	183.8	9.1	174.7	0.0	0.0	0.0	0.0	0.0	0.0	0.0	6.7	76.0	76.0
Net	183.7	9.0	174.7	−668.5	−650.6	−499.5	−478.7	−83.6	−44.2	−26.0	6.7	76.0	100.3
Rate of return on net assets	18.4%				−65.1%		−47.9%		−4.4%		0.7%		10.0%

151

able to the policy to remove patents is that progress from the industry would be stifled.

The adjustment to the removal of both brand names and patents

Drug markets in which market power was originally conferred by brand names are assumed to be affected by the removal of brand names and patents as they would be under a policy to remove brand names alone. As has been said, markets formerly protected by patents would be entered by previously excluded types of firm, and, with the removal of both patents and brand names, prices would be equalized at the level of the lowest mean price charged by any type of firm in the industry after the removal of brand names.

The introduction of this policy is estimated to reduce the large firms' sales of drugs that would be affected (valued at $1,663.7 million before the policy) to $645.8 million. (See Table IX–4.) In the very short run, losses would be incurred on these drugs at the rate of $668.5 million per year, and losses on all drug operations of large firms would be $650.6 million per year. In the short run, a reduction in "cost of goods sold," to reflect the reduction in physical production, would reduce losses on all drug operations to $478.7 million.

It is also assumed that with the removal of brand names and patents drugs produced by all types of sellers would be regarded as homogeneous and that consumers would be free to choose sellers on the basis of price; hence, drug firms might be expected to abandon their promotional efforts. If selling expenditures on all drugs fell to zero, losses on all operations would be reduced to $44.2 million per year. If, in the longer term, "general and administrative" costs associated with drugs affected by the policy could be reduced in proportion to the reduction in production of these drugs, an annual net profit of $6.7 million on all drugs could be earned; this is equivalent to an annual rate of return on original invested capital of 0.7 percent.

With profits at very low levels, and the protection offered by both brand names and patents removed, there is little doubt that firms would be unwilling to finance research and development. The elimination of these costs would permit large firms to earn an annual net profit of approximately $100.3 million, or a 10.0 percent rate of return on original investment. This is approximately the normal rate of return in industry, and it might be concluded, therefore, that large firms could survive the removal of brand names and patents by reacting in the foregoing manner. As with the removal of patent protection alone, however, the introduction of this policy carries with it the cost of halting industry-financed research and development.

Policy outcomes under alternative allocations of costs

Alternative estimates of the outcomes of each of the policies are obtained if the costs of the large firms are allocated in a different manner from that assumed above. It is useful to consider one minor variation in the allocation of costs.

Large firms sell an estimated $86.3 million worth of drugs that would be unaffected by any of the policies. These are drugs which were introduced before 1944 and which are sold by only one firm. Under the assumptions of the model, these drugs are assumed not to owe their market power to brand names, and, since 18 or more years have elapsed by 1961, are also assumed not to be covered by patents. In fact, several possible explanations exist for the observed market structures for these drugs. First, patent protection may not have expired. Second, although the drug may be no longer covered by patent protection, entry to the market may be blocked or hampered by technological difficulties in producing the drug or by insurmountable physician preferences built up over the period when the drug was covered by a patent. Third, the market may be so small that it could not support additional firms. There are also some drugs which the single manufacturer, although he loses money on them, continues to produce as a public service. In the previous analysis of the outcomes of policies, these drugs were assumed to bear their share of selling and research-and-development costs. An alternative is to regard such drugs as bearing no selling costs and no research-and-development costs, and to explain the absence of additional firms in the market on the ground that no more than normal rates of return are earned in these markets.

Assuming that a quantity of net assets proportional to sales is used in the production of these drugs, a normal rate of return on net assets of 9.9 percent would be equivalent to a net rate of return on sales of 5.66 percent. Since total revenues from these drugs are $86.3 million, net profits would be $4.88 million, and total costs other than the corporate income tax would be $76.54 million. (See Table IX–5.) For all drugs sold by large firms the cost-of-goods-sold was estimated to comprise 32.3 percent of total revenues and "general and administrative" costs to comprise 11.0 percent. If costs are allocated to only these two components for drugs un-affected by the introduction of any policy, and if the allocation is weighted by the above proportions, then the cost-of-goods-sold will account for 66.2 percent—$57.1 million—of total revenues; and "general and administrative" costs will account for 22.5 per-cent—$19.4 million. Subtracting these dollar amounts from the original totals for each of the components leaves the amounts available to be allocated to each of these two components for the drugs assumed to be affected by one of the policies. These latter amounts, together with the original amounts to be allocated to selling and to research and development, are allocated to two groups of drugs—those affected by the removal of brand names alone, and those affected by the removal of patents alone—accord-ing to the relative sales of each group of drugs among the sales of all drugs affected by one of the policies. Thus, drugs affected by the removal of brand names alone account for 32.2 percent of the costs of affected drugs, and drugs affected by patent removal alone account for the remaining 66.8 percent of the cost of affected drugs.

With both selling costs and research-and-development costs loaded on to affected drugs, the percentage allocation of total revenues becomes for these drugs:

Cost of goods sold	30.5 percent	
General and administrative	10.4	
Selling	26.3	
Research and development	11.3	
Total costs		78.5
Gross income		21.5
Corporate income tax	10.75	
Net income	10.75	
Total revenues		100.0

IX-5. EXPECTED OUTCOMES OF EACH POLICY WITH RESEARCH AND SELLING COSTS LOADED ON TO DRUGS AFFECTED BY REMOVAL OF SOURCES OF MARKET POWER

	Before Removal of Any Source of Market Power					Policies and Assumed Adjustments					
	Total	Sales affected by				Removal of brand names. No selling effort on affected drugs (1)		Removal of patents. No further research expenditures (2)		Removal of both brand names and patents. No selling or research expenditures by large firms (3)	
		No Policy	Removal of Pats. Brand Names	Removal of Brand Names	Total Affec.	Affected	Total	Affected	Total	Affected	Total
Revenues	1,750.0	86.3	1,111.2	552.7	1,663.7	368.2	1,565.2	572.5	1,211.2	645.8	731.9
Costs											
Goods sold	565.2	57.1	339.4	168.7	508.1	168.7	565.2	179.5	405.3	348.2	405.3
Gen. & adm.	192.5	19.4	115.6	57.5	173.1	57.5	192.5	61.2	138.1	118.7	138.1
Selling	437.5	0.0	292.3	145.2	437.5	0.0	292.3	292.3	437.5	0.0	0.0
Research	187.3	0.0	125.1	62.2	187.3	62.2	187.3	0.0	0.0	0.0	0.0
Total costs	1,382.5	76.5	872.4	433.6	1,306.0	288.4	1,237.3	533.0	980.9	466.9	543.4
Income											
Gross	367.5	9.8	238.8	119.1	357.7	79.9	325.2	39.5	230.3	178.9	188.5
Corp. tax	183.8	4.9	119.4	59.6	178.9	40.0	162.6	19.8	115.2	89.5	94.3
Net	183.7	4.9	119.4	59.5	178.8	39.9	162.6	19.7	115.1	89.4	94.2
Rate of return on net assets	18.4%	9.9%			18.8%		16.3%		11.5%		9.4%

155

Under this allocation of costs, the rate of return on sales for affected drugs becomes 10.75 percent, equivalent to a rate of return on net assets of 18.8 percent.

Table IX–5 considers the probable outcome of each of the policies under these assumptions about the allocation of costs. With the removal of brand names, the rate of return on net assets is reduced by one-tenth of one percent as compared to the outcome under the previous assumptions about the allocation of costs. For the other two policies, these assumptions reduce the rate of return after adjustment to the policies by one half of one percent. Thus the general nature of the outcomes remains unaffected: The removal of brand names would probably not damage the incentive or the willingness of firms to finance research and development whereas the other two policies would probably result in the cessation of industry-financed research and development.

CONCLUSIONS

The significant social costs of the policies arise from their predicted effects upon research and development as it is presently financed and performed. Both the removal of patents alone and the removal of both brand names and patents would undoubtedly entail a substantial reduction in the industry's incentives and capacity to perform research and development, and the introduction of either policy would surely require that alternative arrangements be made for at least the financing of research.

It is not the purpose of this study to suggest the details of possible alternative methods by which research and development in the drug industry could take place. It is sufficient, for our purposes, to suggest that at least one workable alternative exists, which, in combination with one or other of the policies, would yield a net social benefit. This alternative is to have the federal government finance drug research and development through grants or contract arrangements with non-governmental performers—in much the same way that it now does with performers of military and space research. In the drug industry, the non-governmental performers would be, as they now are, the major firms with established research facilities. The results of their research would be made available to all firms wishing to use them.

The research subsidy required from the government would be expected to equal the amount of research—$192 million— financed by the industry in 1961. The net benefits of each policy are calculated as the gross benefits under each policy less the subsidy (as needed) for research. The estimates of the net benefits are shown below in Table IX–6.

IX-6.   NET BENEFITS OF EACH POLICY TO REMOVE MARKET POWER

Policy: Removal of	Gross Benefits	Research Subsidy	Net Benefits
Brand names alone	$228 million	None	$228 million
Patents alone	$274	$192 million	$82
Both brand names and patents	$617	$192	$425

Each policy is predicted to yield a net social gain. The removal of brand names alone would yield a significant social gain without the necessity of changing the institutional arrangements surrounding the performance and financing of research.* The removal of patents alone would yield a much smaller net gain and would require changes in institutional arrangements; as a policy alternative, it is not to be preferred to the removal of brand names alone. Finally, the removal of both patents and brand names together would yield a social gain approximately twice as great as the gain accruing from the removal of brand names alone.

There exists at least one policy through which "the existing misallocation of resources in excessive selling efforts, duplicative research and product development programs, and exceptionally high profit levels"[7] could be remedied. While the removal of brand-name protection or of patent protection—or of both—may seem to some a drastic remedy, it can be pointed out that, with the possible exception of school textbooks, the brand-name protection given to ethical drugs is unique, and that the policy of the United

* As we have seen, this policy would give the consumer a measure of relief from the high cost of drugs, and the manufacturers would in time be able to reattain their pre-policy level of income and continue their research and development without any serious reduction of these activities.

States of granting product patents on drugs, without collateral price control or compulsory licensing provisions, appears to be unique in the world.[8]

The estimates of the effects of the three policies have been obtained under assumptions of price and income inelasticity of demand. While the nature of the commodity suggests that the degree of inelasticity is great in both cases, the assumption of complete inelasticity is not a precise portrayal of reality. Nevertheless, these assumptions can be defended as being the least objectionable. There are no data or previous studies which could be used to obtain an estimate of the values of the coefficients of elasticity. Thus, any non-zero value selected as an estimate of the coefficients would be arbitrary; it would not be known whether the true values lay above or below the estimates. The selection of zero as the value of the coefficient gives estimates of the effects of the policies which are the lower limits of the possible effects. If elasticity of demand were, in fact, zero, then the policies would serve only to reduce the wastes inherent in excessive selling efforts and to redistribute income from stockholders in ethical drug firms to consumers of drugs. If, however, demand is not perfectly inelastic, then the policies will yield, in addition to these effects, an improvement in resource allocation. Since zero elasticity has been assumed, we conclude that the benefits of the policies would be at least as great as the estimates, and probably greater.

APPENDICES

[A] Market-Power Relationships

[B] Classification of Drugs by Type

[C] Classification of Drugs by Year
of Introduction

[D] Estimates of Sales of Individual
Drugs in 1961

[E] Effect of the Removal of Brand
Names upon the Cost of Drugs

[F] Effect of the Removal of Patents
upon the Cost of Drugs

[G] Effect of the Removal of Brand
Names and Patents

[A] Market-Power Relationships[*]

The market power of one type of firm is considered to be less than that of another type of firm if the first type of firm charges significantly (in a statistical sense) lower prices than the second type. A test of significance is to determine whether the geometric mean of the price ratios is significantly less than one. As there is no concept analogous to the standard deviation (which measures typical deviation) from the geometric mean, the test must be applied on the logarithmic mean—the logarithm of the geometric mean—to determine whether the logarithmic mean is significantly less than zero.† Table A–1 shows the "t" values (standardized values) of the difference between zero and the observed value of the logarithmic mean. Values of "t" which are significant at the standard levels of significance for a "one-tailed" test are indicated.

With one exception, the figures in Table–1 support the previously specified hypothesis about the direction of market power

---

* This appendix is co-ordinate with pp. 91–99 of the text.

† Because the groupings of firms are not mutually exclusive in the ten ratios, not all the tests are independent of one another. The ratios S/L, G/B SG/L and SB/L are derived by a weighted pooling of ratios from among the six primary ratios; hence, differences observed in the first six ratios will be reflected in the other four ratios.

between pairs of types of firms; thus, for SG/LB ("Small Firm–
Generic Name"/"Large Firm–Brand Name") the hypothesis that
LB has more market power than SG is borne out by the "t" value
(−4.92). Only for LG/LB does the geometric mean (.9457)
significantly approach one, and for this pair of types of firms it is

A-1. SIGNIFICANCE LEVELS OF LOGARITHMIC MEAN OF
RATIOS

Price Ratio	Logarith- mic Mean	Standard Error	"t" Value	Number of Observations	Geometric Mean
SG/SB	−.5538	.156	−3.56[a]	75	.5748
SG/LG	−.4120	.090	−4.59[a]	106	.6623
SG/LB	−.7623	.155	−4.92[a]	102	.4666
SB/LG	−.0344	.234	−0.15	25	.9662
SB/LB	−.2927	.107	−2.72[a]	76	.7462
LG/LB	−.0558	.125	−0.45	40	.9457
S/L	−.5055	.076	−6.68[a]	185	.6032
G/B	−.5785	.087	−6.67[a]	134	.5607
SG/L	−.5820	.083	−6.98[a]	176	.5588
SB/L	−.2692	.104	−2.59[b]	82	.7640

[a]Significant at 0.005 level.   [b]Significant at 0.01 level.

concluded that there is no significant difference in market power.
It will be noticed that the geometric mean for SB/LG is .9662,
but, as has been said, there is no *a priori* hypothesis for this ratio
because each type of firm symbolized has only one of the bases of
power. Here again, since the value of the ratio closely approaches
unity, the difference in market power between the two types of firm
is not statistically significant.

Market power in relation to time

For the purposes of the present discussion, drug ages are
measured from 1961, and are treated as though no drug had been
introduced before 1900. Since, as has been noted, there is an
inherent inconsistency in taking the arithmetic mean of the values
of the price ratios, the relationship between price ratio and age
was examined by running least-squares regressions between the

A-2. ESTIMATES OF PARAMETERS FOR THE
REGRESSIONS: $\log_e [E(A_i)/E(B_i)] = a + b \times Age_i$

Price Ratio	a*	b*	R^{2*}	d.f.*
SG/SB	−.4750 (−3.82)†	−.00412 (−0.75)	.008	73
SG/LG	−.5160 (−5.52)	+.00357 (+1.28)	.016	102
SG/LB	−.8265 (−6.83)	+.00314 (+0.62)	.004	100
SB/LG	−.1309 (−0.56)	+.00397 (+0.46)	.009	23
SB/LB	−.3749 (−3.51)	+.00490 (+0.96)	.012	74
LG/LB	+.0588 (+0.48)	−.00513 (−1.08)	.030	38
S/L	−.5858 (−7.79)	+.00345 (+1.29)	.009	183
G/B	−.5482 (−6.33)	−.00151 (−0.42)	.001	132
SG/L	−.7748 (−9.49)	+.00769 (+2.82)‡	.044	174
SB/L	−.3710 (+0.10)	+.00581 (+1.24)	.019	80

*"a" and "b" are regression coefficients; "R" is the correlation
coefficient; "d.f." is the number of observations minus 2 ("degrees
of freedom").
†Figures in parentheses are ratios of the value of the estimate to
the standard error of the estimate.
‡Significant at 0.005 level.

natural logarithms of the values of the price ratio for each drug
and age, using the linear form and several nonlinear forms that
related the logarithm of the value to the age. The standard form is

$$\log_e [E (A_i)/E (B_i)] = a + b \times Age_i$$

in which subscript "i" indicates a particular drug, and "a" and "b" are regression coefficients to be estimated. The results of these regressions are shown in Table A–2.

The results are clearly insignificant. Some variation in the logarithms of the price ratios is explained by the age of the drugs, but the largest percentage of variation for any of the price ratios is 4.4, and only four other ratios show as much as 1 percent of the variation explained. If market power did vary inversely with the age of the drugs, the slopes of the regressions as shown on a graph would be expected to be negative; but in fact there is no consistently negative relationship, and only one of the slopes is significantly negative at as much as the 0.05 level. We must conclude that age is irrelevant in explaining variations in price ratios and reject the hypothesis that market power is eroded away by the passage of time.* Accordingly, it would appear that belief in the existence of quality differentials is permanent.

Viewed as a continuum, the age of a drug appears to have no effect on price ratios; but if drug age is divided into two time periods and if the geometric means of the observations falling into each period are determined, we may still observe significant differences among the means.

Drugs may be classified according to whether they were introduced before or after 1944; those introduced before 1944 were more than seventeen years old in 1961, and those introduced after 1944 were seventeen years old or less. As the duration of patent protection is seventeen years, the drugs in the first group are probably no longer covered by patents, whereas those introduced in 1944 or between 1944 and 1961 may still be covered. The difference between the logarithmic means of the observations in each group is computed for each ratio and the results are presented in Table A–3.

Market power in relation to patents

If patents are significant, then market power is expected to be less for drugs introduced before 1944 than for drugs introduced in

* It is to be noted that time-series data might well yield a different conclusion. Further, the conclusion is *not* that age is insignificant in the explanation of the *prices* of drugs, but that it is not significant in the explanation of the *price ratios*.

DIFFERENCES BETWEEN MEANS ACCORDING TO PROBABLE EXISTENCE OF PATENTS

Price Ratio	Before 1944		1944 and After		Difference in means[a]	"t"	d.f.
	Logarithmic mean	Geometric mean	Logarithmic mean	Geometric mean			
SG/SB	-.5725	.5626	-.5306	.5882	-.0446	-0.33	73
SG/LG	-.4243	.6542	-.3793	.6843	-.0445	-0.44	104
SG/LB	-.7423	.4756	-.7846	.4563	+.0414	+0.33	100
SB/LG	-.1661	.8470	+.3827	1.4667	-.5487	-2.90[b]	23
SB/LB	-.2401	.7866	-.3290	.7197	+.0889	+0.69	74
LG/LB	-.0267	.9737	-.0952	.9092	+.0686	+0.56	38
S/L	-.5024	.6051	-.5096	.6008	+.0071	+0.08	183
G/B	-.6002	.5487	-.5541	.5746	-.0461	-0.50	132
SG/L	-.5434	.5808	-.6480	.5231	+.1046	+1.17	174
SB/L	-.2298	.7947	-.3001	.7407	+.0703	+0.58	80

[a]Difference in logarithmic means = Log_e Mean (1944 and after)—Log_e Mean (before 1944).
[b]Significant at 0.005 level.

165

1944 or later. This means that the geometric means for the first group would be greater than the corresponding geometric means for the second group. As the test of the difference between two geometric means must be applied on the logarithmic means, the difference ("1944 and after"–"before 1944") is shown; this value is expected to be positive.

The table shows only one of the differences to be significant at as much as the 0.05 level and indicates no consistency in the sign of the difference. We conclude that, for drugs produced by two or more types of firm, the existence of patents does not explain differences in market power. The one ratio for which the difference between means is significant, SB/LG, is the one ratio for which no *a priori* hypothesis concerning the overall direction of market power could be made. It is a matter of some interest, however, that when the observations for this ratio are classified according to the probable existence of patents, a significant difference between the means is obtained. This suggests that small firms selling under brand names have greater market power during the early life of a drug but that over a period of time large firms selling under generic name are able to accumulate market power relative to small firms selling under brand names.

Market power in relation to method of drug administration

For any pair of types of firms, we hypothesize that the market power will be greater in markets for orally administered drugs than in markets for parenterally administered drugs. To test the hypothesis, the geometric mean and the logarithmic mean were computed for each ratio for oral drugs and parenteral drugs (but not for serums and bulk drugs), and the significance of the difference between the logarithmic means was tested. The difference was constructed by subtracting the logarithmic mean for parenteral drugs from the logarithmic mean for oral drugs; the expected sign of the difference is, therefore, negative. The results are shown in Table A–4. In order to examine the significance of the geometric means for oral drugs and for injectibles, the logarithmic mean was tested against zero; the "t" values shown are the standardized values of the difference between the value of the logarithmic mean and zero.

For oral drugs, in all but the case of SB/LG, the logarithmic

A-4. DIFFERENCE BETWEEN MEANS ACCORDING TO METHOD OF DRUG ADMINISTRATION

Price Ratio	Orally Administered			Parenterally Administered			Difference[a]	"t"	d.f.
	Logarithmic mean	"t"	Geometric mean	Logarithmic mean	"t"	Geometric mean			
SG/SB	−.6713	−4.76[d]	.5110	−.3041	−1.27	.7378	−.3673	−2.68[d]	73
SG/LG	−.6447	−4.87[d]	.5248	−.3703	−1.69	.6905	−.2744	−2.44[c]	74
SG/LB	−.9294	−6.69[d]	.3948	−.4410	−2.13[b]	.6434	−.4884	−3.92[d]	99
SB/LG	+.0697	+0.30	1.0721	−.1161	−0.20	.8904	+.1858	+1.00	23
SB/LB	−.3345	−2.66[d]	.7157	−.1674	−0.76	.8459	−.1671	−1.14	74
LG/LB	−.1377	−0.57	.8713	+.0183	+0.18	1.0185	−.1560	−1.30	38
S/L	−.6712	−6.885[d]	.5111	−.3497	−2.34[c]	.7049	−.3216	−3.21[d]	155
G/B	−.7464	−7.40[d]	.4741	−.3027	−2.25[b]	.7388	−.4437	−5.02[d]	131
SG/L	−.8208	−7.50[d]	.4401	−.4121	−2.76[d]	.6623	−.4088	−4.24[d]	143
SB/L	−.3339	−0.87	.7161	−.1034	−2.29[b]	.9018	−.2305	−1.74	80

[a] Difference between logarithmic means = Log$_e$ Mean$_{(oral)}$ − Log$_e$ Mean$_{(parenteral)}$.

[b] Significant at 0.05 level.
[c] Significant at 0.01 level.
[d] Significant at 0.005 level.

mean of the price ratios is negative. In seven of the nine cases the value of the logarithmic mean is significantly less than zero, indicating a significant difference in market power between the types of firm used in constructing the ratio. For the remaining cases, SB/LG, LG/LB, and SB/L, the logarithmic mean is not significantly less than zero at the 0.05 level, and we conclude that there is no significant difference between pairs of these types of firm in oral-drug markets. For injectible drugs, all but LG/LB have negative logarithmic means, but only five of these cases show significant values at the 0.05 level. Of the seven ratios for which the logarithmic mean was significantly less than zero in oral markets, only four also show significant values in injectible-drug markets. In the case of SB/L, the logarithmic mean is significantly less than zero in injectible-drug markets but not in oral-drug markets.

The difference between logarithmic means is negative in all cases except SB/LG but significant at the 0.05 level in only six cases. The ratios for which the differences are significant all represent small firms selling under generic names, and in all cases where a ratio involves small firms selling under generic names the difference is significant. This evidence supports the hypothesis that drugs sold by large firms or by firms selling under brand names when compared to drugs sold by small firms selling them under their generic names have relatively less market power in markets for injectible drugs than in markets for orally administered drugs. We infer from this that a physician, when purchasing a drug which he would administer to the patient, is more likely to select a firm on the basis of price considerations, and that large firms and small firms selling under brand names adjust their prices to make them competitive with the prices charged by the small firms selling under generic name.

[B] Classification of Drugs by Type*

The following tables, B–1 through B–7, present a typological analysis of sales, pricing, and marketing relationships in the drug industry. Table B–1 (p. 171) classifies drugs belonging to each major group according to: (a) the number of drugs in the major group sold under each market structure and (b) the number of drugs in each major group sold by each type of firm. Table B–2 (p. 172) shows: (a) the proportion of drugs sold under each market structure accounted for by each type of drug and (b) the proportion of drugs sold by each type of firm accounted for by each type of drug. Drugs in major group 40 represent 24.5 percent of all drugs, 27.6 percent of the drugs produced by only one firm, and 20.3 percent of the drugs produced by small firms selling under generic names.

Table B–3 (p. 173) shows for 1961 the proportion of drugs of each type which are sold: (a) under each market structure and (b) by each type of firm. Thus, 42.1 percent of the drugs belonging to major group 10 are sold by only one firm; 44.7 percent of the drugs belonging to this group are sold by small firms selling under

* This appendix is co-ordinate with pp. 15–24 of the text. See in particular Table II–1 (pp.22–23), which classifies drugs and shows the number in use in 1961.

169

generic names. Row entries for type of firm will not add to 100 percent because 227 of the drugs are classified in at least two columns.

Table B–4* presents the value of the price ratios as these ratios are classified into one of the twelve types of drug, and the geometric mean of the observations belonging to each classification is computed. This provides a measure, for each type of drug, of the average benefit of selecting a firm used in the numerator of the price ratio rather than selecting from the type of firm used in the denominator of the ratio. (In other words, if the geometric mean is less than 1.0, it will, on the whole, be to the advantage of the consumer to select the product of the firm symbolized in the numerator of the ratio—e.g., SG rather than SB.)

Effects of the policies upon the sales of drugs by type

Table B–5 presents the estimated sales of each type of drug before the introduction of any policy, and after the introduction of each of the policies. Let the subscript "j" represent the general types of drug and "M" the removal of brand names; then:

TS_j represents the total sales ("TS") of drugs of the jth type before the introduction of any policy;

TSM_j represents the total sales of drugs of the jth type after the removal of brand names.

Similarly, if "P" is used to symbolize the removal of patents and "A" the removal of both brand names and patents, then:

TSP_j represents the total tales of drugs of the jth type after the removal of patents; and,

TSA_j represents the total sales of drugs of the jth type after the removal of brand names and patents.

The table shows the values of TSM_j/TS_j, TSP_j/TS_j and TSA_j/TS_j —the ratio of the estimated sales after the introduction of any given policy to the sales before introduction of the policy. In general, types of drugs which show a relatively large percentage decrease in sales as a result of the introduction of a policy to re-

* Table B-4 appears on p. 174; following text resumes on p. 176.

B-1. CLASSIFICATION OF DRUGS ACCORDING TO TYPE OF DRUG, TYPE OF MARKET STRUCTURE, AND TYPE OF SELLING FIRM

Drug Type	Total No. Drugs in Major Group	Only One Firm	Only One Type of Firm but More Than One Firm	More Than One Type of Firm	Small Firm Generic Name	Small Firm Brand Name	Large Firm Generic Name	Large Firm Brand Name
10	38	16	7	15	17	12	15	18
20	31	11	4	16	15	13	11	13
30	33	26	0	7	9	9	3	20
40	161	104	11	46	46	31	21	123
50	63	43	4	16	13	17	6	46
60	27	19	2	6	5	8	1	20
70	17	7	0	10	11	5	5	10
80	107	58	11	38	41	20	27	70
90	92	37	7	48	46	26	28	72
100	28	20	2	6	4	4	0	28
110	22	14	1	7	7	7	3	17
120	37	22	3	12	13	5	18	13
All drugs	656	377	52	227	227	157	138	450

B-2. DISTRIBUTION OF DRUG TYPES BY TYPE OF MARKET AND TYPE OF FIRM

Drug type	Proportion of all drugs of given type	Proportion of Drugs Sold in Each Type of Market Structure Accounted for by Each Type of Drug			Proportion of Drugs Sold by Each Type of Firm Accounted for by Each Type of Drug			
		Only one firm	Only one type of firm but more than one firm	More than one type of firm	Small firm Generic name	Small firm Brand name	Large firm Generic name	Large firm Brand name
10	.0579	.0424	.1346	.0661	.0749	.0764	.1087	.0400
20	.0473	.0292	.0769	.0701	.0661	.0828	.0942	.0289
30	.0503	.0690	.0000	.0308	.0396	.0573	.0217	.0444
40	.2454	.2758	.2115	.2026	.2026	.1975	.1522	.2733
50	.0960	.1141	.0769	.0701	.0573	.1083	.0435	.1022
60	.0412	.0504	.0385	.0264	.0220	.0510	.0072	.0444
70	.0259	.0186	.0000	.0441	.0485	.0318	.0362	.0222
80	.1631	.1538	.2115	.1674	.1806	.1274	.1957	.1555
90	.1402	.0981	.1346	.2114	.2026	.1656	.2029	.1600
100	.0429	.0531	.0385	.0264	.0176	.0255	.0000	.0622
110	.0335	.0371	.0192	.0308	.0308	.0446	.0217	.0378
120	.0564	.0584	.0577	.0529	.0573	.0318	.1304	.0289
All drugs	1.0000	1.0000	1.0000	1.0000	1.0000	1.0000	1.0000	1.0000

B-3. DISTRIBUTION OF TYPE OF FIRM AND TYPE OF MARKET BY TYPE OF DRUG IN 1961

	Proportion of Each Type of Drug Sold in Each Type of Market			Proportion of Each Type of Drug Sold by Each Type of Firm			
Drug Type	Only one firm	Only one type of firm but more than one firm	More than one type of firm	Small firm Generic name	Small firm Brand name	Large firm Generic name	Large firm Brand name
10	.4210	.1842	.3947	.4474	.3158	.3947	.4737
20	.3548	.1290	.5161	.4839	.4194	.3548	.4194
30	.7879	.0000	.2121	.2727	.2727	.0909	.6061
40	.6460	.0683	.2857	.2857	.1925	.1304	.7640
50	.6825	.0635	.2540	.2063	.2698	.0952	.7302
60	.7037	.0741	.2222	.1852	.2963	.0370	.7407
70	.4118	.0000	.5882	.6471	.2941	.2941	.5882
80	.5421	.1028	.3551	.3832	.1869	.2523	.6542
90	.4022	.0761	.5217	.5000	.2826	.3043	.7826
100	.7143	.0714	.2143	.1429	.1429	.0000	1.0000
110	.6364	.0455	.3181	.3182	.3182	.1364	.7727
120	.5950	.0811	.3243	.3514	.1351	.4865	.3514
All drugs	.5747[a]	.0793	.3460	.3460	.2393	.2104	.6859

[a] Indicates that 58 percent of all drugs in twelve major categories were sold by only one firm.

VALUES OF PRICE RATIOS CLASSIFIED ACCORDING TO TYPE OF DRUG

Type of Drug by Numerical Symbol		SG/SB	SG/LG	SG/LB	SB/LG	SB/LB	LG/LB
10	Number of observations	6	10	6	3	4	7
	Geometric mean	.5432	.7697	.6944	1.0982	1.3986	1.0071
20	Number of observations	4	9	4	4	5	1
	Geometric mean	.4068	.7047	.4340	1.3362	.9587	.9355
30	Number of observations	3	2	3	0	1	0
	Geometric mean	.3267	.5567	.4471		1.0952	
40	Number of observations	14	16	22	2	16	5
	Geometric mean	.4540	.7909	.4461	1.0045	.6624	.8500
50	Number of observations	3	6	7	1	5	1
	Geometric mean	.2847	.8186	.3917	2.4267	.7743	.2166
60	Number of observations	3	1	1	0	3	0
	Geometric mean	.8492	.4292	.4596		.9560	
70	Number of observations	4	5	5	0	4	0
	Geometric mean	.4704	.8610	.3621		.7171	
80	Number of observations	10	21	15	4	9	8
	Geometric mean	1.0906	.7132	.5821	.8303	.5824	1.0840
90	Number of observations	22	23	30	11	20	16
	Geometric mean	.5653	.4213	.4182	.8002	.7272	.9640
100	Number of observations	2	0	4	0	4	0
	Geometric mean	1.1015		.4810		.7486	
110	Number of observations	3	3	5	0	4	2
	Geometric mean	.7299	.6282	.6148		.6828	1.0347
120	Number of observations	1	10	0	0	1	0
	Geometric mean	.8571	.8345			.8082	

B-5. DISTRIBUTION OF TOTAL SALES AMONG TYPES OF DRUGS RESULTING FROM THE INTRODUCTION OF EACH POLICY

Drug Type	TS_j ($ millions)	TSM_j ($ millions)	TSM_j/TS_j	TSP_j ($ millions)	TSP_j/TS_j	TSA_j ($ millions)	TSA_j/TS_j
10	83.70	75.01	89.61%	76.57	91.42%	62.97	75.22%
20	70.30	60.48	86.03%	67.17	95.55%	55.45	78.87%
30	77.82	69.81	89.70%	69.21	88.93%	55.44	71.25%
40	562.44	517.28	91.72%	483.00	85.88%	406.73	72.32%
50	165.25	152.76	92.44%	142.22	86.08%	118.78	71.88%
60	84.24	79.90	94.79%	69.32	82.25%	59.51	70.60%
70	40.91	32.21	78.72%	38.25	93.48%	28.66	70.06%
80	511.35	464.25	90.79%	442.76	86.59%	367.43	71.86%
90	337.36	273.43	81.05%	305.07	90.43%	228.77	67.81%
100	120.48	110.10	91.39%	99.46	82.55%	82.24	68.26%
110	45.15	40.00	88.59%	40.35	89.38%	32.79	72.62%
120	88.89	85.24	95.89%	80.79	90.89%	71.79	80.77%
All drugs	2,188.0	1,960.22	89.60%	1,913.96	87.49%	1,570.33	71.78%

move brand names show a relatively small percentage reduction attributable to the removal of patents.

Table B–6 shows the proportion of total sales accounted for by

B-6.   PERCENTAGE OF TOTAL SALES UNDER EACH
       POLICY ACCOUNTED FOR BY EACH TYPE OF DRUG

Drug Type	TS_j/TS	TSM_j/TSM	TSP_j/TSP	TSA_j/TSA
10	3.83%	3.83%	4.00%	4.01%
20	3.21%	3.09%	3.50%	3.53%
30	3.56%	3.56%	3.62%	3.53%
40	25.71%	26.39%	25.24%	25.90%
50	7.53%	7.79%	7.43%	7.56%
60	3.85%	4.08%	3.62%	3.79%
70	1.87%	1.64%	2.00%	1.83%
80	23.37%	23.68%	23.13%	23.40%
90	15.42%	13.95%	15.94%	14.57%
100	5.51%	5.62%	5.20%	5.24%
110	2.06%	2.04%	2.11%	2.09%
120	4.06%	4.35%	4.22%	4.57%

each type of drug before the introduction of any policy, and after the introduction of each of the policies. These columns are headed: TS_j/TS, TSM_j/TSM, TSP_j/TSP, and TSA_j/TSA.

The proportion of the total sales of industry accounted for by each type of drug, TS_j/TS, shows noticeable deviations from the corresponding distribution for large firms only for the two largest groups—40 and 80—and for the two smallest groups—70 and 110.

The remaining distributions indicate that none of the policies would result in a significant change in the relative importance—in terms of the value of sales—of any type of drug.

Table B–7 shows how the changes in sales, which result from the introduction of each of the three policies, are distributed among the types of drugs. The proportion of the change in total sales, accounted for by each type of drug under each policy, is shown in the columns headed: $CTSM_j/CTSM$, $CTSP_j/CTSP$, $CTSA_j/CTSA$.

B-7. DISTRIBUTION OF CHANGES IN SALES AMONG TYPES OF DRUGS

Drug Type	$CTSM_j^a$ ($ millions)	$\dfrac{CTSM_j}{CTSM}$	$CTSP_j$ ($ millions)	$\dfrac{CTSP_j}{CTSP}$	$CTSA_j$ ($ million)	$\dfrac{CTSA_j}{CTSA}$
10	8.70	4.82%	7.14	2.61%	20.74	3.36%
20	9.83	4.32%	3.13	1.14%	14.86	2.41%
30	8.01	3.52%	8.61	3.15%	22.38	3.63%
40	45.15	19.85%	79.44	29.02%	155.70	25.22%
50	12.49	5.49%	23.02	8.41%	46.47	7.53%
60	4.39	1.93%	14.96	5.47%	24.78	4.01%
70	8.70	3.82%	2.67	0.98%	12.25	1.98%
80	47.10	20.70%	68.59	25.06%	143.91	23.31%
90	63.93	28.10%	32.29	11.80%	108.59	17.59%
100	10.38	4.56%	21.02	7.68%	38.25	6.20%
110	5.15	2.26%	4.80	1.75%	12.36	2.00%
120	3.65	1.60%	8.09	2.96%	17.10	2.77%
All drugs	227.49	100%ᵇ	273.76	100%ᵇ	617.39	100%ᵇ

aCTSMⱼ means the change in total sales of the jᵗʰ type of drug after the removal of brand names. In the other column heads, "P," as noted before, refers to the removal of patents and "A" to the removal of both brand names and patents. The columns which present ratios show the percentage of the change in sales resulting from a policy which is borne by a particular type of drug. Thus, for drug type 10, CTSMⱼ/CTSM equals 4.82% and means that 4.82% of the change in sales arising from the removal of brand names occurs among type-10 drugs.

bThe percentage total shown for each of these columns is a rounded-off figure.

The different policies result in substantial reversals, among the more important groups of drugs, in the proportion of the total change in sales accounted for by each type of drug. Thus, if brand names were to be removed, 28.1 percent of the reduction would be borne by drugs in group 90 and 19.8 percent by drugs in group 40. If, instead, patents were to be removed, the importance of these two groups would be reversed; drugs belonging to group 90 would bear only 11.8 percent of the total change while drugs in group 40 would account for 29.0 percent of the change.

[C] Classification of Drugs by Year of Introduction*

An estimate was made of the year in which each drug was first introduced into commercial use; this characteristic of a drug is referred to as the "year of introduction." For drugs introduced after 1935 the year of introduction was usually available from *New and Nonofficial Drugs: 1962* or *Review of Drugs: 1962*. Drugs introduced prior to 1935 required some estimation. For some of these drugs, explicit information was available in the *Dispensatory*[1] or the *Merck Index*.[2] In the absence of explicit information, the year of introduction is taken to be the date of the first published reference to the drug in the *Dispensatory*.

Several special problems arise in assigning meaningful dates to older drugs. Some drugs have been in existence for many hundreds of years, but their rational use in medicine extends over little more than one hundred years. With two exceptions—digitalis (1785) and the smallpox vaccine (1798)—drugs introduced prior to 1800 were assigned 1800 as the year of introduction. A second problem is that drugs may be introduced for one use but later found to be of more significance in a second, quite different, use. In this case, the drug is classified by type according to the present usage, but the year of introduction is assigned on the basis of the date of

* This appendix is co-ordinate with pp. 91–116 of the text.

commercial introduction for any use. This is done because it is impossible to date the change from the first use to subsequent uses. A final problem, which concerns only a very few drugs, is that a drug which was introduced for a particular use may be later eclipsed as the agent of choice by some other drug. Still later, the merits of using the first drug are rediscovered, and it replaces the other drug or drugs as the agent of choice. This is best exemplified by the ferrous salts that are used in the treatment of some anemias. They were introduced into medicine in the 1870s, but in the 1900s fell into disfavor; within the past thirty years, however, their use has again become common. In the case of drugs of this type, the year of original introduction is used on the ground that the drug probably continued to enjoy some use throughout the whole period even though it was not the agent of choice during some part of the period.

Table C–1 shows the number of drugs introduced in each five-year interval and indicates the number sold (in five year intervals) under each type of market structure as well as the number introduced (in five-year intervals) by each type of firm. Thus, of the 656 drugs that had been produced by the end of 1960, 165 were introduced between the years 1956 and 1960. Also, 337 of the 656 drugs were sold in markets in which there was only one firm, and of these, 136 were introduced in the period 1956–60.

Table C–2 shows (a) for each type of market structure and (b) for each type of firm the proportion of drugs introduced during each five-year period. Thus, 25.2 percent of all drugs were introduced in the period 1956–60, and 36.1 percent of the drugs produced by only one firm were introduced during the same period.

Table C–3 also shows the proportion of drugs introduced in each five-year period that were sold under each type of market structure and by each type of firm. The entries in this table are to be read horizontally. For example, of the drugs that were introduced between 1951 and 1955, and were still being produced in 1961, approximately 73 percent were manufactured by only one firm; approximately 5.3 percent by only one type of firm (but by more than a single firm); and approximately 21.6 percent by more than one type of firm.* Similarly (for the same five-year period),

* Tables C-2, C-3, C-4, and C-5 appear on pp. 181, 182, 183, 184, and 185, respectively; text resumes on p. 186.

C-1. DISTRIBUTION OF DRUGS BY YEAR OF INTRODUCTION

Year of Introduction of Drug	Total number of drugs introduced in period	Number of Drugs Introduced during Specified Period and Sold in Each Type of Market Structure			Number of Drugs Introduced during Specified Period and Sold by Each Type of Firm			
		Only one firm	Only one type of firm but more than one firm	More than one type of firm	Small firm Generic name	Small firm Brand name	Large firm Generic name	Large firm Brand name
Before 1890	10	1	0	9	9	2	9	2
1891-1895	1	0	0	1	1	0	1	0
1896-1900	5	0	1	4	4	2	1	2
1901-1905	4	0	0	4	4	0	3	2
1906-1910	3	0	1	2	3	0	2	1
1911-1915	12	1	1	10	11	2	9	2
1916-1920	8	2	1	5	6	0	4	3
1921-1925	9	1	1	7	7	1	5	3
1926-1930	18	6	1	11	10	6	8	8
1931-1935	32	8	8	16	23	8	11	16
1936-1940	48	8	3	37	38	18	21	28
1941-1945	56	20	5	31	35	20	22	27
1946-1950	114	69	8	37	42	27	24	79
1951-1955	171	125	9	37	26	38	13	141
1956-1960	165	136	13	16	8	33	5	136
All years	656	337	52	227	227	157	138	450

C-2. DISTRIBUTION OF YEAR OF INTRODUCTION BY TYPE OF MARKET AND TYPE OF FIRM

Year of Introduction of Drug	Proportion of all drugs introduced during period	Proportion of Drugs Sold in Each Type of Market Structure Accounted for by Drugs Introduced in Specified Period			Proportion of Drugs Sold by Each Type of Firm Accounted for by Drugs Introduced in Each Period			
		Only one firm	Only one type of firm but more than one firm	More than one type of firm	Small firm Generic name	Small firm Brand name	Large firm Generic name	Large firm Brand name
Before 1890	.0152	.0027	.0000	.0396	.0396	.0127	.0652	.0044
1891-1895	.0015	.0000	.0000	.0044	.0044	.0000	.0072	.0000
1896-1900	.0076	.0000	.0192	.0176	.0176	.0127	.0072	.0044
1901-1905	.0061	.0000	.0000	.0176	.0176	.0000	.0217	.0044
1906-1910	.0046	.0000	.0192	.0088	.0132	.0000	.0145	.0022
1911-1915	.0183	.0027	.0192	.0441	.0485	.0127	.0652	.0044
1916-1920	.0122	.0053	.0192	.0220	.0264	.0000	.0290	.0067
1921-1925	.0137	.0027	.0192	.0308	.0308	.0064	.0362	.0067
1926-1930	.0274	.0159	.0192	.0485	.0440	.0382	.0580	.0178
1931-1935	.0488	.0212	.1538	.0705	.1013	.0510	.0797	.0356
1936-1940	.0732	.0212	.0577	.1630	.1674	.1146	.1522	.0622
1941-1945	.0854	.0531	.0962	.1366	.1542	.1274	.1594	.0600
1946-1950	.1738	.1830	.1538	.1630	.1850	.1720	.1739	.1756
1951-1955	.2607	.3316	.1731	.1630	.1145	.2420	.0942	.3133
1956-1960	.2515	.3607	.2500	.0705	.0352	.2102	.0362	.3022
All years	1.0000	1.0000	1.0000	1.0000	1.0000	1.0000	1.0000	1.0000

C-3. DISTRIBUTION OF TYPE OF MARKET AND TYPE OF FIRM BY YEAR OF INTRODUCTION

Year of Introduction	Only one firm	Only one type of firm but more than one firm	More than one type of firm	Small firm Generic name	Small firm Brand name	Large firm Generic name	Large firm Brand name
Before 1890	.1000	.0000	.9000	.9000	.2000	.9000	.2000
1891-1895	.0000	.0000	1.0000	1.0000	.0000	1.0000	.0000
1896-1900	.0000	.2000	.8000	.8000	.2000	.1000	.2000
1901-1905	.0000	.0000	1.0000	1.0000	.0000	.7500	.5000
1906-1910	.0000	.3333	.6667	1.0000	.0000	.6667	.3333
1911-1915	.0833	.0833	.8333	.9167	.1667	.7500	.1667
1916-1920	.2500	.1250	.6250	.7500	.0000	.5000	.3750
1921-1925	.1111	.1111	.7777	.7777	.1111	.5555	.3333
1926-1930	.3333	.0555	.6172	.5555	.3333	.4444	.4444
1931-1935	.2500	.2500	.5000	.7188	.2500	.3438	.5000
1936-1940	.1668	.0625	.7716	.7919	.3750	.4376	.5835
1941-1945	.3437	.0859	.5328	.6250	.3571	.3929	.4821
1946-1950	.6053	.0675	.3246	.3684	.2368	.2105	.6930
1951-1955	.7312	.0526	.2164	.1520	.2222	.0760	.8246
1956-1960	.8246	.0786	.0968	.0485	.2000	.0303	.8242
Proportion of all drugs sold	.5747	.0793	.3460	.3460	.2393	.2107	.6859

C-4.   VALUES OF PRICE RATIOS CLASSIFIED ACCORDING TO YEAR OF INTRODUCTION

Year of Introduction	SG/SB	SG/LG	SG/LB	SB/LG	SB/LB	LG/LB
Before 1911						
Number of observations	3	15	6	1	3	3
Geometric mean	.5331	.7576	.5291	1.9276	1.3462	.8283
1911-1920						
Number of observations	1	13	2	1	1	1
Geometric mean	.3936	.8031	.3897	1.2900	.4200	.3372
1921-1930						
Number of observations	5	10	3	2	3	2
Geometric mean	.4391	.6074	.5160	1.0693	1.0410	1.1172
1931-1940						
Number of observations	20	27	34	12	17	13
Geometric mean	.5655	.5446	.4450	.7479	.6909	1.0717
1941-1950						
Number of observations	27	36	38	9	25	16
Geometric mean	.5848	.6723	.5051	1.1930	.7169	.8872
1951-1960						
Number of observations	19	5	19	—	27	5
Geometric mean	.6321	.8236	.4179		.7495	1.0434
All Observations						
Number of observations	75	106	102	25	76	40
Geometric mean	.5748	.6623	.4666	.9662	.7462	.9457

C-5. ESTIMATES OF SALES UNDER EACH POLICY ACCORDING TO YEAR OF INTRODUCTION
($ millions)

Year of Introduction	TS_i	TS_i/TS	TSM_i	TSM_i/TSM	TSP_i	TSP_i/TSP	TSA_i	TSA_i/TSA
1960	62.03	2.90%	62.03	3.16%	48.17	2.52%	42.40	2.70%
1959	182.60	8.53%	181.60	9.26%	143.89	7.52%	127.03	8.09%
1958	124.83	5.83%	124.78	6.37%	98.10	5.13%	87.06	5.54%
1957	226.26	10.57%	221.52	11.30%	177.82	9.29%	157.49	10.03%
1956	120.27	5.62%	115.36	5.89%	97.48	5.09%	83.44	5.31%
1955	142.67	6.66%	129.35	6.60%	117.92	6.16%	95.99	6.11%
1954	145.72	6.81%	143.13	7.30%	117.89	6.16%	103.77	6.61%
1953	104.96	4.90%	94.11	4.80%	89.14	4.66%	70.04	4.46%
1952	79.47	3.71%	74.79	3.82%	70.48	3.68%	58.81	3.75%
1951	44.97	2.10%	42.03	2.14%	37.64	1.97%	30.69	1.95%
1950	48.70	2.27%	45.60	2.33%	40.60	2.12%	33.41	2.13%
1949	99.78	4.66%	82.95	4.23%	90.92	4.75%	69.18	4.41%
1948	54.13	2.53%	50.20	2.56%	47.22	2.47%	40.12	2.56%
1947	57.82	2.70%	46.45	2.37%	54.25	2.83%	40.10	2.55%
1946	57.29	2.68%	47.59	2.43%	53.03	2.77%	40.32	2.57%
1945	33.54	1.57%	28.55	1.46%	27.47	1.44%	21.23	1.35%
1944	22.35	1.04%	13.99	0.71%	21.60	1.13%	12.90	0.82%
1943[a]	580.56	27.11%	456.54	23.29%	580.56	30.33%	456.54	29.07%
All years	2,188.0	100%	1,960.22	100%	1,913.96	100%	1,570.33	100%

[a]Data for 1943 and previous years included.

185

15.2 percent of the drugs introduced were produced by small firms selling under generic names, 22.2 percent by small firms selling under brand names, 7.6 percent by large firms selling under generic names, and 83 percent by large firms selling under brand names.

Table C–4 presents the value of the price ratios as these ratios are classified according to ten-year periods. The geometric mean of each ratio provides a measure, for each ten-year period, of the average benefit of selecting a firm used in the numerator of the price ratio rather than selecting from the type of firm used in the denominator of the ratio. Here again, if the geometric mean is less than 1.0, it will, on the whole, be to the advantage of the consumer to select the product of the firm symbolized in the numerator of the ratio (e.g., SG rather than SB).

Table C–5 presents the estimates of total sales accounted for by drugs introduced in each year before the introduction of any policy and after the introduction of each of the three policies. There are 18 "years of introduction," and the letter "i" is used to represent any given year; accordingly,

TS_i represents the total sales ("TS") of drugs introduced in the ith year before the introduction of any policy;

TSM_i represents the total sales of drugs introduced in the ith year after the removal of brand names;

TSP_i represents the total sales of drugs introduced in the ith year after the removal of patent protection;

TSA_i represents the total sales of drugs introduced in the ith year after the removal of both brand names and patents.

The values TS_i/TS, TSM_i/TSM, TSP_i/TSP, and TSA_i/TSA indicate the proportion of total sales accounted for by drugs introduced in the ith year before the introduction of any policy and after the introduction of the various policies.

Notice that, for 1960, TSM_i is equal to TS_i, because in that year no drugs were introduced which would be affected by the removal of brand names. For "1943 and previous years," TSP_i is equal to TS_i, since drugs introduced prior to 1944 are considered to be no longer covered by patent protection, and, hence, not affected by the policy to remove patents.

Table C–5 also shows that, as the years of introduction become more distant from the present, the total sales of drugs introduced in each year decline. This is to be expected. None of the policies appears to result in a radical change in the proportion of total sales accounted for by drugs introduced in a particular year.

Table C–6 shows the distribution of sales of drugs according to year of introduction. The estimates for the sales of large firms differ from those made by the Pharmaceutical Manufacturers Association.[3]

In particular, P.M.A. estimates that drugs introduced prior to 1951 accounted for 31.4 percent of the sales of large firms, while our estimate for the industry as a whole is 44.6 percent.* Drugs introduced in 1943 or earlier—those drugs which, it is assumed, are no longer covered by patents—are estimated to account for 21.8 percent of the sales of large firms and 45.3 percent of the sales of small firms.

Tables C–7, C–8, and C–9 present the effects on drugs of policies to remove brand names, patents, and both patents and brand names, according to the year of introduction of the drug.

Table C–10 shows the percentage distribution and the cumulative percentage distribution, according to the year of introduction, of the ratio of the change accounted for by each year to the total change resulting from the introduction of a policy. These columns are headed: $CTSM_i/CTSM$, $CTSP_i/CTSP$, and $CTSA_i/CTSA$.

The three policies have quite different distributions. In the case of the removal of brand names, over 50 percent (54.5 percent) of the reduction effected by the policy is accounted for by drugs introduced prior to 1944. In the case of patent removal, over 55 percent of the reduction is accounted for by drugs introduced subsequent to 1955, when patent protection is assumed to be still in effect.

---

* The effect of the higher estimate is probably to overstate the effect of the removal of brand names upon large firms and to understate the effect of removing patent protection.

C-6. DISTRIBUTION OF SALES AND NUMBER OF DRUGS BY YEAR OF INTRODUCTION
(Large firms only)

Year of Introduction i	Percent of Sales of Large Firms Accounted for by Drugs Introduced in Year i	Number of Drugs Sold by Large Firms Introduced in Year i	Percent of Drugs Sold by Large Firms Introduced in Year i	Number of Drugs Sold by Large Firms under Brand Name Introduced in Year i	Percent of Drugs Sold by Large Firms under Brand Name Introduced in Year i	Number of Drugs Sold by Large Firms under Generic Name Introduced in Year i	Percent of Drugs Sold by Large Firms under Generic Name Introduced in Year i
1960	4.6%	9	1.64%	8	1.78%	1	0.72%
1959	10.5%	37	6.75%	36	8.00%	1	0.72%
1958	7.3%	26	4.74%	26	5.78%	0	0.0%
1957	15.1%	37	6.75%	34	7.56%	3	2.17%
1956	6.6%	28	5.11%	28	6.22%	0	0.0%
1955	8.2%	25	4.56%	25	5.56%	1	0.72%
1954	8.1%	34	6.20%	33	7.33%	1	0.72%
1953	4.7%	32	5.84%	30	6.67%	3	2.17%
1952	2.9%	29	5.29%	26	5.76%	4	2.90%
1951	0.6%	28	5.11%	27	6.00%	3	2.17%
1950[a]	31.4%	263	47.99%	177	39.33%	121	87.68%
All years		548		450		138	

[a]Data for 1950 and previous years included.

C-7. DISTRIBUTION OF SALES BY YEAR OF INTRODUCTION AFTER REMOVAL OF BRAND NAMES
($ millions)

Year of Introduction	Total Sales before Removal of Brand Names: All Drugs	Total Sales after Removal of Brand Names: All Drugs	Sales after Removal as Percent of Sales before Removal: All Drugs	Total Sales before Removal of Brand Names: Affected Drugs	Total Sales after Removal of Brand Names: Affected Drugs	Sales after Removal as Percent of Sales before Removal: Affected Drugs	Changes in Sales Attributable to Removal of Brand Names	Cumulative Changes in Sales Attributable to Removal of Brand Names
1960	62.03	62.03	100.00%	0.00	0.00		0.00	0.00
1959	182.60	181.60	99.45%	18.65	17.65	94.65%	1.00	1.00
1958	124.83	124.78	99.96%	9.43	9.38	99.52%	0.05	1.05
1957	226.26	221.52	97.91%	32.18	27.44	85.27%	4.74	5.79
1956	120.27	115.36	95.91%	25.41	20.49	80.64%	4.92	10.71
1955	142.57	129.35	90.60%	45.02	31.64	70.22%	13.42	24.13
1954	145.72	143.13	98.22%	26.42	23.83	90.20%	2.59	26.72
1953	104.96	94.11	89.67%	32.15	21.30	66.26%	10.86	37.58
1952	79.47	74.79	94.13%	27.09	22.41	82.73%	4.68	42.26
1951	44.97	42.03	93.48%	11.36	8.43	74.18%	2.93	45.19
1950	48.70	45.60	93.62%	6.71	3.60	53.70%	3.11	48.30
1949	99.78	82.95	83.13%	55.10	38.27	69.45%	16.83	65.13
1948	54.13	50.20	92.74%	21.52	17.59	81.73%	3.93	69.09
1947	57.82	46.45	80.33%	35.96	24.59	68.38%	11.37	80.43
1946	57.29	47.59	83.06%	33.34	23.63	70.89%	9.71	90.14
1945	33.54	28.55	85.10%	16.89	11.90	70.41%	5.00	95.14
1944	22.35	13.99	62.58%	18.58	10.21	54.98%	8.36	103.50
1943[a]	580.56	456.54	78.63%	467.26	343.23	73.46%	124.01	227.50
All years	2,188.0	1,960.22	89.60%	883.04	655.56	74.24%		

[a]Data for 1943 and previous years included.

189

C-8. DISTRIBUTION OF SALES BY YEAR OF INTRODUCTION AFTER REMOVAL OF PATENTS
($ millions)

Year of Introduction	Total Sales before Removal of Patents: All Drugs	Total Sales after Removal of Patents: All Drugs	Sales after Removal as Percent of Sales before Removal: All Drugs	Total Sales before Removal of Patents: Affected Drugs	Total Sales after Removal of Patents: Affected Drugs	Sales after Removal as Percent of Sales before Removal: Affected Drugs	Change in Sales Attributable to Removal of Patents	Cumulative Change in Sales Attributable to Removal of Patents
1960	62.03	48.17	77.66%	62.03	47.17	77.66%	13.85	13.85
1959	182.60	143.89	78.80%	161.80	123.09	76.08%	38.71	52.56
1958	124.83	98.10	78.59%	113.63	86.90	76.48%	26.73	79.29
1957	226.26	177.82	78.59%	192.78	144.34	74.87%	48.44	127.73
1956	120.27	97.98	81.05%	93.91	71.11	75.73%	22.80	150.52
1955	142.67	117.92	82.66%	97.62	72.87	74.65%	24.74	175.27
1954	145.72	117.89	80.90%	119.30	91.47	76.68%	27.83	203.10
1953	104.96	89.14	84.93%	72.81	56.99	78.28%	15.82	218.92
1952	79.47	70.48	88.69%	52.38	43.39	82.85%	8.98	227.90
1951	44.97	37.64	83.70%	33.60	26.28	78.19%	7.33	235.23
1950	48.70	40.60	83.36%	40.14	32.04	79.81%	8.10	243.33
1949	99.78	90.92	91.12%	44.69	35.82	80.16%	8.87	252.20
1948	54.13	47.22	87.23%	29.31	22.40	76.42%	6.91	259.11
1947	57.82	54.25	93.83%	20.19	16.62	82.33%	3.57	262.68
1946	57.29	53.03	92.56%	22.66	18.39	81.18%	4.26	266.94
1945	33.54	27.47	81.89%	16.65	10.58	63.51%	6.08	273.02
1944	22.35	21.60	96.64%	3.76	3.02	80.08%	0.75	273.77
1943[a]	580.56	580.56	100.00%	0.00	0.00		0.00	273.77
All years	2,188.0	1,913.96	87.49%	1,177.16	903.41	76.75%		

[a]Data for 1943 and previous years included.

C-9. DISTRIBUTION OF SALES BY YEAR OF INTRODUCTION AFTER REMOVAL OF BRAND NAMES AND PATENT PROTECTION
($ millions)

Year of Introduction	Total Sales before Removal of Brand Name and Patents: All Drugs	Total Sales after Removal of Brand Names and Patents: All Drugs	Sales after Removal as Percent of Sales before Removal: All Drugs	Total Sales before Removal of Brand Names and Patents: Affected Drugs	Total Sales after Removal of Brand Names and Patents: Affected Drugs	Sales after Removal as Percent of Sales before Removal: Affected Drugs	Change in Sales Attributable to Removal of Brand Names and Patents	Cumulative Change in Sales Attributable to Removal of Brand Names and Patents
1960	62.03	42.40	68.36%	62.03	42.40	68.36%	19.63	19.63
1959	182.60	127.03	69.57%	180.45	124.88	69.21%	55.57	75.20
1958	124.83	87.06	69.74%	123.06	85.29	69.31%	37.77	112.97
1957	226.26	157.49	69.61%	224.96	156.19	69.43%	68.77	181.74
1956	120.27	83.44	69.38%	119.32	82.49	69.13%	36.83	218.57
1955	142.67	95.99	67.28%	142.67	95.99	67.28%	46.68	265.25
1954	145.72	103.77	71.21%	145.72	103.77	71.21%	41.95	307.20
1953	104.96	70.04	66.73%	104.96	70.04	66.73%	34.91	342.11
1952	79.47	58.81	74.00%	79.47	58.81	74.00%	20.66	362.77
1951	44.97	30.69	68.26%	44.97	30.69	68.26%	14.27	377.04
1950	48.70	33.41	68.60%	46.85	31.56	67.36%	15.29	392.33
1949	99.78	69.18	69.33%	99.78	69.18	69.33%	30.60	422.93
1948	54.13	40.12	74.13%	50.84	38.83	72.45%	14.01	436.94
1947	57.82	40.10	69.36%	56.15	38.44	68.45%	17.72	454.66
1946	57.29	40.32	70.38%	56.99	39.02	69.69%	16.97	471.63
1945	33.54	21.23	63.29%	33.54	21.23	63.29%	12.32	483.95
1944	22.35	12.90	57.71%	22.35	12.90	57.71%	9.45	493.40
1943[a]	580.56	456.54	78.64%	467.26	343.24	73.46%	124.01	617.41
All years	2,188.0	1,570.33	71.78%	2,060.15	1,442.76	70.03%		

[a]Data for 1943 and previous years included.

C-10.   PERCENTAGE OF CHANGE IN SALES BY YEAR OF INTRODUCTION

Year of Introduction	$\frac{CTSM_i}{CTSM}$	Cumula- tive	$\frac{CTSP_i}{CTSP}$	Cumula- tive	$\frac{CTSA_i}{CTSA}$	Cumula- tive
1960	0.0%	0.0%	5.06%	5.06%	3.18%	3.18%
1959	0.44%	0.44%	14.14%	19.20%	9.00%	12.18%
1958	0.02%	0.46%	9.76%	28.96%	6.12%	18.30%
1957	2.08%	2.55%	17.70%	46.66%	11.14%	29.44%
1956	2.16%	4.71%	8.33%	54.99%	5.97%	35.40%
1955	5.90%	10.60%	9.04%	64.03%	7.56%	42.97%
1954	1.14%	11.74%	10.17%	74.19%	6.80%	49.76%
1953	4.77%	16.51%	5.78%	79.79%	5.66%	55.41%
1952	2.06%	18.57%	3.28%	83.25%	3.35%	58.76%
1951	1.29%	19.86%	2.68%	85.93%	2.31%	61.07%
1950	1.37%	21.22%	2.96%	88.89%	2.48%	63.55%
1949	7.40%	28.62%	2.52%	91.41%	4.96%	68.51%
1948	1.73%	30.35%	1.30%	92.72%	2.27%	70.71%
1947	5.00%	35.35%	1.56%	94.27%	2.87%	73.64%
1946	4.27%	39.61%	3.78%	90.05%	2.75%	76.79%
1945	2.20%	41.81%	2.02%	100.07%	2.00%	78.39%
1944	2.68%	45.49%	0.27%	100.34%	1.53%	79.92%
1943[a]	54.51%	100.00%	0.00%	100.34%	20.08%	100.00%

[a] Data for 1943 and previous years included

[D] Estimates of Sales of Individual Drugs in 1961*

The Pharmaceutical Manufacturers Association has estimated the proportion of the 1960 sales of large firms which were accounted for by drugs introduced in each year from 1951 to 1960.[1] These estimates are presented in Table D–1. As explained in Chapter I, drugs introduced in 1961 are not included in the study, and references to the 1961 sales of the industry, or of any subdivision of the industry, should be understood to mean the total quantity of drugs produced in 1960 and evaluated at 1961 prices. Under this definition of 1961 sales, the proportion of sales accounted for in 1960 by drugs introduced in each of the years between 1951 and 1960 is used for the proportion of sales accounted for in 1961 by each year of introduction during the same period.

Again, the reader should understand that no data are available to the author for the total sales of individual drugs or total sales income. To estimate sales of individual drugs, data concerning the sales of particular groupings of drugs are used under a set of assumptions which seem the most reasonable for the purpose. These assumptions, and the estimates which they yield, are examined in detail below.

Drugs introduced in a particular year (or over a longer period, in the case of drugs introduced prior to 1951) are assumed to have

* This appendix is co-ordinate with pp. 100–109 of the text.

D-1.   DISTRIBUTION OF SALES AND NUMBER OF DRUGS BY YEAR OF INTRODUCTION[a]
(Large firms only)

Year of Introduction i	Percent of Sales of Large Firms Accounted for by Drugs Introduced in Year i	Number of Drugs Sold by Large Firms Introduced in Year i	Percent of Drugs Sold by Large Firms Introduced in Year i	Number of Drugs Sold by Large Firms under Brand Name Introduced in Year i	Percent of Drugs Sold by Large Firms under Brand Name Introduced in Year i	Number of Drugs Sold by Large Firms under Generic Name Introduced in Year i	Percent of Drugs Sold by Large Firms under Generic Name Introduced in Year i
1960	4.6%	9	1.64%	8	1.78%	1	0.72%
1959	10.5%	37	6.75%	36	8.00%	1	0.72%
1958	7.3%	26	4.74%	26	5.78%	0	0.0%
1957	15.1%	37	6.75%	34	7.56%	3	2.17%
1956	6.6%	28	5.11%	28	6.22%	0	0.0%
1955	8.2%	25	4.56%	25	5.56%	1	0.72%
1954	8.1%	34	6.20%	33	7.33%	1	0.72%
1953	4.7%	32	5.84%	30	6.67%	3	2.17%
1952	2.9%	29	5.29%	26	5.76%	4	2.90%
1951	0.6%	28	5.11%	27	6.00%	3	2.17%
1950[b]	31.4%	263	47.99%	177	39.33%	121	87.68%
All years		548		450		138	

[a] For the convenience of the reader, this table is repeated from the preceding appendix (p. 188).

[b] Data for 1950 and previous years included.

equal sales. Since there is undoubtedly considerable variation in the sales of drugs introduced in a particular year, this assumption will probably yield substantial understatements of the sales of a few drugs and moderate overstatements of the sales of the remaining drugs. Nevertheless, some assumption about the distribution of sales of drugs must be made, and since no information exists which would permit the assumption of some other distribution, this assumption appears to be the only one available. There will be a distortion in the estimate of the sales of individual drugs, since our primary concern is with the total sales of all drugs, but the assumption is not so restrictive as it appears.

Allocation of the sales of large firms

The sales by large firms of the kth drug (that is, any of the 548 drugs produced by large firms and introduced in the year i) are here represented as SL_k. Then, using the information given in Table D–1, we estimate these sales by means of the following formula:

$$SL_k = \frac{\begin{array}{c}\text{Total sales of} \\ \text{large firms}\end{array} \times \begin{array}{c}\text{Proportion of sales of large} \\ \text{firms accounted for by drugs} \\ \text{introduced during the } i^{th} \text{ year}\end{array}}{\begin{array}{c}\text{No. of drugs introduced during } i^{th} \text{ year} \\ \text{which were sold by large firms in 1961}\end{array}}$$

Referring again to Table D–1, we estimate the total sales of a drug introduced in 1955 as follows:

$$SL_k = (\$1{,}750 \text{ million} \times 0.082)/25 = \$5.74 \text{ million}$$

Here, $1,750 million represents the domestic sales of ethical drugs in 1961, and 8.2 is the percent of these sales accounted for by drugs introduced in 1955; further, 25 drugs were introduced in 1955. (This procedure for estimating the sales of a drug by large firms will be referred to as Assumption G. A summary list of the assumptions used in Appendix D is given on pp. 202–203.

In constructing a price index of ethical drugs for the Pharmaceutical Manufacturers Association, John Firestone determined the proportion of sales of large firms in 1960 accounted for by

D-2.   DISTRIBUTION OF SALES AND NUMBER OF DRUGS BY TYPE OF DRUG
(Large firms only)

Drug Type	Percent of Sales of Large Firms Accounted for by Drugs of Type j	Number of Type j Drugs Sold by Large Firms	Percent of Drugs Sold by Large Firms Which are Type j	Number of Type j Drugs Sold under Brand Names by Large Firms	Percent of Drugs Sold under Brand Names by Large Firms Which are Type j	Number of Type j Drug Sold under Generic Name by Large Firms	Percent of Drugs Sold under Generic Name by Large Firms Which are Type j
10	3.13%	26	4.74%	18	4.00%	15	10.87%
20	3.38%	23	4.20%	13	2.89%	11	7.97%
30	3.38%	23	4.20%	20	4.44%	3	2.17%
40	23.90%	139	25.36%	123	27.33%	21	15.22%
50	7.18%	51	9.31%	46	10.22%	6	4.35%
60	3.96%	21	3.83%	20	4.44%	1	0.72%
70	1.33%	15	2.74%	10	2.22%	5	3.62%
80	27.50%	89	16.24%	70	15.56%	27	19.62%
90	14.50%	84	15.33%	72	16.00%	28	20.29%
100	6.78%	28	5.11%	28	6.22%	0	0.0%
110	1.33%	17	3.10%	16	3.56%	3	2.17%
120	3.63%	32	5.84%	14	3.11%	18	13.04%
All drugs		548		450		138	

drugs of various types to the total sales of all firms.[2] Adapting his data to our classification, we obtain the results shown in Table D–2.* The proportion of sales by large firms according to type of drug can be used as a second basis for estimating the sales of an individual drug by large firms. Again, sales are assumed to be equally distributed among all drugs of a given type. To estimate the sales of the kth drug, if it belongs to the jth type (that is, to any given type of the 12 major types), the following computation is performed:

$$SL_k = \frac{\begin{array}{c}\text{Total sales,}\\\text{large firms}\end{array} \times \begin{array}{c}\text{Proportion of sales of large}\\\text{firms accounted for by drugs}\\\text{of the } j^{th} \text{ type}\end{array}}{\begin{array}{c}\text{No. of drugs of the } j^{th}\\\text{type sold by large firms}\end{array}}$$

Thus, an estimate of the sales by large firms of a drug belonging to type 20 would be:

$$SL_k = \$1{,}750 \text{ million} \times 0.038/23 = \$2.57 \text{ million}$$

Estimates of the sales based on the type of drug are referred to as Assumption H.

A third estimate (referred to as Assumption I) of the sales of an individual drug by large firms can be obtained by combining the information on proportion of sales accounted for by different years of introduction and different types of drug. Drugs are classified according to both variables, and all drugs that are of the same type and that have been introduced in the same year are assumed to have equal sales. On this basis the sales of an individual drug are computed as follows:

$$SL_k = \frac{\begin{array}{c}\text{Total sales,}\\\text{large firms}\end{array} \times \begin{array}{c}\text{Proportion of total}\\\text{sales accounted}\\\text{for by drugs intro-}\\\text{duced in year } i\end{array} \times \begin{array}{c}\text{Proportion of}\\\text{total sales}\\\text{accounted for}\\\text{by type } j \text{ drugs}\end{array}}{\begin{array}{c}\text{No. of type } j \text{ drugs introduced in}\\\text{the year } i \text{ and sold by large firms}\end{array}}$$

* A summary of the drug types considered in this study is given in Chapter II, pp. 22–23.

This procedure would be consistent (that is, the sum of the individual sales would add to the total sales) if there were at least one drug in each cell of the cross-classification. This is not the case, however; of the 132 cells, 32 are empty. As it stands, the procedure allocates sales to cells for which there are no drugs and hence underestimates the sales of cells which are occupied. If we estimate the sales of each drug and total these, we obtain $1,610.89 million, or 92.051 percent of the previously accepted figure of $1,750 million. To correct for this discrepancy, we divide each estimate of the sales of an individual drug by 0.92051. Thus, the estimated sales of a drug introduced in 1957 and belonging to type 40 would be:

$$\text{SL}_k = (\$1,750 \text{ million} \times 0.151 \times 0.239)/(17 \times 0.92051)$$
$$= \$4.04 \text{ million}$$

In this equation 0.151 is derived from the percentage of sales (15.1) of large firms accounted for by drugs introduced in 1957 (see Table D–1), and 0.239 is derived in the same way from the percentage given in Table D–2 for the sales of large firms accounted for by type-40 drugs. The decimal in the denominator is the correction factor, and 17 is the number of j-type (type 40) drugs introduced in the year i (1957) and sold by large firms. Without the correction factor, the estimated sales of this drug would be $3.72 million.

Allocation of sales of large firms among large firms selling under brand names and large firms selling under generic names

If a drug is sold by large firms under both a brand name and the generic name, we wish to allocate the total sales by large firms to these two types of firm. This is done by assuming that the sales of the drug are equally distributed among all large firms. Suppose that there are NL_k large firms selling the kth drug and that, of these, NLG_k firms sell it under the generic name and NLB_k sell it under a brand name. The share of total sales of this drug held by firms selling it under generic name is $\text{NLG}_k/(\text{NLG}_k + \text{NLB}_k)$, and the share held by firms selling under brand name is $\text{NLB}_k/(\text{NLG}_k + \text{NLB}_k)$.

Estimation of sales of individual drugs by
small firms selling under brand names

No data exist concerning the sales of this type of firm. To estimate the sales of an individual drug by small firms selling it under
brand names, any one of four assumptions might be made. First
(Assumption C), the total sales of this group of firms could be
assumed to be equally distributed among the 157 drugs which
they produce. On this basis the estimate of the sales of an individual drug would be:

$$\text{SSB}_k = \$204 \text{ million}/157 = \$1.30 \text{ million}.$$

Second (Assumption D), the distribution of the sales of large
firms, according to the year of introduction of the drugs sold, might
be assumed to be relevant to small firms selling under brand name.
This distribution, together with the assumption that all drugs introduced in a given year have equal sales, is used to estimate the sales
of individual drugs. The distribution of drugs sold by small firms
under brand names according to the year of introduction is shown
in Table D–3. The procedure, after appropriate changes for this
type of firm, is the same as that used in Assumption G.

Third (Assumption E), the distribution of the sales of large
firms according to type of drug can be assumed to be applicable
to small firms selling under brand name. The distribution of drugs
sold by small firms selling under brand names is shown according
to type of drug in Table D–4. The procedure, after the necessary
changes have been made for the type of firm, is the same as that
used in Assumption H.

Fourth (Assumption F), an estimate of the sales of individual
drugs is made by combining the information concerning proportion
of sales accounted for by the various years of introduction and by
the various types of drug. The procedure is that used in Assumption I. As was the case with large firms, the procedure assigns sales
to cells which contain no drugs. Under this assumption total sales,
before correction, are \$139.08 million, or 68.177 percent of the
previously determined value of \$204 million. Each estimate is
therefore corrected by dividing it by 0.68177. (Text continues on
p. 202.)

D-3. DISTRIBUTION OF SALES AND NUMBER OF DRUGS BY YEAR OF INTRODUCTION
(Small firms only)

Year of Introduction	Number of Drugs Sold by Small Firms under Brand Name Which Were Introduced in Year i	Percent of Drugs Sold by Small Firms under Brand Name Which Were Introduced in Year i	Number of Drugs Sold by Small Firms under Generic Name Which Were Introduced in Year i	Percent of Drugs Sold by Small Firms under Generic Name Which Were Introduced in Year i
1960	2	1.27%	0	0.0%
1959	11	7.01%	2	0.88%
1958	7	4.46%	2	0.88%
1957	5	3.18%	6	2.64%
1956	8	5.10%	2	0.88%
1955	10	6.37%	8	3.52%
1954	6	3.82%	2	0.88%
1953	11	7.01%	6	2.64%
1952	9	5.73%	7	3.08%
1951	3	1.91%	3	1.32%
1950[a]	85	54.1%	189	83.3%
All years	157		227	

[a]Data for 1950 and previous years included.

D-4. DISTRIBUTION OF SALES AND NUMBER OF FIRMS BY TYPE OF DRUG
(Small firms only)

Drug Type	Number of Drugs Sold by Small Firms under Brand Names Which Are of Type j	Percent of Drugs Sold by Small Firms under Brand Names Which Are of Type j	Number of Drugs Sold by Small Firms under Generic Names Which Are of Type j	Percent of Drugs Sold by Small Firms under Generic Names Which Are of Type j
10	12	7.64%	17	7.49%
20	13	8.28%	15	6.61%
30	9	5.73%	9	3.96%
40	31	19.75%	46	20.25%
50	17	10.83%	13	5.73%
60	8	5.10%	5	2.20%
70	5	3.18%	11	4.85%
80	20	12.74%	41	18.06%
90	26	16.56%	46	20.26%
100	4	2.55%	4	1.76%
110	7	4.46%	8	3.52%
120	5	3.18%	12	5.29%
All drugs	157		227	

Estimation of sales of individual drugs by
small firms selling under generic names

Two alternative assumptions are made in estimating the sales of individual drugs by this type of firm. Under Assumption A, the total sales are assumed to be equally distributed among the 227 drugs produced by this type of firm. The sales of any drug are estimated to be:

$$\text{SSG}_k = \$234 \text{ million}/227 = \$1.03 \text{ million}$$

Under Assumption B, the data for the sales of large firms accounted for by each type of drug are used in estimating the sales of individual drugs by small firms selling under generic names. Here, it is assumed that all drugs of a given type have equal sales.

In summary, to estimate the sales of individual drugs, two assumptions have been made about how drug sales are distributed among drugs for small firms selling under generic names; four assumptions for small firms selling under brand names; and three for large firms. These assumptions are summarized in algebraic form herewith.*

A $\text{SSG}_k = \text{SSG}/227$

B $\text{SSG}_k = (\text{SSG} \times \text{PTYPE}_j)/\text{NSG}_j$

C $\text{SSB}_k = \text{SSB}/157$

D $\text{SSB}_k = (\text{SSB} \times \text{PTYPE}_j)/\text{NSB}_j$

E $\text{SSB}_k = (\text{SSB} \times \text{PYEAR}_i)/\text{NSB}_i$

F $\text{SSB}_k = (\text{SSB} \times \text{PYEAR}_i \times \text{PTYPE}_j)/(\text{NSB}_{ij} \times 0.68177)$

G $\text{SL}_k = (\text{SL} \times \text{PTYPE}_j)/\text{NL}_j$

H $\text{SL}_k = (\text{SL} \times \text{PYEAR}_i)/\text{NL}_i$

I $\text{SL}_k = (\text{SL} \times \text{PYEAR}_i \times \text{PTYPE}_j)/(\text{NL}_{ij} \times 0.92051)$

  $\text{SLG}_k = \text{SL}_k \times (\text{NLG}_k)/(\text{NLG}_k + \text{NLB}_k)$

  $\text{SLB}_k = \text{SL}_k \times (\text{NLB}_k)/(\text{NLG}_k + \text{NLB}_k)$

* Text continues on p. 204.

Explanation of Symbols

SSG, SSB, SL, SLG, SLB

Total sales of drugs sold by small firms under generic names; by small firms under brand names; by large firms; by large firms under generic names; and by large firms under brand names, respectively.

SSG_k, SSB_k, SL_k, SLG_k, SLB_k

Sales of the kth drug by small firms selling under generic names; by small firms selling under brand names; by large firms; by large firms selling under generic names; and by large firms selling under brand names, respectively.

NLG_k, NLB_k

Number of large firms selling under generic names, and number of large firms selling under brand names, respectively, selling the kth drug.

NSG_j, NSB_j, NL_j

Number of drugs of type j sold under generic names by small firms, under brand names by small firms, and by large firms, respectively.

NSB_i, NL_i

Number of drugs introduced in year i and sold under brand names by small firms, and by large firms, respectively.

NSB_{ij}, NL_{ij}

Number of drugs of type j introduced in year i sold by small firms under brand names, and sold by large firms, respectively.

$PTYPE_j$

Proportion of the total sales of large firms accounted for by drugs of type j.

$PYEAR_i$

Proportion of total sales of large firms accounted for by drugs introduced in year i.

Under each assumption the total sales of all drugs by a given type of firm remain at the previously estimated values of $234 million, $204 million, and $1,750 million. In the case of large firms, the three assumptions affect the distribution of sales between large firms selling under generic names and large firms selling under brand names. Table D–6 shows that the largest sales assigned to large firms selling under generic names occur under Assumption G (year of introduction) and that the smallest occur under Assumption I (years of introduction and types of drug). Table D–5 shows, as well, the sales of drugs which, it is assumed, would be affected by removal of brand names and by the removal of patents according to each assumption.

Estimation of the total sales of an individual drug

The total sales of a drug are obtained by adding together the estimates of the sales by each type of firm:

$$\text{SSG}_k + \text{SSB}_k + \text{SLG}_k + \text{SLB}_k$$

Since SSG_k can be estimated in two ways, SSB_k in four ways, and SL_k (which yields SLG_k and SLB_k) in three ways, the total sales of a drug can be estimated in twenty-four ways, the product of separate estimates for each type of firm. The ways in which Assumptions A through I can be combined to obtain these estimates are shown in Table D–6.

For each drug, an estimate of total sales is obtained according to each of the twenty-four procedures. The mean of these twenty-four estimates is computed, and that value is taken as the overall estimate of the total sales of the drug.

$$\text{TS}_k = \sum_{r=A}^{B} \sum_{s=C}^{D,E,F} \sum_{t=G}^{H,I} (\text{SSG}_{k,r} + \text{SSB}_{k,s} + \text{SL}_{k,t})/24$$

Table D–7 shows the distribution of drugs according to the values of TS_k. Although not shown in Table D–7, five drugs are estimated to have sales equal to or greater than $12 million and to have mean sales of $14.68 million. Suppose that four of these five drugs had sales of exactly $12 million; the sales of the remaining drug would be $25.42 million. The maximum value that this procedure can estimate is therefore in the neighborhood of $25 million. This is

D-5. ESTIMATES OF SALES OF TYPES OF FIRMS PROVIDED BY ASSUMPTIONS ABOUT DISTRIBUTION OF SALES

Type of Firm	Assumption	Total Sales	Sales Affected by Removal of Brand Names	Sales Affected by Removal of Patents
Small firm Generic name	A	234.0[a]	199.90	0.0[a]
Small firm Generic name	B	234.0[a]	200.82	0.0[a]
Small firm Brand name	C	204.0[a]	129.94	67.94
Small firm Brand name	D	204.0[a]	134.99	59.85
Small firm Brand name	E	204.0[a]	120.02	78.70
Small firm Brand name	F	204.0[a]	135.04	60.97

Type of Firm	Assumption	Total Sales	Brand Names	Patents
Large firm Generic name	G	369.04	307.86	37.18
Brand name		1,380.95	350.92	948.55
Total		1,750.0[a]	658.78[b]	985.73[b]
Large firm Generic name	H	277.71	216.80	44.20
Brand name		1,472.28	291.46	1,124.41
Total		1,750.0[a]	508.26[b]	1,168.61[b]
Large firm Generic name	I	266.78	214.89	92.51
Brand name		1,483.21	276.20	1,146.64
Total		1,750.0[a]	491.09[b]	1,179.15[b]

[a]The value is defined earlier (Table I-2, p. 8) rather than estimated here.

[b]These figures represent the total sales that would be realized by large firms after the removal of brand names or patents.

D-6. COMBINATIONS OF ASSUMPTIONS FOR TOTAL SALES

SSGk	SSBk	SLk	Estimate Number

D-7.   DISTRIBUTION OF INDIVIDUAL DRUG SALES

Individual Sales—TS_k ($ millions)	Number of Drugs	Cumulative Percentage of Drugs
0.0-1.0	42	6.4%
1.0-1.5	53	14.5%
1.5-2.0	48	21.8%
2.0-2.5	76	33.4%
2.5-3.0	77	45.1%
3.0-3.5	90	58.8%
3.5-4.0	62	68.3%
4.0-4.5	67	78.5%
4.5-5.0	69	89.0%
5.0-5.5	24	92.7%
5.5-6.0	5	93.4%
6.0-6.5	15	95.7%
6.5-7.0	9	97.1%
7.0-7.5	7	98.2%
More than 7.5	12	100.0%
Total	656	

probably an underestimate of the sales of the leading drug in 1961. As well, the procedure probably overestimates the sales of some drugs, particularly those classified as bulk drugs. In general, the procedure undoubtedly underestimates the variance of the distribution, and the skewness is probably more to the right than the distribution shows it to be.

[E] Effect of the Removal of Brand Names upon the Cost of Drugs*

For the purpose of computing the effects of brand-name removal upon the revenues of drug manufacturers, the mean prices charged by each type of firm have been used rather than the prices charged by individual firms. As has been said, the expected effect of the policy would be to reduce the prices charged by the various firms in the market to the level charged by the firm offering the lowest price, and it is assumed that mean prices would better represent the probable hypothetical price in a state of market equilibrium.

The mean price charged by each type of firm for a common unit of the kth drug is represented by the following variables: PSG_k, PSB_k, PLG_k, PLB_k, in which "P" means the price of the kth drug sold, respectively, by small firms under generic names, by small firms under brand names, by large firms under generic names, and by large firms under brand names.

These values are positive if a particular type of firm sells the drug and undefined if the given type of firm does not. The physical quantity (measured in terms of the common unit) sold by each type of firm is obtained by dividing the estimate of the sales of that type of firm by the respective prices. Thus, QSG_k (the quantity of the kth drug sold by a small firm under a generic name) equals SSG_k (sales by the same firm of the kth drug) divided by PSG_k (price of the kth drug sold by SG). This and the following equa-

* This appendix is co-ordinate with pp. 102–103 of the text.

208

tions are used in determining the quantities sold by the four types of firm:

$$QSB_k = SSB_k/PSB_k \quad QLG_k = SLG_k/PLG_k \quad QLB_k = SLB_k/PLB_k$$

The total quantity sold is found by combining the right-hand side of each of these four equations. Hence, $Q_k = QSG_k + QSB_k + QLG_k + QLB_k$. The minimum price charged for the kth drug can be represented as $PMIN_k$, the smallest positive value of PSG_k, PSB_k, PLG_k, or PLB_k.

Since the demand for drugs is assumed to be perfectly inelastic, the reduction in price will not affect the quantity demanded, and it is assumed that it will not affect the distribution of the quantity sold by various types of firm in the market. The total sales of each type of firm after the removal of brand names is obtained by multiplying the quantity sold by each type of firm by $PMIN_k$. Symbolically:*

$$SSGM_k = QSG_k \times PMIN_k \qquad SLGM_k = QLG_k \times PMIN_k$$

$$SSBM_k = QSB_k \times PMIN_k \qquad SLBM_k = QLB_k \times PMIN_k$$

Before the removal of brand names, the total sales by each type of firm of drugs which would be affected by the removal of brand names is computed according to the following definitions.†

* The letter "M," as has been noted, is used to represent the policy of removing brand names. Added to the symbol for a variable, as here, M means that we are considering the value of the variable after the removal of brand names. Thus SSG_k represents the value of the sales of the kth drug by small firms selling under generic names *before* brand names are removed, and $SSGM_k$ represents the sales of the same drug *after* brand names have been removed.

† Used as a superscript with a variable representing a total, M means that we are considering all the drugs in one—and only one—category, the category of drugs that would be affected by the removal of brand names. Thus, SSG^M refers to the total sales of those drugs that would be affected by the removal of brand names *before* the policy went into effect, and $SSGM^M$ would express the total sales of the same drugs *after* the policy went into effect.

$$SSG^M = \sum_{k \in M} SSG_k \qquad SLG^M = \sum_{k \in M} SLG_k$$

$$SSB^M = \sum_{k \in M} SSB_k \qquad SLB^M = \sum_{k \in M} SLB_k$$

E-1.   SALES OF AFFECTED DRUGS BEFORE REMOVAL OF
BRAND NAMES

Variable Estimated	Number of Estimates	Mean of Estimates ($ millions)	Standard Error of Estimates	Coefficient of Variation	Number of Drugs
SSG^M	2	200.4	0.42	0.002	194
SSB^M	4	130.0	6.12	0.047	100
SLG^M	3	246.5	43.38	0.176	116
SLB^M	3	306.2	32.23	0.105	133
TS^M	24	883.0	75.58	0.086	227

The total sales of all affected drugs are computed by adding together the totals for each type of firm. Thus:

$$TS^M = SSG^M + SSB^M + SLG^M + SLB^M$$

The values obtained for these five totals depend upon the assumptions that are used in computing the sales of the individual drug
(see pp. 202–203). For each total, individual values were computed under each relevant assumption and the mean of these
estimates obtained. The results are shown in Table E–1.

Estimates of the sales of affected drugs after the removal of
brand names are computed according to the following definitions,
and the estimates are presented in Table E–2.

E-2.   SALES OF AFFECTED DRUGS AFTER REMOVAL OF
BRAND NAMES

Variable Estimated	Number of Estimates	Mean of Estimates ($ millions)	Standard Error of Estimates	Coefficient of Variation
SSG^M	2	194.3	0.58	0.003
SSB^M	4	93.0	6.51	0.070
SLG^M	3	179.5	30.66	0.171
SLB^M	3	188.8	14.73	0.078
TS^M	24	655.6	45.56	0.069

$$SSGM^M = \sum_{k \in M} SSGM_k \qquad SLGM^M = \sum_{k \in M} SLGM_k$$

$$SSBM^M = \sum_{k \in M} SSBM_k \qquad SLBM^M = \sum_{k \in M} SLBM_k$$

$$TSM^M = SSGM^M + SSBM^M + SLGM^M + SLBM^M$$

The change in sales of each type of firm, attributable to the removal of brand names, is computed by subtracting the sales of affected drugs before removal from the sales of affected drugs after removal of brand names. The definitions are shown below, and the results are presented in Table E–3.*

E-3.   CHANGES IN SALES OF AFFECTED DRUGS ATTRIBUTABLE TO REMOVAL OF BRAND NAMES

Variable Estimated	Number of Estimates	Mean of Estimates ($ millions)	Standard Error of Estimates	Coefficient of Variation
CSSGM	2	− 6.1	0.99	0.162
CSSBM	4	− 37.0	3.19	0.086
CSLGM	3	− 67.0	12.83	0.191
CSLBM	3	−117.4	17.68	0.151
CTSM	24	−227.5[a]	30.56	0.134

[a]Negative numbers have been used here to represent reductions in total sales in order to avoid the use of such numbers to represent increases in total sales at a later point in the discussion (Table E-4).

$$CSSGM = SSGM^M - SSG^M \qquad CSLGM = SLGM^M - SLG^M$$
$$CSSBM = SSBM^M - SSB^M \qquad CSLBM = SLBM^M - SLB^M$$
$$CTSM = TSM^M - TS^M$$

The sales of all drugs following the removal of brand names are determined by subtracting from the original sales the change in sales attributable to the removal of brand names. The definitions are given below and the results presented in Table E–4.

$$SSGM = \sum SSGM_k = SSG + CSSGM$$
$$SSBM = \sum SSBM_k = SSB + CSSBM$$
$$SLGM = \sum SLGM_k = SLG + CSLGM$$
$$SLBM = \sum SLBM_k = SLB + CSLBM$$
$$TSM = \sum TSM_k = TS + CTSM$$

* In the following equations, "CS" means change in sales, and "CTS" means change in total sales.

It is estimated that the removal of brand names would reduce the total sales of the industry to $1,960 million, or to 89.6 percent of the level existing under brand names. The sales of those drugs affected by the policy are estimated to fall from $883 million to $656 million, or to 74.2 percent of the old level. The brunt of the change falls on the large firms. Of a reduction of $227.5 million, they account for $184.3 million, or 80.6 percent. Drugs sold by large firms and affected by the policy are estimated to experience a decline in sales to two-thirds of their old level. Small firms selling under generic names are relatively unaffected by the policy, as theirs is almost always the lowest mean price in the market for a drug. Small firms selling under brand names suffer a greater per-

E-4.   SALES OF ALL DRUGS AFTER REMOVAL OF BRAND NAMES[a]

Variable Estimated	Number of Estimates	Mean of Estimates ($ millions)	Standard Error of Estimates	Coefficient of Variation
SSGM	2	227.9	0.98	0.004
SSBM	4	167.0	3.19	0.019
SLGM	3	237.5	33.33	0.140
SLBM	3	1,328.0	63.53	0.048
TSM	24	1,960.2	30.63	0.016

[a]Notice again that differences are obtained by adding since reductions have already been defined to be negative quantities.

centage reduction on the sales of all their drugs than do large firms, but on the sales of affected drugs only the reduction is 28.5 percent (71.5 percent of the old level), or approximately the same as the reduction on drugs sold under generic names by large firms. Other relationships are shown in Table E–5, which summarizes the effects of the policy upon the various types of firm.*

The change in the total sales of an individual drug, $CTSM_k$, is determined by subtracting the sales of the drug before removal of brand names from the sales after removal; thus:

$$CTSM_k = TSM_k - TS_k$$

* Table E–5 is also used as Table VI–1 on p. 104.

E-5. EFFECT OF REMOVAL OF BRAND NAMES UPCN SALES OF THE INDUSTRY

Type of Firm	Total Sales before Removal of Brand Names: All Drugs	Total Sales after Removal of Brand Names: All Drugs	Sales after Removal as Percent of Sales before Removal: All Drugs	Total Sales before Removal of Brand Names: Affected Drugs	Total Sales after Removal of Brand Names: Affected Drugs	Sales after Removal as Percent of Sales before Removal: Affected Drugs	Change in Sales Attributable to Removal of Brand Names
Small firm Generic name	234.0[a]	227.89	97.93%	200.3?	194.29	96.95%	−6.11
Small firm Brand name	204.0[a]	166.98	81.86%	130.0?	92.98	71.53%	−37.01
Large firm Generic name	304.51	237.49	77.99%	246.5?	179.50	72.82%	−67.01
Large firm Brand name	1,445.31	1,327.95	91.88%	306.1?	188.82	61.67%	−117.37
Subtotal Large firms	*1,750.0[a]*	*1,565.44*	*89.45%*	*552.69*	*368.32*	*66.64%*	*−184.34*
Totals	2,188.0[a]	1960.22	89.60%	883.04	655.56	74.24%	−227.48

[a]The value is defined earlier (see Table I-2, p. 8) rather than estimated here. Figures printed in italic are not included in totals.

E-6.   DISTRIBUTION OF SALES AFTER REMOVAL OF
BRAND NAMES TO SALES BEFORE

TSM_k/TS_k	Number of Drugs	Cumulative Percentage of Drugs	Sales before Removal of Brand Names	Cumulative Percentage of Sales before Removal of Brand Names	Sales after Removal of Brand Names
Below 0.40	8	1.2%	39.88	1.8%	14.47
0.40-0.45	12	3.1%	52.67	4.2%	22.78
0.45-0.50	10	4.6%	40.17	6.1%	19.20
0.50-0.55	7	5.7%	26.75	7.3%	13.83
0.55-0.60	14	7.8%	57.34	9.9%	32.41
0.60-0.65	23	11.2%	83.47	13.7%	52.30
0.65-0.70	20	14.3%	77.32	17.3%	52.14
0.70-0.75	14	16.5%	56.84	19.9%	41.00
0.75-0.80	19	19.4%	74.37	22.5%	41.00
0.80-0.85	8	20.6%	25.74	23.6%	21.24
0.85-0.90	21	23.8%	84.13	27.5%	73.49
0.90-0.95	27	27.9%	102.08	32.1%	94.81
0.95-1.00	32	32.8%	123.18	37.8%	120.74
No change	441	100%	1,344.07	100%	1,344.07

It would be possible to present the distribution of $CTSM_k$, but this would give very little insight into the effect of the policy upon individual drugs. Instead, the value TSM_k/TS_k is computed for each drug. This shows the ratio of the sales of an individual drug (the kth drug) after the removal of brand names to the sales before removal.

Table E–6 presents the distribution of this value. The table also shows the sales of all drugs, having a value of TSM_k/TS_k in a particular range, before and after removal of brand names. The distribution shows that, on the whole, it is the more important drugs which are affected by the removal of brand names, since, for all groups, the cumulative proportion of sales accounted for by the drugs is greater than the cumulative percentage of drugs.

There are 227 drugs that are likely to be affected by the removal of brand names and, thus, 429 which will not be affected. The table shows that 441 register no change as a result of the policy. This implies that twelve drugs are produced by two or more types of firm and that the mean prices charged by each type are identical.

[F] Effect of the Removal of Patents upon the Cost of Drugs[*]

Several assumptions have been made about the effect of patent removal upon market power in the drug industry and the prices of drugs. Thus, it is expected that if patent protection is removed from a drug produced by only one type of firm, the other three types of firms—those that were previously excluded from the market—will be free to enter it and that the entering firms will continue to sell—as the case may be—under generic names or brand names. It is further assumed that an entering firm will capture a physical share of the market equal to the average share obtained in markets in which it competed with at least one other type of firm and finally that entry into the market for these newer drugs will be on the same terms as those for older drugs.

With these assumptions it is possible to estimate what 1961 sales would have been had patent protection been removed. To do so, it is necessary to determine the average market share held by each type of firm in markets where two or more different types of firm existed. The physical quantity sold of a given drug is determined as the sum of the quantities sold by each of the four types of firm. This relationship can be represented by the following equation:

$$Q_k = SSG_k/PSG_k + SSB_k/PSB_k + SLG_k/PLG_k + SLB_k/PLB_k$$
$$Q_k = QSG_k + QSB_k + QLG_k + QLB_k,$$

[*] This appendix is co-ordinate with pp. 103–107 of the text.

Here Q_k symbolizes the quantity sold of the kth drug, and the ratios represent the total sales of the kth drug by each type of firm (for example, the sales of "k" by small firms selling under generic names) divided by the price charged for the kth drug by each type of firm (e.g., PSG_k). In other words, by performing each of the divisions we can determine the quantity of the kth drug sold by SG, SB, LG, and LB. Hence, where the terms are zero, the kth drug is not produced by a particular type of firm. Since the physical units of one drug are rarely commensurable with those of another drug, the average share of market power must be ascertained by means of an index number. To determine this, we establish a ratio for the proportionate share held by each type of firm in the kth market; thus: QSG_k/Q_k; QLG_k/Q_k; QSB_k/Q_k; QLB_k/Q_k, where QSG_k/Q_k is the ratio of the quantity of the kth drug produced by SG to the total quantity produced by all four types of firm.

Each market share is then weighted by the total sales of the kth drug, and this procedure is repeated for all drugs produced by two or more types of firm. For each type of firm the weighted terms are totalled, and the sum is divided by the sum of the sums for all types of firm. Thus, for small firms selling under generic names, these operations reduce to the following expression:

$$\sum \frac{QSG_k}{Q_k} \times TS_k / \sum TS_k$$

The market share estimated for one type of firm (for example, SG in the preceding equation) depends upon the sales of the three remaining types of firm, but these sales depend upon the assumptions made in estimating the sales of individual drugs (see Appendix D, pp. 193–207). There are also twenty-four combinations of assumptions that can be used to estimate total sales and therefore as many estimates of overall market share held by each type of firm. Further, since significant differences in price ratios have been observed among different methods of drug administration, market shares have been computed for orally administered drugs, parenterally administered drugs, and serums and bulk drugs, for each of which twenty-four estimating procedures have been used. A summary of the results is presented in Table F–1.

F-1.   THE PHYSICAL SHARES OF MARKETS OBTAINED BY
TYPES OF FIRMS FOR MARKETS IN WHICH TWO OR MORE
TYPES OF FIRM OPERATE

Estimate Number	Small Firm Generic Name	Small Firm Brand Name	Large Firm Generic Name	Large Firm Brand Name
1	.301	.131	.280	.289
2	.341	.148	.223	.283
3	.346	.151	.230	.274
4	.296	.142	.277	.285
5	.336	.157	.226	.280
6	.340	.163	.228	.270
7	.303	.121	.282	.294
8	.343	.141	.230	.285
9	.348	.142	.232	.278
10	.297	.139	.277	.287
11	.337	.157	.226	.280
12	.340	.162	.228	.270
13	.298	.133	.281	.288
14	.332	.151	.231	.285
15	.343	.153	.231	.272
16	.294	.143	.279	.284
17	.328	.159	.229	.284
18	.338	.164	.229	.269
19	.300	.123	.284	.293
20	.335	.144	.234	.288
21	.346	.144	.233	.276
22	.295	.140	.279	.286
23	.329	.158	.229	.284
24	.339	.163	.229	.269

The geometric means of the price ratios have been recomputed and grouped together under the two methods of administration (oral and parenteral) and serums and bulk drugs. These are shown in Table F–2. It is assumed that when patents are removed, the type of firm originally in the market will continue to sell at its existing price and that the prices charged by entering firms of another type will bear the same relation to the existing price as the ratios of the mean prices computed between the prices of the original type of firm (in the denominator) and the prices of each of the other types of firm (in the numerator). Zero elasticity of demand is again assumed for the market, so that although con-

F-2.   GEOMETRIC MEANS OF PRICE RATIOS[a]

Types of Firm in Market before Removal of Patent Protection (Dominator of ratio)

		SG	SB	LG	LB
		Orally administered drugs			
	SG	1.000	0.511	0.525	0.395
	SB	1.957	1.000	1.072	0.716
	LG	1.905	0.933	1.000	0.871
	LB	2.533	1.397	1.148	1.000
		Parenterally administered drugs			
	SG	1.000	0.738	0.691	0.643
	SB	1.355	1.000	0.890	0.846
	LG	1.448	1.123	1.000	1.018
	LB	1.554	1.182	0.982	1.000
		Serums and bulk drugs			
	SG	1.000	–	0.916	1.000
	SB	–	–	–	–
	LG	1.092	–	1.000	–
	LB	1.000	–	–	1.000

Types of Firm in Market after Removal of Patent Protection. (Numerator of ratio)

[a]The geometric means are derived by reading the left-hand letters as numerator equivalents and the uppermost letters as denominator equivalents in the price ratios: Small firm (Generic name)/Large firm (Brand name) = 0.395.

sumers now face four different prices instead of only one, there is no increase in the quantity consumed of the drug. As an example, suppose a large firm sells an orally administered (and patented) drug under a brand name at the price PLB_k. With the removal of patent protection, prices charged by other types of firm entering the same market can be calculated as the product of the appropriate geometric mean and the existing price—PLB_k. Thus, in Table F–2, under "Orally administered drugs" in the column headed by LB, we note that the geometric mean for PLB_k is 1.000; and, multiplying this by the existing price, we obtain PLB_k ($1.000 \times$ PLB_k) as the price charged by the existing firm. The same relationship holds for the other three types of firm—SG, SB, and LG. For instance, the price charged by an entering firm of the SG type will be (from Table F–2) $0.395 \times PLB_k$ (the existing price), or PSG_k; in the same way,

$$PSB_k' = 0.716 \times PLB_k \qquad PLG_k' = 0.871 \times PLB_k$$

With the same example in mind, suppose that total sales of the kth drug by firms of the LB type before the removal of patents are estimated (under Estimate 1, Assumptions A, C, and G, pp. 202–203) to be $4.0 million. Under the same assumptions, but after the removal of patents, it is estimated that each type of firm will obtain the following market shares (represented by the prefix "W"):

$$WSG = 0.312 \qquad WLG = 0.198$$
$$WSB = 0.152 \qquad WLB = 0.337$$

The relative prices charged by each type of entering firm after the removal of patents are determined from the table of geometric means, F–2. Total sales for each type will be:

$$SSGP_k = TS_k \times WSG \times E[E(SG)/E(LB)]$$
$$= \$4.0 \times 0.312 \times 0.395 = \$0.493 \text{ million}$$

$$SSBP_k = TS_k \times WSB \times E[E(SB)/E(LB)]$$
$$= \$4.0 \times 0.152 \times 0.176 = \$0.435 \text{ million}$$

$$SLGP_k = TS_k \times WLG \times E[E(LG)/E(LB)]$$
$$= \$4.0 \times 0.198 \times 0.871 = \$0.690 \text{ million}$$

$$SLBP_k = TS_k \times WLB \times E[E(LB)/E(LB)]$$
$$= \$4.0 \times 0.337 \times 1.000 = \$1.348 \text{ million}$$

Adding these values together to obtain the total revenue from the sales of the kth drug (TSP_k), we get $2.966 million. In this example, the brand-name sale of k by the hypothetical large firm (before the removal of patents, the only firm in the market) are reduced from $4.0 to $1.35 million, and the sales of the other types of firm are increased, upon their entry into the market after the removal of patents, from zero to the figures shown.

These values have been obtained by using only Estimate 1; actual values are obtained by repeating the estimation process with each of the twenty-four combinations of assumptions about the distribution of the sales of a drug. Letting "Y"* represent the general type of firm in the denominator before the removal of patents, the procedure for computing TSP_k can be shown as:

$$TSP_k = \tfrac{1}{24} \times \sum_{r=1}^{24} \Big[TS_{k,r} \times \big(WSG_r \times E[E(SG)/E(Y)] $$
$$+ WSB_r \times E[E(SB)/E(Y)] + WLG_r \times E[E(LG)/E(Y)] $$
$$+ WLB_r \times E[E(LB)/E(Y)] \big) \Big]$$

The format used in showing the results of the removal of brand names is also used here in presenting estimates of the effects of patent removal. Each term is defined and is followed by a tabular presentation of the estimates of its value. The letter "P" as a suffix and as a superscript has the same interpretation for patents as the letter "M" had for brand names (see Appendix E, p. 209).

The original sales of all drugs which would be affected by the removal of patents are computed according to the definitions below, and the estimates obtained are presented in Table F–3.

F-3.   SALES OF AFFECTED DRUGS BEFORE REMOVAL OF PATENTS

Variable Estimated	Number of Estimates	Mean of Estimates ($ millions)	Standard Error of Estimates	Coefficient of Variation	Number of Drugs
SSG^P	0				0
SSB^P	4	66.12	6.12	0.083	50
SLG^P	3	37.97	4.32	0.074	14
SLB^P	3	1,073.10	77.99	0.068	290
TS^P	12	1,177.16	75.59	0.058	354

$$SSG^P = \sum_{k \in P} SSG_k = 0 \text{ (by assumption)}$$
$$SSB^P = \sum_{k \in P} SSB_k \qquad SLG^P = \sum_{k \in P} SLG_k$$
$$SLB^P = \sum_{k \in P} SLB_k$$
$$TS^P = SSG^P + SSB^P + SLG^P + SLB^P$$

* In other words, "Y" stands for whichever type of firm happens to be in the market before the removal of patents.

Among the four types of firm, there are substantial differences between the proportion of original sales that would be affected by the removal of patents and by the removal of brand names. Of the sales of large firms, 63.5 percent would be affected by the removal of patents, but only 29.9 percent by the removal of brand names. Of the sales of drugs sold by large firms under generic names, 12.5 percent would be affected by patent removal, but 81.0 percent by the removal of brand names; for the sales of drugs sold under brand names, the corresponding figures are 74.3 percent and 21.2 percent. For small firms selling under brand name, 63.7 percent of sales would be affected by a removal of brand names and 32.4 percent by a removal of patents. Since drugs sold by small firms selling under generic name are excluded, the removal of patents would have no effect upon the original sales of this type of firm; but 85.6 percent of the sales of such firms would be affected by a policy which removed brand names.

The sales of drugs affected by the removal of patents are computed as follow, and the estimates of these sales, are given after patent removal, in Table F–4.

F-4.   SALES OF AFFECTED DRUGS AFTER REMOVAL OF PATENTS

Variable Estimated	Number of Estimates	Mean of Estimates ($ millions)	Standard Error of Estimates	Coefficient of Variation
SSGP^P	24	179.7	22.87	0.107
SSBP^P	24	151.3	22.53	0.142
SLGP^P	24	196.8	18.04	0.083
SLBP^P	24	375.7	14.94	0.034
TSP^P	24	903.4	39.52	0.038

$$\text{SSGP}^P = \sum_{k \in P} \text{SSGP}_k \qquad \text{SLGP}^P = \sum_{k \in P} \text{SLGP}_k$$
$$\text{SSBP}^P = \sum_{k \in P} \text{SSBP}_k \qquad \text{SLBP}^P = \sum_{k \in P} \text{SLBP}_k$$
$$\text{TSP}^P = \text{SSGP}^P + \text{SSBP}^P + \text{SLGP}^P + \text{SLBP}^P$$

The changes in the sales of each type of firm which result from removing patents are computed from the following equation, and the results are shown in Table F–5.

F-5. CHANGES IN SALES OF AFFECTED DRUGS ATTRIBUTABLE TO THE REMOVAL OF PATENTS

Variable Estimated	Number of Estimates	Mean of Estimates ($ millions)	Standard Error of Estimates	Coefficient of Variation
CSSGP	24	+170.7	22.85	0.127
CSSBP	24	+ 85.1	25.34	0.298
CSLGP	24	+158.8	18.24	0.115
CSLBP	24	−697.4	68.74	0.099
CTSP	24	−273.8	36.38	0.133

$$CSSGP = SSGP^P - SSG^P \qquad CSLGP = SLGP^P - SLG^P$$
$$CSSBP = SSBP^P - SSB^P \qquad CSLBP = SLBP^P - SLB^P$$
$$CTSP = TSP^P - TS^P$$

Following patent removal, the total sales of all drugs are computed according to the procedures shown below, and the estimates of these sales are shown in Table F–6.

F-6. SALES OF ALL DRUGS AFTER REMOVAL OF PATENTS

Variable Estimated	Number of Estimates	Mean of Estimates ($ millions)	Standard Error of Estimates	Coefficient of Variation
SSGP	24	413.7	22.85	0.055
SSBP	24	289.1	25.34	0.088
SLGP	24	463.3	59.72	0.129
SLBP	24	747.9	25.24	0.034
TSP	24	1,914.0	36.39	0.019

$$SSGP = \sum_k SSGP_k = SSG + CSSGP$$
$$SSBP = \sum_k SSBP_k = SSB + CSSBP$$
$$SLGP = \sum_k SLGP_k = SLG + CSLGP$$
$$SLBP = \sum_k SLBP_k = SLB + CSLBP$$
$$TSP = SSGP + SSBP + SLGP + SLBP$$

[G] Effect of the Removal of Brand Names and Patents[*]

With the removal of brand names and patents, drugs that are potentially affected by the removal of brand names are expected to behave as they did when brand names alone were removed. For drugs affected by the removal of patents the results of the policy are predicted to be more drastic. First, the removal of patents permits the entry of all four types of firm, and the entering firms will behave as though market power were conferred by brand names alone. Second, the removal of brand names will cause all prices to become equal to the lowest mean price charged by any type of firm after the removal of patents. The drugs that are considered to be affected by the policy of removing both brand names and patents are those which are assumed to be affected by either one of the two policies. There are 581 such drugs (out of a total of 656); the remaining 75 are assumed to be not affected.

In the following analysis the letter symbol "A" used as a suffix or superscript has the same meaning for the policy to remove both brand names and patents that the letter symbols "M" and "P" have for the two policies taken separately (see Appendix E, p. 209). We consider first the effect of removing brand names from drugs that are not patented, that are affected by the removal of

* This appendix is co-ordinate with chapters VI and IX in the text.

brand names, and that are produced by two or more types of firm. The effect of the policy upon this group of drugs is estimated by equating total sales after the removal of brand names with total sales after the removal of both brand names and patents ($TSM_k = TSA_k$).

For drugs assumed to be covered by patents, TSP_k is computed for each drug. TSA_k is then determined by assuming that the prices charged by each type of firm will become equal to the lowest mean price charged by any type of firm after the removal of patent protection. These values can be obtained from Table F–2 (p. 219); examination of this table shows that the prices—referred to here as $PMIN_k$—will always equal the mean price charged by small firms selling under generic names. Using the letter symbol "Y" to represent whichever type of firm happens to be in the market before the removal of patents, we define $PMIN_k$ as the smallest positive value of:

$$E[E(SG)/E(Y)] \qquad E[E(SB)/E(Y)]$$
$$E[E(LB)/E(Y)] \qquad E[E(LG)/E(Y)]$$

Then the sales of each drug by each type of firm after the removal of brand names will be

$$SSGA_k = SSGP_k \times (PMIN_k/E[E(SG)/E(Y)]$$
$$SSBA_k = SSBP_k \times (PMIN_k/E[E(SB)/E(Y)]$$
$$SLGA_k = SLGP_k \times (PMIN_k/E[E(LG)/E(Y)]$$
$$SLBA_k = SLBA_k \times (PMIN_k/E[E(LB)/E(Y)]$$
$$TSA_k = SSGA_k + SSBA_k + SLGA_k + SLBA_k$$

The sales of the four types of firm—before the removal of brand names and patents—of drugs that would be affected by this policy were determined by means of the definitions listed below. Estimates of these sales are given in Table G–1.

$$SSG^A = \sum_{k \in M} SSG_k \qquad SLG^A = \sum_{k \in P} SLG_k$$
$$SSB^A = \sum_{k \in P} SSB_k \qquad SLB^A = \sum_{k \in P} SLB_k$$
$$TS^A = SSG^A + SSB^A + SLG^A + SLB^A$$

For the industry as a whole, 94.2 percent of the original sales and 88.6 percent of the drugs would be affected by this policy. There

G-1.   SALES OF AFFECTED DRUGS BEFORE REMOVAL
OF BRAND NAMES AND PATENT PROTECTION

Variable Estimated	Number of Estimates	Mean of Estimates ($ millions)	Number of Drugs
SSG^A	2	200.4	194
SSB^A	24	196.1	150
SLG^A	24	284.5	130
SLB^A	24	1,379.3	423
TS^A	24	2,060.2	581

is little variation among types of firm in the proportion of sales
involved. Small firms selling under generic names have 85.6 percent of their sales involved; for each of the remaining classifications of firm, approximately 95 percent of the sales are subject to
the policy.

G-2.   SALES OF AFFECTED DRUGS AFTER
REMOVAL OF BRAND NAMES AND PATENT
PROTECTION

Variable Estimated	Number of Estimates	Mean of Estimates ($ millions)
SSGA^A	24	586.7
SSBA^A	24	210.3
SLGA^A	24	290.2
SLBA^A	24	355.6
TSA^A	24	1,442.8

Estimates of the sales of the 581 drugs that are affected by the
policy are shown in Table G–2. These estimates were calculated
by means of the following equations:

$$SSGA^A = \sum_{k \in A} SSGA_k \qquad SLGA^A = \sum_{k \in A} SLGA_k$$
$$SSBA^A = \sum_{k \in A} SSBA_k \qquad SLBA^A = \sum_{k \in A} SLBA_k$$
$$TSA^A = SSGA^A + SSBA^A + SLGA^A + SLBA^A$$

G-3.   CHANGES IN SALES ATTRIBUTABLE TO REMOVAL OF BRAND NAMES AND PATENTS PROTECTION

Variable Estimated	Number of Estimates	Mean of Estimates ($ millions)
CSSGA	24	+386.3
CSSBA	24	+14.2
CSLGA	24	+5.7
CSLBA	24	−1,023.6
CTSA	24	−617.4

Table G–3 gives the changes in the sales of each type of firm that are attributable to the policy. The relevant definitions are:

$$CSSGA = SSGA^4 - SSG^4 \qquad CSLGA = SLGA^4 - SLG^4$$
$$CSSBA = SSBA^4 - SSB^4 \qquad CSLBA = SLBA^4 - SLB^4$$
$$CTSA = TSA^4 - TS^4$$

G-4.   SALES OF ALL DRUGS AFTER REMOVAL OF BRAND NAMES AND PATENT PROTECTION

Variable Estimated	Number of Estimates	Mean of Estimates ($ millions)
SSGA	24	620.3
SSBA	24	218.2
SLGA	24	310.2
SLBA	24	421.7
TSA	24	1,570.3

Total sales of all drugs after introduction of the policy appear in Table G–4. The procedures used in deriving the estimates were:

$$SSGA = SSG + CSSGA \qquad SLGA = SLG + CSLGA$$
$$SSBA = SSB + CSSBA \qquad SLBA = SLB + CSLBA$$
$$TSA = TS + CTSA$$

Table VI–3 (p. 110 in the text) summarizes the effects of the policy on all four types of firm.

NOTES

CHAPTER ONE

1. Seymour Harris, *The Economics of American Medicine* (New York, 1964), p. 6.

2. Henry Steele, "Monopoly and Competition in the Ethical Drugs Market," *Journal of Law and Economics* 5 (Oct. 1962): 164.

3. U.S., Congress, Senate, Subcommittee on Antitrust and Monopoly of the Committee on the Judiciary, *Hearings on Administered Prices in the Drug Industry,* 86th Cong., 2nd sess., 1960, pt. 22, pp. 12141–44.

4. Pharmaceutical Manufacturers Association, *Prescription Drug Industry Fact Book* (Washington, D.C., 1962), sec. 1, p. 3.

5. Ibid., p. 1.

6. Jesse Markham, "Economic Incentives in the Drug Industry," in *Drugs in Our Society,* ed. Paul Talalay (Baltimore, 1964), pp. 167–68.

7. Odin W. Anderson, Patricia Collette, and Jacob J. Feldman, *Changes in Family Medical Care Expenditures and Voluntary Health Insurance: A Five Year Resurvey* (Cambridge, Mass., 1963).

CHAPTER TWO

1. On the appropriate procedures for assigning generic names and the mechanism by which generic names become official, see the testimony of Lloyd C. Miller (Director of Revision, *United States Pharmacopeia*), U.S., Congress, Senate, Subcommittee on Antitrust and Monopoly of the Committee on the Judiciary, *Hearings on Administered Prices: Drugs,* 86th Cong., 2nd sess., 1960, pt. 21, pp. 11674–75.

CHAPTER THREE

1. Carl Kaysen and Donald F. Turner, *Antitrust Policy: A Legal and Economic Analysis* (Cambridge, Mass., 1959), p. 75.

2. *Physician's Desk Reference* (Oradell, N. J., annually).

3. In personal conversations with doctors and officials of the large drug firms, I have heard brand names defended on the grounds that they save the physician's valuable time. It is interesting to see how socially valuable the physician's time must be if this argument is true. Suppose that, in the actual writing of the prescription, the use of the generic name, rather than a brand name, added thirty seconds to the time required. Suppose further that the typical prescription calling for the brand name product of a large firm costs the patient $4.50. If the mark-up used by the pharmacist in arriving at this price is 50 percent, then the cost to the pharmacist is $3.00. In cases where small firms selling a drug under its generic name and large firms selling the same drug under a brand name exist in the same market, the former charge, on the average, 46.7 percent of the price charged by the latter (*see* Chapter V). The cost to the pharmacist of the drug from a small firm selling under generic name would be $1.40; adding 50 percent to this gives a retail price of $2.10. If the physician were to spend an additional thirty seconds, he could save the patient $2.40. However, the value of his time in some other use is greater than this (or would be if there were some compensation mechanism by which the patient could pay the physician for taking the additional time). If we use $2.40 per thirty seconds as a wage rate, the annual gross income of the physician would be expected to be in the neighborhood of $576,000 (taking a year to be 250 eight-hour days). In fact, the annual income of physicians is little more than one-twentieth of this.

Although the above example is contrived, the argument that brand names save time is specious on other grounds. If it does save time, it is only because large firms have assigned awkward generic names in the first place.

4. As a recent example of a variant of this, consider the following: "A $500,000 suit was filed in federal court yesterday by a Monterey, Tenn., man against an Indianapolis drug manufacturer for the death of his wife allegedly caused from taking a drug . . . [The suit] alleged that Eli Lilly represented Delvex as a 'safe and proper chemical for effective treatment of various infestations of intestinal parasites in human beings,' and particularly for treating the parasitic infestation known as roundworms. The complaint said the firm represented that the drug could be

taken without danger. . . . The complaint alleged that the drug caused the deaths of several persons prior to the spring of 1965, and the defendant knew or should have known this. . . . Notwithstanding this, the complaint said, the defendant continued to sell the drug and hold it out to the public and the medical profession as a fit, safe and proper drug for use in treatment of parasitic infections" *Nashville Tennessean,* 12 July 1966. While the press report of this suit makes no mention of a doctor, it seems likely that most such suits would include the doctor as a co-defendant.

5. Henry Steele, "Monopoly and Competition in the Ethical Drugs Market," *Journal of Law and Economics* 5 (Oct. 1962): 164.

6. William S. Comanor, "Research and Competitive Product Differentiation in the Pharmaceutical Industry in the United States," *Economica,* n.s., 31 (Nov. 1964): 375.

7. William S. Comanor, "Research and Technical Change in the Pharmaceutical Industry," *The Review of Economics and Statistics,* 47 (May 1965): 190.

8. National Science Foundation, *Research and Development in Industry: 1961* (Washington, D.C., 1964), p. 90, Table A-28.

9. Ibid., p. 84, Table A-22

10. U.S., Congress, Senate, Subcommittee on Antitrust and Monopoly of the Committee on the Judiciary, *Report, Administered Prices: Drugs,* 87th Cong., 1st sess., 1961, S. Rept. 448, p. 157. (Hereafter cited as *Report* or *Minority Report.*)

11. On this, see Edith Penrose's comments as cited by Comanor, "Research and Competitive Product Differentiation," p. 375.

12. E. D. Pellegrino, M.D. (Professor of Medicine, University of Kentucky Medical College), "The State Medical Journal as an Educational Instrument," *Medical Times,* 92 (Nov. 1964): 1112, Table I.

13. Ibid., pp. 1113–14.

14. Henry A. Davidson, M.D. (Editor, *Journal of the Medical Society of New Jersey*), "Our State Medical Society Journals: Can They Survive? Should They Survive?" *Journal of the Medical Society of New Jersey* 61 (Jan. 1964): 13–14.

15. Ibid., p. 14.

16. Ben Gaffin and Associates, "The Fond du Lac Study, A Basic Marketing Study Made for the American Medical Association" (Chicago, 1956); reprinted in U.S., Congress, Senate, Subcommittee on Antitrust and Monopoly of the Committee on the Judiciary, *Hearings on Drug Industry Antitrust Act,* 87th Cong., 1st sess., 1961, pt. 2, pp. 697–806. (Hereafter cited as *1961 Hearings.*) The above figure is computed from evidence submitted on each of the four drugs.

17. Davidson, "Our State Medical Society Journals," pp. 13–14.

18. *Report,* p. 31.

19. First National City Bank of New York, *Monthly Economic Letter* (April 1959).

20. Scale computed by:

$$5.83 = 100 - \frac{66.6 + 0.344 \times (84.4 + 15.6/\text{scale})}{1.13}$$

21. $89.2 = 80.0 / (100 - 10.32) \times 100$

22. James E. Bowes, M.D., U.S., Congress, Senate, Subcommittee on Antitrust and Monopoly of the Committee on the Judiciary, *Hearings on Administered Prices: Drugs,* 86th Cong., 2nd sess., 1960, pt. 18, pp. 10453–54.

23. Ibid., p. 10455. The city is Salt Lake City.

24. See Oliver E. Williamson, "Selling Expense as a Barrier to Entry," *Quarterly Journal of Economics* 77 (Feb. 1963): 112–28.

25. Nationwide Insurance Company, "The Consumer's Stake in Drugs" (Columbus, Ohio, n.d.); reprinted in *1961 Hearings,* 2nd sess., pt. 3. p. 1646.

26. *Report,* p. 105.

27. Kaysen and Turner, *Antitrust Policy,* p. 166.

28. Paul de Haen, *New Product Survey 1950–59;* reprinted in *1961 Hearings,* 2nd sess., pt. 3, p. 1656.

29. Computed by counting such drugs listed in Pharmaceutical Manufacturers Association, "Review of Drugs, 1941–1961: Single Chemical Entities Introduced in the United States," mimeographed (Washington, 1962).

30. J. P. Miller, "Measures of Monopoly Power and Concentration: Their Economic Significance," in *Business Concentration and Price Policy,* ed. George J. Stigler (Princeton, 1955), pp. 123–29.

CHAPTER FOUR

1. Barbara Moulton, M.D., U.S., Congress, Senate, Subcommittee on Antitrust and Monopoly of the Committee on the Judiciary, *Hearings on Administered Prices: Drugs,* 86th Cong., 2nd sess., 1960, pt. 22, p. 12040. (Hereafter cited as *1960 Hearings.*)

2. Henry Steele, "Monopoly and Competition in the Ethical Drugs Market," *Journal of Law and Economics* 5 (Oct. 1962): 134.

3. Canada, Restrictive Trade Practices Commission, *Material Collected for Submission to the Restrictive Trade Practices Commission in the Course of an Inquiry under Section 42 of the Combines Investigation Act Relating to the Manufacture, Distribution and Sale of Drugs;*

reprinted as Appendix Q in Canada, Restrictive Trade Practices Commission, *Report Concerning the Manufacture, Distribution and Sales of Drugs* (Ottawa, 1963). (Hereafter cited as *Green Book.*)

4. Ibid., p. 106.

5. Ibid., p. 145. Other estimates of the cost of quality control in Canada have been made. The Canadian Pharmaceutical Manufacturers Association (C.P.M.A.) states: ". . . According to some manufacturers, these painstaking, comprehensive quality safeguards are responsible for from 10 to 15 percent of production costs." C.P.M.A., *Facts About Pharmaceutical Manufacturing,* as quoted in *Green Book,* p. 145. Dr. Arthur Grieve (Director of Control for Ayerst) is quoted as saying that quality control amounts to less than 10 percent of the cost of manufacturing a drug in Canada. Vancouver *Sun,* 12 April 1960, as quoted in *Green Book,* p. 145.

6. "The Pharmacopeia serves medicine in two ways. First, it gives the practicing physician his most effective voice in determining the quality of drugs he prescribes . . . . To fulfill [this function], the Pharmacopeia must reflect with fidelity the best standards of medicine and pharmacy in providing standards of purity and potency for drugs of established merit and necessity." *United States Pharmacopeia,* 16th ed. rev. (Easton, Pa., 1960), p. xiv. (Hereafter cited as *U. S. P. XVI.*)

7. Ibid., p. 2.

8. Walter Modell, M.D. (Associate Professor of Pharmacology, Cornell University Medical College), *1960 Hearings,* 2nd sess., pt. 21, p. 11610.

9. As the most comprehensive evidence of the variations which the *U.S.P.* permits, consider the following specifications for tablet weights. "The average weight of uncoated tablets conforms to the tolerances given in the accompanying table unless otherwise provided in the individual monograph.

"Weigh individually 20 whole tablets, and calculate the average weight: the weights of not more than two of the tablets differ from the average weight by more than the percentage listed and no tablet differs by more than double the percentage." (*U.S.P. XVI,* p. 962).

Average weight of tablets mg.	*Percentage difference*
13 or less	15
from 13 through 130	10
from 130 through 324	7.5
more than 324	5

10. Of the drugs produced by small firms selling under generic name, 85 percent were introduced prior to 1950; only 38.4 percent of the

drugs sold by large firms under brand names were introduced before 1950. This can be derived from the figures in Table C-I.

11. *1960 Hearings*, 1st sess., p. 9242, as quoted in U.S., Congress, Senate, Subcommittee on Antitrust and Monopoly of the Committee on the Judiciary, *Report, Administered Prices: Drugs,* 87th Cong., 1st sess., 1961, S. Rept. 448, p. 293. (Hereafter cited as *Report* or *Minority Report.*)

12. *Minority Report*, p. 292.

13. Leonard Engel, *Medicine Makers of Kalamazoo* (New York, 1961), p. 27.

14. Herman Kogan, *The Long White Line: The Story of Abbott Laboratories* (New York, 1963), pp. 47–48. The period described is about 1900.

15. Austin Smith, M.D., *1960 Hearings*, 2nd sess., pt. 19, p. 10738.

16. Ibid., p. 10623.

17. Ibid., pp. 10703–04. See below for a discussion of the quality and sources of the physician's information about drugs.

18. Steele, "Monopoly and Competition," p. 142.

19. *1960 Hearings*, 2nd sess., pt. 21, p. 11713.

20. Newell Steward (Executive Vice-President of the National Pharmaceutical Council), *1960 Hearings*, 2nd sess., pt. 21, p.11699.

21. John T. Connor, *1960 Hearings*, 1st sess., pt. 14, p. 8198.

22. *1960 Hearings*, 2nd sess., pt. 21, p. 11606.

23. "In 1960 the Subcommittee on Generic Terms of the Los Angeles County Medical Association sent a letter to each of the 82 medical schools in the United States. Within three weeks 77 responses arrived from the departments of pharmacology of those schools answering these questions:

"1. Do you teach the prescription of drugs by generic terms?
"2. Do you favor the continuation of this practice?

"Sixty-four replied that they taught only generic terminology; 3 taught both generic and trade names; 10 used trade names under certain circumstances such as when a drug is exclusively monopolized under a patent." *Report*, p. 226.

24. Walter Modell, M.D., *1960 Hearings*, 2nd sess., pt. 21., pp. 11608–27, *passim*.

25. Solomon Garb, M.D., "Teaching Medical Students to Evaluate Drug Advertising," *Journal of Medical Education*, 35 (Aug. 1960) : 736.

26. *1960 Hearings*, 2nd sess., pt. 18, p. 10477.

27. Ibid., p. 10476.

28. August H. Groeschel, M.D. (Associate Director of the New York Hospital), *1960 Hearings*, 2nd sess., pt. 21, pp. 11566–89, *passim*.

29. Herman R. Fahlbusch (Captain, U.S.N., and Deputy-Director, Military Medical Supply Agency), *1960 Hearings*, 2nd sess., pt. 21, pp. 11544–66, *passim*.

30. *Report*, pp. 248–49.

31. Alvin G. Brush (President, American Home Products Corp.), *1960 Hearings*, 1st sess., pt. 16, p. 9242.

32. Osler L. Peterson, et al., "An Analytical Study of North Carolina General Practice: 1953–1954," *Journal of Medical Education* 31 (Dec. 1956): 1–165.

33. Ibid., p. 13.

34. Ibid., pp. 40–44.

35. Kenneth F. Clute, M.D., *The General Practitioner: A Study of Medical Education and Practice in Ontario and Nova Scotia* (Toronto, 1963).

36. Ibid., p. 347 (italics in original). Results are shown in tables 89 and 90, pp. 348 and 349. The teaching of approximately half of the medical school subjects was found unsatisfactory by a greater proportion of respondents, and half by a smaller proportion. Dermatology was the most strongly condemned and bacteriology the least strongly condemned.

37. Ibid., p. 351.

38. Ibid., pp. 353–55.

39. Ibid., p. 163.

40. Ben Gaffin and Associates, "The Fond du Lac Study, A Basic Marketing Study Made for the American Medical Association" (Chicago, 1956); reprinted in U.S., Congress, Senate, Subcommittee on Antitrust and Monopoly of the Committee on the Judiciary, *Hearings on Drug Industry Antitrust Act*, 87th Cong., 1st sess., pt. 2, 1961. (Hereafter cited as *1961 Hearings*.) With respect to the first study in the series of studies for the A.M.A., completed in 1953, the "Fond du Lac Study," states: "Utilization of the study findings netted the AMA a return of 3600% in increased pharmaceutical advertising for each dollar spent on the [study] research.

"The survey of pharmaceutical advertisers played a part in bringing about a number of policy changes: the institution of an index of advertisers, the exclusion of cigarette advertising, and the eventual dropping of the 58-year old Council Seal of Acceptance Program" (pt. 2, p. 702).

41. Peterson, et al., "Study of General Practice," p. 103.

42. Charles E. Silberman, "Drugs: The Pace is Getting Furious," *Fortune*, May 1960, p. 276.

43. Gaffin and Associates, "Fond du Lac Study," *1961 Hearings*, 1st sess., pt. 2, pp. 783, 792.

44. Louis Lasagna, M.D., *The Doctors' Dilemmas* (New York, 1962), pp. 135–36. A. Dale Console (former Medical Director of E. R. Squibb & Co.) asked: "How can legitimate education compete with . . . the carefully contrived distortions driven home by the triphammer effect of weekly mailings, the regular visits of the detail man, the two-page spreads, and the ads which appear six times in the same journal, not to mention the added inducement of the free cocktail party and the golf outing complete with three golf balls stamped with the name of the doctor and the company in contrasting colors?"

Console went on to say: "There are far too many physicians who must still be taught the differences between a free golf ball, the magnetic personality of a detailman, and a scientific fact as criteria for the evaluation of a drug." *1960 Hearings*, 2nd sess., pt. 18, pp. 10374–75.

45. William S. Merrell Co., "Drug Instruction Manual for 'Kevadon Hospital Clinical Program' " (Cincinnati, 1960); reprinted in U.S., Congress, Senate, Subcommittee on Reorganization and International Organizations of the Committee on Government Operations, *Hearings on Interagency Coordination in Drug Research and Regulation*, 88th Cong., 2nd sess., 1963, pt. 1, pp. 259–70. (Hereafter cited as *1963 Hearings*.)

46. Ibid., p. 264.

47. George P. Larrick (Commissioner of Food and Drugs), *1960 Hearings*, 2nd sess., pt. 22, pp. 12107–212. In particular, see pp. 12137–65, tables 1–21.

48. U.S., Federal Trade Commission, *Concentration Ratios in American Industry* (Washington, D.C., 1963), p. 229, Table 5.

49. *Report*, p. 251. As examples of the allocation of resources in the agency, consider the following regulatory actions from the FDA's 1964 submission to the House Appropriations Subcommittee (p. 235). U.S., Congress, House, Subcommittee on the Departments of Labor, and Health, Education, and Welfare of the Committee on Appropriations, *Hearings on Appropriations for 1965*, 88th Cong., 2nd sess., 1964, pt. 1 (hereafter cited as *1964 Hearings*).

Product: Dr. Reeves' Special Foot Cream for Diabetics

Shipper, manufacturer: Chemical Commodities, Inc., Olathe, Kans.

Charge: Misbranded by false claims in the label that the article was an adequate and effective treatment for impaired foot circulation and would prevent corns and calluses.

Disposition: Decree entered, destroyed December 31, 1962 (p. 235).

Product: Sumner County Margarine

   Shipper: Lever Brothers, Hammond, Ind.

Charges: Charged misbranded in that the label statement "High-Nutritional" and labelling statements are false and misleading because they imply, contrary to fact, that the product is significantly higher in nutrition than margarine and similar spreads available; that it contributes a significantly greater nutrient content than butter, and significant amounts of ascorbic acid, niacin, [etc.], for special dietary use. In addition the label statements 'made especially for growing children' and 'you get the good things growing children need every day' are also false and misleading, since they imply, contrary to fact, that this product is of special value in promotion of growth of children, and that it contains significant amounts of all nutrients needed by growing children to maintain good health.

Disposition: Consent decree March 26, 1963. Product turned over to charity April 26, 1963 (p. 223).

Product: Magnetic Bracelets

   A metal expansion bracelet consisting of eight enclosed magnets.

Each magnet engraved with the word 'RELAX' and the design of playing-card clubs. The bracelet is gold-colored on the outside and silver-colored on the inside.

In possession of: Rimar, Inc., San Juan, P. R.

Charges: Misbranding while held for sale after shipment in interstate commerce. False and misleading claims represented the device as adequate and effective treatment for providing longer and more active life, relieving arthritis, and inhibiting bacterial growth.

Disposition: Default decree, February 12, 1963. Merchandise destroyed (p. 229).

   As a digression on the overall allocation of resources in society, it is of interest that one witness before an earlier subcommittee pointed out that, while there was no continuous government inspection in the manufacture of pharmaceuticals, there is, and has been for over 50 years, such inspection for some meats, and since 1958, for poultry products, and there is also some federal government inspection of canned meats for dogs and cats. Herbert B. Bain, Director of Public Information, American Meat Institute, to Dr. Solomon Garb, Albany Medical College; reprinted in *1960 Hearings,* 2nd sess., pt. 18, p. 10584.

   The witness presented to the subcommittee an advertisement for a dog food: "The headline—up here says, 'All Dog Foods Do Not Have a Wholesome Meaty Aroma' and then in big red letters, 'U.S. Government Inspected Ideal Dog Food Does.' " The witness concluded: "If we can afford continuous Government inspection and certification for dog and cat food, we can afford continuous Government inspection of pharmaceutical manufacturing." Solomon Garb, M.D., *1960 Hearings,* 2nd sess., pt. 18, p. 10480.

50. Clair Wilcox, *Public Policies Toward Business,* 2nd ed. (Homewood, Ill., 1960), p. 768.

51. George Larrick to Congressman Melvin R. Laird (R., Wis.), 6 March 1964, as quoted in *1964 Hearings,* pp. 1314–15. Figure of 1,150 medical, etc., personnel derived by using 1963 accession rates of these persons—cited by Larrick on p. 213.

52. Wilcox, *Public Policies,* p. 766. Congressman Laird pointed out the problem to Larrick in a letter of 17 January 1964—cited in *1964 Hearings,* pp. 1313–14. "We in Congress faced up to this issue long ago in respect to Defense Department personnel. A statute was passed prohibiting career military personnel from working on defense matters for private industry until at least 2 years had passed following their retirement. I strongly incline toward a requirement of this same kind in respect to FDA personnel."

53. Barbara Moulton, M.D., *1960 Hearings,* 2nd sess., pt. 22, p. 12030.

54. Ibid., p. 12025.

55. ". . . he said that he had just come from a private conference with a member of our General Counsel's office, about another seized product, and had reached an agreement whereby his client would be able to resume almost identical promotion without fear of further FDA action, although, of course, this was a gentleman's agreement between the two lawyers and nothing was or would be put in writing." Ibid., p. 12029.

56. *Report,* p. 250.

57. "In the recent Congressional investigation of the cost of drugs, it was repeatedly stated by executives of pharmaceutical companies that a major expenditure in the promotion of drugs was the cost of 'educating' physicians to use the products—and they mean doing what has always been expected of medical institutions." Charles D. May, M.D. (Professor of Pediatrics, New York University College of Medicine), "Selling Drugs by 'Educating' Physicians," *Journal of Medicine Education* 36 (Jan. 1961); reprinted in *1961 Hearings,* 1st sess., pt. 2, p. 948.

58. "U.S. District Judge Matthew M. McGuire fined Richardson-Merrell, New York, and William S. Merrell Co., Cincinnati, . . . [$80,000]. The two were charged with withholding information and making false statements [in connection with a new drug application] about the composition of MER/29 (triparanol)." *Wall Street Journal,*

5 June 1964. *See also* Morton Mintz, *The Therapeutic Nightmare* (Boston, 1965), chap. 11.

59. "It may be of interest to the committee to know that a substantial number of so-called medical scientific papers that are published on behalf of these drugs are written within the confines of the pharmaceutical houses concerned. Frequently the physician involved merely makes the observations and his data, which is sometimes skecthy and uncritical, is submitted to a medical writer employed by the company. The writer prepares the article which is returned to the physician who makes the overt effort to submit it for publication. The article is frequently submitted to one of the journals which looks to the pharmaceutical company for advertising and rarely is publication refused. The particular journal is of little interest inasmuch as the primary concern is to have the article published any place in order to make reprints available. . . .

"Of further interest may be the existence of a journal, recently founded, called 'Current Therapeutic Research,' which appears to be devoted entirely to pharmaceutical promotion. It accepts no advertising as such. However, there is a fee per page for any article published and publication is very prompt. The publisher's major source of income presumably is the lucrative reprint market." Haskell J. Weinstein, M.D., *1960 Hearings,* 2nd sess., pt. 18, pp. 10244–45.

60. On this, see the exhibits relating to the Medical and Pharmaceutical Information Bureau (hereafter cited as MPIB) in *1961 Hearings,* 2nd sess., pt. 7. As examples: (*a*) from a medical column called "Spotlight on Health" which appeared in several newspapers in early 1956—magnesium trisilicate—"Among these antacids such as gelusil [Warner-Chilcott brand name for magnesium trisilicate—introduced to clinical use about 1936] are probably most widely used. A drug has been developed for the excruciatingly painful heart condition called angina pectoris. . . . This may be prevented by a drug called peritrate [Warner-Chilcott brand name for pentaerythritol tetranitrate—introduced in 1950] that exerts a protective action that lasts from four to six hours." *1961 Hearings,* 2nd sess., pt. 7, p. 3544. (*b*) from the script of the *Today* show of Monday, 15 December 1958—"Today, this is the story . . . . the new drug decadron [Merck brand name for dexamethasone] . . . . the most powerful of that test tube's descendants [reference to the test tube in which cortisone was discovered]." *1961 Hearings,* 2nd sess., pt. 7, p. 3581 (ellipses in original). The exhibits contain the correspondence between MPIB and the firms arranging these plants.

61. *Report,* p. 220.

62. Henry Dolger, M.D. (Chief of Diabetes and Associate Attending

Physician for Metabolic Diseases, Mount Sinai Hospital, New York), *Report*, p. 216.

63. *Report,* pp. 193–94.

64. Ibid., p. 194 (emphasis in original).

65. Ibid., p. 195.

66. Ibid., p. 196.

67. Haskell J. Weinstein, M.D., *1960 Hearings,* 2nd sess., pt. 18, p. 10244.

68. *1960 Hearings,* 2nd sess., pt. 18, p. 10372.

69. A. Dale Console, M.D., *1960 Hearings,* 2nd sess., pt. 18, p. 10379.

70. Martin A. Seidell, M.D. (Associate Medical Director, Riker Laboratories, and formerly Medical Director of the Roerig Division of Pfizer), *1960 Hearings,* 2nd sess., pt. 18, p. 10288.

71. Charles D. May, M.D., *1961 Hearings,* 1st sess., pt. 2, pp. 958–59.

72. Lasagna, *Doctors' Dilemmas,* p. 142.

73. A. Dale Console, M.D., *1960 Hearings,* 2nd sess., pt. 18, p. 10368.

74. Ibid., pp. 10372–73.

CHAPTER FIVE

1. Since the same three firms produce almost all the pharmaceuticals in the category of bulk drugs, the evidence for this inference is admittedly weak.

CHAPTER SIX

1. There must surely be cases in which a small firm was established to produce a drug, under generic name, on which a patent had been obtained. These cases are probably rare, however, and, in any case, unidentifiable.

CHAPTER SEVEN

1. In most large centers the distribution chain also includes a wholesaler who distributes pharmaceuticals to the local pharmacists. In all but the very largest metropolitan areas, the number of wholesalers in the market is very small, a not unusual structure being a branch of McKesson and Robbins and one or two local firms. The pharmacist has the

option of dealing with the wholesaler or ordering directly from the manufacturer. Very little information is available about the behavior of wholesalers in drug markets, and for the purpose of obtaining crude estimates of how the consumer might benefit from the introduction of the policies, we ignore this participant in the market.

CHAPTER EIGHT

1. All data in this section are taken from National Science Foundation, *Research and Development in Industry: 1961* (Washington, D.C., 1964).

Industrial research and development can be performed by industrial firms, or it can be performed by independent contractors outside the industrial sector. Such research can be financed by industrial firms or it can be financed by other sources of support, e.g., governments, philanthropic foundations, etc. Thus industrial firms can figure in industrial research and development in any of three ways: they can (*a*) perform the research and development but not finance it; (*b*) finance the industrial research and development but not perform it; (*c*) both perform and finance the work.

2. Data obtained from National Academy of Science-National Research Council, *Industrial Research Laboratories of the United States,* 9th ed., 11th ed. (Washington, D.C., 1950; 1960).

3. Duplicate single chemical entities accounted for 17 percent of all new products introduced during the period 1950-60. *See* Table VIII-3. It must not be assumed that each of these duplicates was introduced because a firm was able to patent around the existing patent, i.e., that the *duplicate* product required some research-and-development expenditure. To the extent that duplicate products are the result of research-and-development expenditures, they probably enter the market by avoiding existing patents. However, the majority of the duplicate products enter the market through licensing agreements.

4. American Medical Association, *Report of the Commission on the Cost of Medical Care* (Chicago, 1964), I, 111–19.

5. U.S., Congress, Senate, Subcommittee on Antitrust and Monopoly of the Committee on the Judiciary, *Hearings on Drug Industry Antitrust Act,* 87th Cong., 2nd sess., 1962, pt. 4, p. 2480, Table V.

6. Ibid., p. 2481, Table VII.

7. An indication of the extent of the conservatism of the estimate of the annual benefits of drug research and development is obtained by a comparison with Weisbrod's findings. He estimated the total loss attributable to deaths and new cases in 1954 of cancer, tuberculosis, and

poliomyelitis to be approximately $3 billion. Losses from premature deaths were discounted at 10 percent. *See* Burton A. Weisbrod, *Economics of Public Health: Measuring the Impact of Diseases* (Philadelphia, 1961), pp. 48–98.

CHAPTER NINE

1. U.S., Congress, Senate, Subcommittee on Antitrust and Monopoly of the Committee on the Judiciary, *Report, Administered Prices: Drugs,* 87th Cong., 1st sess., 1961, S. Rept. 448, p. 31. (Hereafter cited as *Report.*)

2. Pharmaceutical Manufacturers Association, *Prescription Drug Industry Fact Book* (Washington, D.C., 1962), sec. 1, p. 2.

3. The primary functions of research establishments maintained abroad are to serve as a liaison with foreign medical research communities and to arrange clinical trials of drugs in foreign countries. The latter are necessary in some countries if a new drug is to receive approval by the country's drug agency. They may also be helpful in gaining acceptance of a new drug in a particular country if clinical trials have been performed by persons known to the medical community of the country.

Some of the discrepancy between the National Science Foundation estimate of the amount of research performed in the industry in 1961—$196 million—and the estimate made by P.M.A.—$227 million—may be accounted for by differences in definitions of terms; some of the difference may be accounted for by the fact that some research and development is performed abroad.

4. From the First National City Bank of New York, *Monthly Economic Letter,* April 1962. *See also,* "Survey of the 500 Largest Industrial Firms: 1961," *Fortune,* July 1962.

5. See *Monthly Economic Letter* and "Survey of Industrial Firms."

6. See *Monthly Economic Letter* and "Survey of Industrial Firms." For the 500 largest manufacturing firms, *Fortune,* July 1962, reports a rate of return of 8.3 percent.

7. Steele, "Monopoly and Competition in the Ethical Drugs Market," *Journal of Law and Economics* 5 (Oct. 1962): 164.

8. See *Report,* pp. 105–07.

APPENDIX C

1. A. Osol, A. E. Farrar, and R. Pratt, *The Dispensatory of the United States of America,* 1960 ed. (Philadelphia, 1960).

2. *The Merck Index of Chemicals and Drugs,* 7th ed. rev. (Rahway, N.J., 1960).

3. U.S., Congress, Senate Subcommittee on Antitrust and Monopoly of the Committee on the Judiciary, *Hearings on Drug Industry Antitrust Act,* 87th Cong., 2nd sess., 1962, pt. 4, p. 2525.

APPENDIX D

1. U.S., Congress, Senate, Subcommittee on Antitrust and Monopoly of the Committee on the Judiciary, *Hearings on Drug Industry Antitrust Act,* 87th Cong., 2nd sess., 1962, pt. 4, p. 2525. The estimates were made for the Association by Arthur D. Little, Inc., and cover the sales of the 33 largest firms in the industry.

2. Ibid., p. 2465.

SELECTED BIBLIOGRAPHY

American Medical Association. *Distribution of Physicians in the United States*. Chicago: American Medical Association, 1965.
———. *Report of the Commission on the Cost of Medical Care*. 4 vols. Chicago: American Medical Association, 1964.
American Medical Association Council on Drugs. *New and Nonofficial Drugs: 1962*. Philadelphia: J. B. Lippincott Co., 1962.
Anderson, Odin W.; Collette, Patricia; and Feldman, Jacob J. *Changes in Family Medical Care Expenditures and Voluntary Health Insurance: A Five Year Resurvey*. Cambridge, Mass.: Harvard University Press, 1963.

Canada. Restrictive Trade Practices Commission. *Report Concerning the Manufacture, Distribution and Sale of Drugs*. Ottawa: Queen's Printer, 1963.
Clute, Kenneth F. *The General Practitioner: A Study of Medical Education and Practice in Ontario and Nova Scotia*. Toronto: University of Toronto Press, 1963.
Comanor, William S. "The Economics of Research and Development in the Pharmaceutical Industry." Ph. D. dissertation, Harvard University, 1963.
———. "Research and Competitive Product Differentiation in the Pharmaceutical Industry in the United States." *Economica*, n.s. 31 (November 1964): 372–84.
———. "Research and Technical Change in the Pharmaceutical Industry." *Review of Economics and Statistics* 47 (May 1965): 182–90.

Davidson, Henry A. "Our State Medical Society Journals: Can They Survive? Should They Survive?" *Journal of the Medical Society of New Jersey* 61 (January 1964): 13–14.

Drug Topics Red Book: 1962. New York: Topics Publishing Company, 1961.

Engel, Leonard. *Medicine Makers of Kalamazoo.* New York: McGraw-Hill Book Company, 1961.

First National City Bank of New York. *Monthly Economic Letter.* 1950–65.

"The Fortune Directory: The 500 Largest U.S. Industrial Corporations." *Fortune Magazine.* 1960–65.

Garb, Solomon. "Teaching Medical Students to Evaluate Drug Advertising." *Journal of Medical Education* 35 (August 1960): 729–39.

Grollman, Arthur. *Pharmacology and Therapeutics.* 5th ed. rev. Philadelphia: Lea & Febiger, 1962.

Harris, Richard. *The Real Voice.* New York: The MacMillan Company, 1964.

Harris, Seymour. *The Economics of American Medicine.* New York: The Macmillan Company, 1964.

Kaysen, Carl, and Turner, Donald F. *Antitrust Policy: A Legal and Economic Analysis.* Cambridge, Mass.: Harvard University Press, 1959.

Kogan, Herman. *The Long White Line: The Story of Abbott Laboratories.* New York: Random House, 1963.

Lasagna, Louis. *The Doctors' Dilemmas.* New York: Harper & Brothers, 1962.

Merck Index of Chemicals and Drugs. 7th ed. rev. Rahway, N.J.: Merck & Company, Inc., 1960.

Mintz, Morton. *The Therapeutic Nightmare.* Boston: Houghton Mifflin Company, 1965.

Nashville Tennessean. 12 July 1966.

National Academy of Science-National Research Council. *Industrial Research Laboratories of the United States.* 9th ed.; 11th ed. rev. Washington D.C.: National Research Council, 1950; 1960.

National Science Foundation. *Research and Development in Industry: 1961.* Washington, D.C.: U.S. Government Printing Office, 1964.

Osol, A.; Farrar, A. E.; and Pratt, R. *Dispensatory of the United States of America.* 1960 ed. Philadelphia: J.B. Lippincott Co., 1960.

Pellegrino, E. D. "The State Medical Journal as an Educational Instrument. *Medical Times* 92 (November 1964): 1111–18.
Peterson, Osler L.; Andrews, Leon P.; Spain, Robert S.; and Greenburg, Bernard G. "An Analytical Study of North Carolina General Practice." *Journal of Medical Education* 31 (December 1956): 1–165.
Pharmaceutical Manufacturers Association. *Prescription Drug Industry Fact Book.* Washington D.C.: Pharmaceutical Manufacturers Association, 1962.
———. "Review of Drugs, 1941–61: Single Chemical Entities Introduced in the United States." Mimeographed. Washington, D.C.: Pharmaceutical Manufacturers Association, 1962.
Physicians' Desk Reference. Oradell, N.J.: Medical Economics, Inc., 1947–65.

Silberman, Charles E. "Drugs: The Pace is Getting Furious." *Fortune Magazine,* May 1960, pp. 138–41.
Steele, Henry. "Monopoly and Competition in the Ethical Drugs Market." *Journal of Law and Economics* 5 (October 1962): 131–63.
———. "Patent Restrictions and Price Competition in the Ethical Drugs Industry." *Journal of Industrial Economics* 12 (July 1964): 198–223.
Stigler, George J., ed. *Business Concentration and Price Policy.* Princeton, N.J.: Princeton University Press, 1955.
"Survey of the 500 Largest Industrial Firms: 1961." *Fortune Magazine,* July 1962, pp. 171–90.

Talalay, Paul, ed. *Drugs in Our Society.* Baltimore: Johns Hopkins University Press, 1964.

United States. Congress. House. Subcommittee on the Departments of Labor, and Health, Education, and Welfare of the Committee on Appropriations. *Hearings on Appropriations for 1965.* 88th Cong., 2nd sess., 1964.
United States. Congress. Senate. Subcommittee on Antitrust and Monopoly of the Committee on the Judiciary. *Hearings on Administered Prices: Drugs.* 86th Cong., 1st sess., 2nd sess., 1959; 1960.
United States. Congress. Senate. Subcommittee on Antitrust and Monopoly of the Committee on the Judiciary. *Hearings on Drug Industry Antitrust Act.* 87th Cong., 1st sess., 2nd sess., 1961; 1962.
United States. Congress. Senate. Subcommittee on Reorganization and International Operations of the Committee on Governmental Opera-

tions. *Hearings on Interagency Coordination in Drug Research and Regulation.* 87th Cong., 2nd sess., 1963.

United States. Congress. Senate. Subcommittee on Antitrust and Monopoly of the Committee on the Judiciary. *Report, Administered Prices: Drugs.* 87th Cong., 1st sess., 1961, S. Rept. 448.

United States. Federal Trade Commission. *Concentration Ratios in American Industry.* Washington, D.C.: U.S. Government Printing Office, 1963.

United States. Federal Trade Commission-Securities and Exchange Commission. *Quarterly Financial Report for Manufacturing Corporations.* Washington, D.C.: U.S. Government Printing Office. 1956–65.

United States Pharmacopeia. Easton, Pa.: Mack Publishing Co., 1960.

Wall Street Journal. 5 June 1964.

Weisbrod, Burton. *The Economics of Public Health: Measuring the Impact of Diseases.* Philadelphia: University of Pennsylvania Press, 1961.

Wilcox, Clair. *Public Policies Toward Business.* 2nd ed. rev.; 3rd ed. Homewood, Ill.: Richard D. Irwin, Inc., 1960; 1966.

Williamson, O. E. "Selling Expense as a Barrier to Entry." *Quarterly Journal of Economics* 77 (February 1963): 112–28.

Index

Abbott Laboratories: advertising techniques of, 60

Achromycin (drug): advertising of, 73

ACTH (drug), 70

Advertising and promotion of drugs: criticized, 3, 12, 65, 83–88; to physicians, 3, 4, 5, 33, 39–40, 42–47, 64–65, 73, 75, 82–88, 89; to the public, 4, 84; direct mail, 33, 39–40, 41, 42, 46–47, 64–65, 72; costs, 38–39, 41–45; in medical journals, 39–43, 45–46, 72–73, 234n40; unethical, 65, 83–88, 89; in lay press, 84, 238n60; estimated effect of brand-name removal on, 147, 152; on television, 238n60

Aldactone (drug), 72

Aldosterone (drug), 72

American Medical Association: recommends prescribing by generic name for welfare patients, 67; study of drug marketing, 73; Council Seal of Acceptance Program, 234n40

Anemia: treatment of, 68–69; side effect of chloramphenicol, 85

Antibiotics: batch inspection of, 24; indiscriminate use of, 68

Anti-substitution laws. *See* Laws, anti-substitution

Aspirin, 34

Atomic Energy Commission: regulates raidoactive drugs, 16

Ayerst (drug firm): reported quality-control costs, 57

Assumptions used in estimating drug sales, 202–206, 210, 217, 220

Bacteriology: medical school course in, 234n36

Bain, Herbert B., 236n49

Bain's measure of market power, 53

Barriers to entry of new firms into drug markets, 29, 34, 35, 42

Batch inspection of drugs, 24, 83, 90, 98

Batch method in drug manufacture, 36–37, 90

Bowes, James E., M.D.: quoted on physicians' response to direct-mail ads, 47, 231n23

Brand names, drug: contribute to market power of drug firms, 3, 4, 13, 51, 96, 100; defined, 6n, 18; compared to generic names, 6n, 18–20, 33, 61–62; in advertising, 13, 33, 51, 64–65, 71–73; legal

Merrell, William S., Co. (drug firm): promotes Kevadon, 75; fined for false advertising, 237n58

Methazolamide (drug), 18

Military Medical Supply Agency: purchases drugs competitively by generic name, 66–67

Modell, Walter, M.D.: quoted on USP standards, 58, 232n8; quoted on method of teaching therapeutics, 63

Monopoly in drug industry: 2, 12, 19, 48–51, 117, 123–24

Moulton, Barbara, M.D.: quoted on drug safety, 55–56, 231n1; quoted on processing new drug applications, 81, 237n53,54; quoted in criticism of FDA action on dangerous drugs, 83n

National Association of Retail Druggists: opposes price competition among pharmacists, 118

National Formulary, 58, 59

National Opinion Research Centre: surveyed use of medical services, 10

National Pharmaceutical Council: promotes anti-substitution laws, 61, 62, 63n

National Research Council: warning on chloramphenicol, 85–86

National Science Foundation: estimate of expenditures on research, 126–27, 129n, 143

New and Nonofficial Drugs, 31, 64, 72

New York Hospital: uses formulary system of dispensing drugs, 65–66

North Carolina study of physicians, 67–70, 73

Nova Scotia: general practitioners in, 70–72

Nuclear medicine, 135

Official drugs: defined, 58–59

Oligopoly, 12, 47, 109

Ontario: general practitioners in, 70–72

Over-the-counter drugs: defined, 4

Panmycin (drug), 18

Panray (drug firm): reported quality-control costs, 56

Papandreou's measure of market power, 53

Parenterals, 21, 98

Parke-Davis (drug firm): 61; misleading advertising of, 85–86

Patent litigation, 49

Patent Office, 48

Patents: contribute to market power, 3, 12, 35, 48–51, 100, 164–66; on manufacturing processes, 48–49; quantity of, 50; for ethical drugs, are unique, 157–58

Patents, removal of: estimated effect on research, 3, 14, 150, 152–53, 156; estimated effect on drug sales, 103–104, 106–109, 113, 115, 152, 185–86, 190; estimated effect on prices, 103, 109, 115, 118–23, 148 152, 218–19; estimated effect on large firms, 109–12, 148–52, 156, 157, 222; estimated effect on small firms, 106–108, 110–11; estimated effect on consumer, 117, 119–23

Pathology, 135

Pellegrino, E. D., M.D.: survey of state medical journals, 40, 230n13

Penicillin: use of, 68, 70

Peritrate (drug): advertised, 238n60

Peterson, Osler L.: study of general practitioners in North Carolina, 67–70, 73

Pfizer (drug firm): advertising methods, 73–74; promotion of Diabinese, 85

Pharmaceutical industry. See Drug industry

Pharmaceutical Manufacturers Association: 6; counts drug firms,

Research and development (*cont.*)
57; proposed government aid, 14,
156–57; economies of scale in, 37–
38; expenditures on, 38, 126–33,
142–44; result in many useless
drugs, 39, 88; existing government
aid, 126–27; magnitude of, 126–
29; compared with total industrial
effort, 126–29; estimated social
benefit, 131–33, 135–41; medical
benefits of, 133–35; estimated effects of brand-name removal on,
148; duplicative, 157
Research establishments abroad,
241n3
Reserpine (drug): 25; price of, 26
Retail drug prices, 117–23
Richardson-Merrell (drug firm):
fined for false advertising, 237n*58*
Rothschild's measure of market
power, 53

Sales, drug: estimated effect of
brand-name removal on, 102–104,
109–15, 119, 122–24, 145–47, 152,
153–55, 209–15; estimated effect
of patent removal on, 103, 106–15,
119, 122–24, 148–49, 151, 152,
153–55, 209–15; estimated effect
142–44, 153, 193–95
Salesmen, drug, 33, 39–40, 42, 44–
47, 72–73, 86
Samples of drugs: used in promotion,
71, 73; tested by FDA, 76, 78–79,
98
Senate Judiciary Committee, 2
Serums: 21; inspected by Public
Health Service, 24, 90, 98; estimated effect of brand-name and
patent removal on, 113, 114, 121,
123, 217–19
Side effects of drugs, 55–56, 70, 85
Silberman, Charles E.: quoted on influence of advertising on physicians, 73, 234n*42*

Small drug firms. *See* Drug firms,
small
Smallpox vaccine, 179
Smith, Austin, M.D.: quoted on drug
quality and brand names, 60–61,
233n*15–17*
Steclin (drug), 18
State medical associations, 40–41
Steele, Henry: quoted on necessity
for regulation of drug industry, 3;
quoted on batch methods in drug
production, 36*n;* quoted on small
physical volume of each drug produced, 37; quoted on quality of
low-priced products, 61; quoted on
variations in treatment for drug
quality violations, 79–80
Steward, Newell: quoted on variations between drugs with same
generic name, 62, 233n*20*
Subcommittee on Antitrust and Monopoly: 2, 9, 36, 78, 79, 142–44;
quoted on process patents, 49;
quoted on success of large firms
in opposing use of generic names,
82; quoted on competitive purchasing of drugs by generic names, 66;
quoted on omitting information on
dangerous side effects in drug promotion, 85
Sulfathiazole (drug), 63
Syphilis, 137

Television advertising of drugs,
238n*60*
Testimonials in drug promotion, 85,
86–87
Tetrabon (drug), 18
Tetracycline (drug), 18, 73
Textbooks on drugs, 17, 64, 72
Therapeutics courses in medical
schools: criticised, 63; use generic
names of drugs, 64
Tolbutamide (drug), 85
Trademarks, 6, 18